AMERICAN
LEGAL AND
CONSTITUTIONAL
HISTORY ★ A Garland
Series of
Outstanding
Dissertations

Edited by
HAROLD HYMAN
William P. Hobby Professor of History,
Rice University

STUART BRUCHEY
Allan Nevins Professor of American
Economic History, Columbia University

RUNNING
THE GAUNTLET ★ Cultural Sources
of Violence
Against the I.W.W.

John Clendenin Townsend

Garland Publishing, Inc.
New York & London ★ 1986

Library of Congress Cataloging-in-Publication Data

Townsend, John Clendenin, 1939–
  Running the gauntlet.

  (American legal and constitutional history)
  Bibliography: p.
  1. International Workers of the World. I. Title.
II. Series.
HD8055.I56T68   1986   331.88′6   86-25632
ISBN 0-8240-8298-2

All volumes in this series are printed on acid-free,
250-year-life paper.

Printed in the United States of America

RUNNING THE GAUNTLET:
CULTURAL SOURCES OF VIOLENCE
AGAINST THE I.W.W.

RUNNING THE GAUNTLET:
CULTURAL SOURCES OF VIOLENCE
AGAINST THE I.W.W.

These [months of imprisonment] are all a part of the premium that one gets and has always received, for his services to his fellow man. For the world is the same now that it always was, and if a man is so insane that he wants to go out in the wilderness and preach and work for the poor and the oppressed and the despised, for the men who do not own the tools, the newspapers, and the courts, and the machinery, and the organization of society, these are the wages that he receives today, and which he has received from the time the first foolish man commenced to agitate for the uplifting and the upbuilding of the human race.

> -- Clarence Darrow for the defense,
> 1906 Haywood trial.

During the visit of the Industrial Workers of the World they will be accorded a night and day guard of honor, composed of citizens armed with rifles. The Coroner will be in attendance at his office every day.

> -- Los Angeles _Times_, 1912

TABLE OF CONTENTS

*

PART ONE

VIGILANTES AND THE HOBO MENACE

Member of I.W.W. desires to sell his home;
reason, police persecution. Splendid opportunity
for some patriotic citizen. Address 35-D, R-1.
San Diego.

> -- Classified Ad, San Diego
> Union, May 12, 1912.

Hanging is none too good for them and they would
be much better dead; for they are absolutely
useless in the human economy; they are waste
material of creation and should be drained off in
the sewer of oblivion there to rot in cold
obstruction like any other excrement.

> -- San Diego Tribune, 1912

CHAPTER 1

INTRODUCTION:
ANTI-WOBBLY VIOLENCE
AND THE STRESS OF INDUSTRIALISM

The I.W.W. can be profitably viewed only as a
psychological byproduct of the neglected child-
hood of industrial America.

> -- Carleton Parker, Atlantic
> Monthly, November, 1917)

The Industrial Workers of the World, the most radical
union America had seen, was the object of repeated attacks
and vilification throughout the decade and a half of its
effective existence, 1905-1919. The rough treatment and
abuse endured by the Wobblies came from every segment of
society; Socialists, Progressives, liberals, conservatives,
labor, business, the church, the press, and state and local
authoritico all participated in the attack, which culminated
in the massive Federal campaign to suppress the IWW. In
nearly every state in the Union, Wobblies were clubbed,
tarred and feathered, deported, shot, tortured, maimed,
occasionally lynched, and universally despised. Newspapers
of every description depicted them as a gang of irrational

3

saboteurs, vile agents of corruption and free love, destroyers of the church and the family, unconscionable traitors
and, during the World War, agents of the Hun. The organization's initials were variously interpreted as "I Want to
Wreck," "I Won't Work," "Imported Weary Willies," and "Impe-
rial Wilhelm's Warriors."[1] Paul F. Brissenden, whose contemporary history still is among the most comprehensive
studies of the IWW, described its distorted public image:

> Though nowadays well aware of the existence of the
> I.W.W., the public still knows little about the organi-
> zation and its members. Moreover, a great deal of what
> it does know is false. For thirteen years the I.W.W
> has been rather consistently misrepresented -- not to
> say vilified -- to the American people. The public has
> not been told the truth about the things the I.W.W. has
> done or the doctrines in which it believes. The papers
> have printed so much fiction about this organization
> and maintained such a nation-wide conspiracy of silence
> as to its real philosophy -- especially as to the
> constructive items of this philosophy -- that the popu-
> lar conception of this labor group is a weird unreal-
> ity. The current picture is of a motley horde of
> hoboes and unskilled laborers who will not work and
> whose philosophy is a philosophy simply of sabotage and
> the violent overthrow of "capitalism," and whose
> actions conform to that philosophy.[2]

Journalistic animus toward the IWW was not subtle --
during a 1910 free-speech fight, the Fresno Herald proposed
that "a whipping post and a cat-o-nine tails well seasoned
by being soaked in salt water is none too harsh a treatment
for peace-breakers."[3] Such suggestions were all too often
translated into shocking incidents of anti-IWW violence such
as the mass deportations into the Arizona desert, or the
Everett massacre, or the sadistic murders of Wesley Everest
and Frank Little. But more common were beatings, "water

4

treatment" with firehoses, the "third-degree" in town and
county jails -- and the vigilante gauntlet:

> The first thing on the program was to kiss the flag.
> "You son of a B----, Come on Kiss it, G-- Damn You."
> As he said it I was hit with a wagon spoke all over,
> when you had kissed the flag you were told to run the
> gauntlet. 50 men being on each side and each man being
> armed with a gun and a club and some had long whips.
> When I started to run the gauntlet the men were ready
> for action, they were in high spirits from booze. I
> got about 30 feet when I was suddenly struck across the
> knee. I felt the wagon spoke sink in splitting my
> knee. I reeled over. As I was lying there I saw other
> fellow workers running the gauntlet. Some were bleed-
> ing freely from cracked heads, others were knocked down
> to be made to get up to run again. Some tried to break
> the line only to be beaten back. It was the most cow-
> ardly and inhuman cracking of heads I ever witnessed.[4]

The fury of enraged citizens shocked outside observers.
Harris Weinstock, head of a Commission appointed to investigate the disturbances at San Diego in 1912, commented:

> Your Commissioner has visited Russia and while there
> has heard many horrible tales of high-handed proceed-
> ings and outrageous treatment of innocent people at the
> hands of despotic and tyrannic Russian authorities.
> Your Commissioner is frank to confess that when he
> became satisfied of the truth of the stories, as re-
> lated by these unfortunate men, it was hard for him to
> believe that he still was not sojourning in Russia,
> conducting his investigation there, instead of in this
> alleged "land of the free and home of the brave."
> Surely these American men, who as the overwhelming
> evidence shows, in large numbers assaulted with weapons
> in a most cowardly and brutal manner their helpless and
> defenseless fellows, were certainly far from "brave"
> and their victims far from "free."[5]

The Wobblies were the subject of a hysteria which saw
them as a generalized force with extraordinary power to
undermine community life. To some, they were so evil that
they ceased to be human. "In considering such a movement as
the I.W.W," declared the St. Louis _Republic_ in 1912, "there

is no need to pause over its history. . . . Nor is it necessary to consider the philosophy. It has none. It is mere brute ferocity. The tiger which springs on the traveler in the jungle has no philosophy -- only a thirst for blood. He cannot be reasoned with -- he must be overcome."[6] The Wobbly had become a public enemy sans pareil. In a statement on the Senate floor in 1918, Senator William E. Borah pictured the IWW as an invisible conspiracy: "You cannot destroy the organization. That is an intangible proposition. It is something you can not get at. You can not reach it. You do not know where it is. It is not in writing. It is not in anything else. It is a simple understanding between men, and they act upon it without any evidence of existence whatever."[7] As events would demonstrate, Senator Borah's concern about the IWW's indestructibility proved groundless.

What accounts for the intense hostility to the Industrial Workers of the World? Why did those who spoke and acted with so much force apparently fear this organization above all others? What beliefs and values seemed so jeopardized that only violent repression could preserve them? From its birth in 1905 until its effective demise following the mass trials in 1918, the Industrial Workers of the World was the victim of violent repression at the hands of employers, vigilante committees, local, state, and federal authorities; the question is: why? What ideas justified violence against this segment of the working class? Who espoused such ideas? Who participated in the violence and under what circumstances? How were such ideas sanctioned by the culture? How were they influenced by social and economic development? This study explores American cultural perceptions of radicals, workers and immigrants, and relates them to economic and social developments of this period. It examines how the expression of ideas and attitudes about Wobblies and the "labor question" created a climate for violence.

During its brief but colorful existence, the IWW participated in many strikes and free speech fights in cities and towns across the nation. Typically, the confrontations took place in a small city or town, usually in the West or Midwest. Ordinarily there was a bona fide labor grievance at the bottom of it -- scab labor or job sharks or wage cuts. But such an issue quickly became overshadowed as stereotyped responses from both sides precluded compromise and escalated confrontation. The business community usually rallied quickly and showed little restraint in expressing their opposition to the Wobblies. The police, with few exceptions, actively joined in, as did the local press, again with few and usually short-lived exceptions. Dissenters, especially businessmen, were ostracized and pressured to conform. The authorities typically adopted a conspiracy theory of events, blaming professional agitators and searching for ringleaders. Protesters were viewed as riff-raff, ignorant foreigners, radicals and scum, although occasionally seen as misguided youth led on by devious and cowardly agitators. Rumor and misinformation ran rampant, sometimes augmented by the activities of <u>agents</u> <u>provocateurs</u>. Negotiation was not considered until well after the conflict had escalated into violence and polarized the community. For their part, the Wobblies responded with increased rhetorical defiance, non-violent resistance, calls for more martyrs to fill the jails, and mockery for the angry vigilantes who ran them out of town.

Although a pattern for IWW free speech fights and strikes can be discerned, motives for IWW antagonists' behavior are less clear. For example, were there differences between towns that resolved their quarrel with the IWW quickly and fairly and those that did not? Little evidence of such counter-models survives beyond brief mention or what may be inferred. Despite the utility of the few historical community studies that have looked at conflicts with the IWW, answers to such economic and demographic questions are hard to come by.[8] Securing socio-economic data even for the present day is difficult; finding them for times past, or measuring historical state-of-mind variables, is even more so. Granted these limitations, there are useful sources that reveal the psychological and cultural context of anti-Wobbly violence. In addition to aggregate economic data showing the impact of corporate industrialism, they include contemporary local newspaper stories, editorials, and letters to the editor; articles and editorials in labor papers, trade journals, and popular weekly magazines; verbatim records of governmental hearings and reports of investigations into violent episodes and industrial conditions; trial transcripts and reports of trials involving the IWW; autobiographies, memoirs and reminiscences; contemporary commentary on industrial conditions, violence, socialism, radicals, the "labor question," etc.

Analysis of these sources is limited to the years prior to America's entry into World War I. With this event and the revolution in Russia, the campaign against the IWW reached a peak of hysteria and took on a new character. In addition, the Federal government moved to halt IWW disruptions, because of war-time need for sustained production and rational markets. This federal activity affected the IWW drastically: the nationwide dragnet arrests, raids, deportations, and mass trials for treason, sedition, sabotage, and conspiracy to violate the Selective Service and Espionage Acts converted the IWW from a fighting union to a harried defense organization. For these reasons, and because the story of the war-time suppression of the IWW has been chronicled by others, pre-World War I America is a logical setting for this study.[9]

Fear of internal subversion, religious or political, has influenced American culture since Colonial days; the paranoia that helped crush the IWW continued into the 20th century. The Civil War augmented such fears; before it, traditional values more effectively restrained dissent and other offenses against community norms. But the war demonstrated that great harm could come from dissent, and all opinion advocating change came under greater suspicion. In a crisis, negative elements of identity, ordinarily repressed, are projected onto others; the acute hatred and fear provoked by Wobblies suggest that they threatened psychic stability as well as social stability. These fears were intensified by social and economic changes in pre-World War I America, which affected many individuals' self-image. During the last quarter of the century attitudes toward radicalism were colored by European immigration, and by such events as the railroad strikes of 1877 and 1884, the Haymarket affair of 1886, the labor wars in the mining districts of the West and the Appalachians, the attempted assassination of Henry Clay Frick in 1892, and the assassination of President McKinley in 1901. These events and others helped create the image of the bomb-throwing anarchist who threatened the American way of life.

At bottom, the IWW threatened certain individuals' identity by challenging the way authority was structured in America. The individual's struggle for independence and a place in the culture determines what roles the individual

adopts to form an identity. This striving leads to the
formation of interest groups, which shape the authority
relations embodied in social, political, and economic institutions, and which influence the culture's acceptance or
rejection of political, social, scientific and technological
ideas.[10] The growth and subsequent repression of the IWW
is at root a function of changing authority relations in the
context of post-Civil War modernization and industrialization. This idea can be clarified by briefly discussing
these questions: What is the nature of authority in an
industrial setting? How did changes in the organization of
American industry shift the locus of authority? What effect
did these shifts have on the IWW and their opponents?

Knowledge is the source of authority in industrial
societies.[11] The formation and transmission of knowledge
is a key characteristic of the industrializing process,
affecting all facets of social life. One of the most important of these is the occupational structure, in which occupations are ranked in relation to the creation, administration and distribution of knowledge. The industrial occupational structure is meritocratic, creating groups and
classes based on function rather than on traditional ideologies or interests. The ascendence of knowledge-based groups
over interest-based groups results in new social and political alignments; generally, functional industrial occupations
replace traditional occupations. Since various functional
occupations are also rendered obsolete by new knowledge,

11

industrialism continually creates marginal groups whose opportunities for social mobility and economic participation are more or less diminished.

The pre-World War I years saw unprecedented and unpredictable change -- the rise of big business, frequent and damaging fluctuations in the economy, several waves of immigration, numerous episodes of labor unrest, rapid invention of new technologies in communication and transportation, to name but a few. This rapidly changing industrial development displaced or threatened the functionality of certain groups within the middle and working classes. In particular, workers in extractive industries and small businessmen -- Wobblies and their main opponents -- were downwardly mobile.[12] The economic historian Alfred Chandler, summarizing the major features of this change, pointed out that:

> By the beginning of the twentieth century, many more companies were making producers' goods, to be used in industry rather than on the farm or by the ultimate consumer. Most of the major industries had become dominated by a few large enterprises. These great industrial corporations no longer purchased and sold through agents, but had their own nation-wide buying and marketing organizations. Many, primarily those in the extractive industries, had come to control their own raw materials. In other words, the business economy had become industrial. Major industries were dominated by a few firms that had become great vertically integrated, centralized enterprises.[13]

The typical nineteenth century business was a small regional firm owned and managed by the same individual or partnership, producing a single product for a limited market. By 1900, as part of the long-term shift from an agricultural to an industrial economy, the small firm had given

12

way to a bureaucratically-organized corporation marketing a wide range of products on a national scale. Decision making shifted away from local control as Wall Street increasingly controlled each corporation and a few large corporations controlled each industry.[14] The result was a national urban market. Prior to the Civil War, the economy served agriculture; but after the war, urban population expanded, providing a market for industrial products and a concentrated labor supply. By 1900, urban population was 40 per cent of the total.[15] The growing national railroad network played a significant part in establishing a national market, providing reliable long-distance bulk transport and a model for large-scale organization and financing. In addition, machine production and labor and machine specialization made economies of scale possible; this and severe competition encouraged vertical integration, as corporations sought to control raw materials, manufacture and marketing. Legal, political and social factors also contributed to corporate development by means of patent law, protective tariffs, 14th Amendment protection of corporate property rights; judges, legislators, governors, cabinet officers and Presidents sympathetic to business interests; and values exalting private property, free enterprise, thrift, hard work and Social Darwinism.[16]

The existence of a large capital market and a favorable political climate facilitated the growth of mergers and trusts.[17] Finance capitalism had developed in the post-

Civil War period to fund industrial, agricultural and commercial growth. Technological innovations in industry and agriculture and a shift of industry to the West and South called for large-scale investment which local bankers were unable to supply; the demand for financing could only be met by houses like J.P. Morgan's.[18] New York investment bankers, commercial banks, insurance companies, and investment trusts collected savings and sold them to enterprises that could not fund their own capital requirements. Though typically thought of as financial middlemen bringing savers and capital users together, they often insisted on controlling the firms they invested in; some, like Morgan, had extensive power over many industries, giving rise to public outcries against the "Money Trust."[19] "The history of this country," declared a businessman to the U.S. Industrial Commission in 1900,

> gives examples of poor boys who became great men, beginning at splitting rails, tanning hides, driving canal horses, etc., and we all know personally some illustration of self-made men; we have listened to the stories of father and grandsire, telling the younger generation of early struggles, and many instances have been cited where a few thousand dollars started them upon a career to fame and fortune. Trusts have come, however, as a curse for this generation and a barrier to individual enterprise. What will be the prospects for our children? God-Almighty alone knows.[20]

As federal regulation and centralized business monopoly increased, local power brokers became more dependent upon the cooperation of the federal government and the corporate power structure, leaving local authority feeling vulnerable to outside forces. In particular, industrial violence and

14

revolutionary rhetoric were perceived as great threats, although industrial violence during the Progressive years was probably no greater in the United States than elsewhere.[21]

Thus a perception of disorder accompanied the shift in the locus of authority. In the first two decades of the twentieth century, America changed from a society in which farmers, small businessmen, mechanics and artisans had place and function, to a society in which such groups were increasingly marginal. A concern arose for reform of political and corporate abuses and regulation of industrial conflicts.[22]

But the need to legitimize and regulate labor conflict was not welcomed by all during the score of years under consideration. Although trade union strength had grown, it did so in the teeth of determined employer opposition. The economic down-turn of 1903-04 gave employers' associations the chance to crack down on unionism with an open-shop drive.[23] The IWW made its appearance at the same time, calling for a large-scale organization of industrial workers that echoed corporate organization. The IWW's experiences with industrialism had convinced it that there would be no quarter given, and so it rejected political action: "the working class and the employing class have nothing in common."[24] Progressives, too, although ready to exploit the threat of violence for the sake of social reform, were unwilling to accept the IWW.[25] After the great IWW-led strike at Lawrence, Massachusetts, in 1912, an editorial in the Progressive _Survey_ asked:

> Is this a new thing in the industrial world? . . . Are
> we to see another serious, perhaps successful, attempt
> to organize labor by whole industrial groups instead of
> by trades? Are we to expect that instead of breaking
> out into lawless riot which we know well enough how to
> deal with, the laborers are to listen to a subtle
> anarchistic philosophy which challenges the fundamental
> idea of law and order, inculcating such strange doc-
> trines as those of "direct action," "sabotage," "syndi-
> calism," "the general strike," and "violence?" . . . .
> We think that our whole current morality as to the
> sacredness of property and even of life is involved in
> it.[26]

Many who confronted this "new thing" felt the same way.

The following chapters examine interrelated themes: the pressures brought to bear upon the culture by the rapid development of corporate industrialism; the role of language in degrading the IWW; the psychological motives and social roles that sanctioned violence against them; the beliefs and values of the typical anti-Wobbly businessman; and the human and cultural costs of prejudice against the Wobblies and those they spoke for.

CHAPTER 2

THE SAN DIEGO FREE SPEECH FIGHT
HARD WORDS, HARD WORK

> But even during the kingdom of Christ those
> people who do not belong to the community of
> believers, who do not love him, and whom he does
> not love, stand outside this tie. Therefore a
> religion, even if it calls itself the religion of
> love, must be hard and unloving towards those who
> do not belong to it. Fundamentally indeed every
> religion is in this same way a religion of love
> for all those whom it embraces; while cruelty and
> intolerance towards those who do not belong to it
> are natural to every religion.
>
>   -- Sigmund Freud, Group Psychology
>   and the Analysis of the Ego

The most brutal and protracted anti-IWW activity occured in San Diego during the winter and spring of 1911-
1912.[1] The trouble began at a secret night meeting held in
the U.S. Grant Hotel early in December of 1911. Members of
the San Diego Grand Jury and other prominent businessmen met
with General Harrison Grey Otis, owner of the Los Angeles
Times, and his colleague, Secretary Zeehandelaar of the
adamantly open-shop Merchants and Manufacturers Association
of Los Angeles. Although details of this conference were
never publicized, it was commonly understood that discussion

17

centered on IWW propaganda and the need for its suppression.[2]

A few days earlier, on December 1st, two labor leaders, the McNamara brothers, had stunned organized labor by confessing to having dynamited the Los Angeles Times building. The spectacular bombing had focused the nation's attention to an even greater degree upon radicalism and the labor question; for instance, this event led directly to the formation of the Commission on Industrial Relations. The McNamaras' admission robbed Los Angeles Socialists of an assured victory in the mayoral race, halted union drives in that city and elsewhere, and insured that Los Angeles would remain a bastion of the open-shop movement.[3] Their confession was a major setback for organized labor and increased the public's prejudice against radicals.

There is little doubt that General Otis, buoyed by this news, imparted a crusader's zeal to his audience. The first result was a petition, presented to the Common Council on December 8, 1911, to prohibit street speaking in a 7-block district of downtown San Diego, including a corner traditionally used for open-air meetings of all sorts. Eighty-five citizens, mostly merchants, signed this petition; they considered the street speaking to be "a nuisance and detriment to the public welfare of this, our city."[4]

These words probably best expressed the true extent of the Wobbly menace, for San Diego was not a hot spot of labor or radical trouble. It is likely that the community-minded

18

citizens assembled at the U.S. Grant were not particularly angry, but merely annoyed and apprehensive; however, having been invited to a clandestine meeting and addressed by one of the country's most well-known and influential business-men, their indignation was no doubt heightened. Here was General Otis, monied, tough as a nut, calling on them for dedication and bravery, suggesting that it was not only advisable to fear and despise the IWW but morally correct to threaten and harass them.

Sitting next to one another, speaking out on the IWW menace, these men perhaps felt impelled to enhance their prestige, perhaps expressed themselves in stronger terms because of General Otis' presence, perhaps exaggerated a bit for the rhetorical effect, recounting stories and rumors about other towns' efforts to rid themselves of the Wob-blies. What emerged was a conviction that the IWW really was a threatening force, and a determination to do something about it.

Although, like Otis, these men felt their economic interests threatened, they rarely referred to an economic motive for denying the IWW the right to speak. There was rather a seige mentality, as if San Diego were repelling a barbarian attack, with community pride, manhood, womanhood, and the American way of life at stake. Such upwelling of patriotic ardor and righteousness was common to other cities and towns that confronted the Wobblies (see Appendix I).

Of the fifty IWW free-speech fights or strike actions

19

in the years under consideration, the great majority took place in cities like San Diego with a population of fifty thousand or less, and most occurred in the West and Midwest.[5] Typically, these communities were not factory towns, but agricultural, mercantile or, less often, mining centers. Business life had not yet been as completely altered by vertical integration of industry, absentee ownership, corporate bureaucracy, and federal regulation as it would be during and after the Great War. In most cases, the social order was unchanged since the Civil War. And with work forces dispersed in mill, forest, mine or farm, these towns were without a large and concentrated working-class quarter to balance the dominant influence of the merchants.

Community affairs were in the hands of local bankers, lawyers, doctors, merchants, small manufacturers, and the occasional timber baron or other rich entrepreneur who made his home in the locality -- men whose business operations were on a modest and traditional scale. By and large, they did not require a room full of clerks and files, or specialized accounting or marketing knowledge; they paid their laborers by the day, knew them by name, and were generally on the job themselves day in and day out; they knew the details of their business and could have run that of others as well, so generalized and relatively simple were their business procedures.

Compared to businessmen in the large cities where corporations and bureaucratic organization had already gained a foothold, the sole proprietors and partners in these smaller towns and cities were like the artisans of a generation earlier; they took pride in their work, had a paternal relationship with their employees, and took an interest in the welfare of each other and the community. Moreover, there was usually a geographic center where trade and service activities were carried on, which meant that most businessmen not only knew each other and shared a familiar neighborhood, they shared the idea of a neighborhood. The people of these towns had a sense of self-sufficiency that stemmed from their everyday life -- most families, even in town, had a cow or chickens, probably a horse, certainly a garden; many chopped their own wood or drew water from their own well, and most made and mended their own clothes.

But new forms of machinery, transport, advertising, market configurations, and other signs of progress were altering these independent patterns of life. A community's enthusiasm to expand commerce, to pave the streets and extend the gasworks, to see horseless carriages or moving pictures was accompanied by vexation over manipulated railroad rates and other unchecked monopoly practices, by fear of governmental encroachment into local affairs, and by mistrust of union agitation and strikes. With the resurgence of the open-shop movement, lobbies like the Citizens' Industrial Alliance, the National Association of Manufacturers, and local Merchants and Manufacturers Associations had sprung up everywhere to combat unionism and promote their own communities.

These feelings, the natural result of shared values, shared neighborhoods, and shared business interests, put pressure on merchants, politicians, clergy and editors to support the suppression of the IWW[6] (see Appendix II). San Diegans had protected common interests before: like most of California, the city had a history of violence and discrimination against Indians, Mexicans, Negroes and Chinese, much of it recent.[7] The people of such communities took pride in running their own affairs and bridled at interference by either the IWW or the state. (Curiously, in almost every vigilante action against Wobblies, cities like San Diego, which resented state interference, sought federal help, demanding deportation of radicals and petitioning for federal troops, as if harking back to a time when the king protected the commons. State militias were thought to be ineffective; perhaps the call for federal troops gratified a fantasy of total annihilation of the enemy).

For six months intolerance and mounting violence would disturb the peace of San Diego. But although threats, intimidation, jailings, beatings, torture, kidnappings, a dynamite plot, the destruction of a newspaper office, death

22

lists and allegations of murder would soon excite newspaper readers, the affair got off to a slow start. The anti-street-speaking petition was presented to the Common Council on December 8, 1911. A few days later, 250 signed a counterpetition. Things were peaceful until January 6th, when a scuffle broke out between police and a gathering of Socialists and Single-Taxers. This event provoked the Common Council to pass the January 8th ordinance prohibiting street speaking in downtown San Diego. Caution still prevailed, however, for in spite of the declaration of an emergency, the City Attorney advised a thirty day delay to comply with a recent California court decision in a similar case. During this period, while the police merely kept an eye on street speakers, the California Free Speech League -- an organization of Wobblies, Socialists, labor leaders and unfashionable clergymen -- put out a leaflet condemning the ordinance.[8]

Had the street confrontation turned violent immediately, the shock of it might have brought a more responsible attitude to bear. As it was, the delay fostered expectations of a conflict. The town's informal conversation networks gave scope to the desire to be either the conductor of, or at least the audience for, the latest news, with the result that indignant speech became a familiar habit. The idea of vigilante action gained currency over a month's time.

By early February, threats were appearing in the newspapers. The San Diego _Union_ printed this suggestion by

former parks commissioner Clark Braly:

> Determined, representative men of San Diego should meet
> those fellows at the city limits, if they come, and
> drive them back with horsewhips as an expression from
> the people direct that they will not tolerate any of
> the disorder which these same fellows have created in
> other cities. . . . If good representative citizens
> volunteer to be deputized for this work, these fellows
> can take it as an expression from the people direct
> that we are determined to run our own affairs here and
> they can't raise the cry that good honest workingmen
> are persecuted and run down by the police who do not
> represent the real wishes of the people of our city.
> These fellows believe in popular government. Now let's
> give it to them if they come.

Braly stressed another concern of the business community:

> San Diego is approaching an important period in her
> history and with the development and progress now going
> on we can't afford to take any chances with these
> lawless troublemakers and get the disagreeable notori-
> ety that they have brought other cities. . . . I don't
> believe that guns and bloodshed are necessary. Horse-
> whips are enough to deal with these fellows.[9]

Thus, battle lines were drawn, sides chosen, pressure

mounted. Tolerance for the street speakers dwindled as

impatience to enforce the ordinance grew; the delay clouded

the reality of the violence that was contemplated. Then, on

Friday, February 9th, when the thirty day moratorium had

expired, forty one persons were arrested during a demonstra-

tion protesting the ordinance.

With this event, the local newspapers took an active

interest. Four papers served San Diego: the San Diego

Union, _Evening Tribune_, _Sun_, and _Herald_. The _Union_ and the

Evening Tribune were both against the IWW from the outset.

The _Sun_ for a time called for fair play when it learned of

24

the mistreatment of prisoners, but its criticisms soon became low-key and inoffensive. The _Herald_ alone printed the Wobblies' side of the story until the kidnapping and attempted murder of the editor and destruction of type forms silenced it. (Aside from the _Herald_, there were several weeklies that supported the free-speech fights -- _Free Speech_, published by the California Free Speech League; two labor weeklies, the San Francisco _Bulletin_ and the _Labor Leader_; and the IWW's _Solidarity_ and _Industrial Worker_.)

The newspapers opposed to the Wobblies echo back the angry words of editors, officials and citizens.[10] They also display a certain unthinking enthusiasm, much in the spirit of children tying cans to a dog's tail. For example, in an early story, the San Diego _Union_ parodied the free-speechers as if they were pagans sacrificing themselves on an altar:

> The first victim to mount the sacrificial box was on deck at 7 o'clock. . . . Early in the proceeding, someone with hoofs of the Chicago girl dimensions had planted them lightly on the box and wrecked it. But the demolished "altar" of "free speech" rather intensified the frenzy of its devotees and they offered up their voices and themselves from the level of the cobbles. (February 12, 1912, p. 7)

This circus atmosphere culminated in the fire hose incident of Sunday, March 10th, when police and citizens turned the fire brigade's hoses on a crowd of 3000 peaceful demonstrators. The papers treated it lightly:

> Numbers of citizens actually rushed into the street and helped carry the lines whenever required. Some even held the nozzle and directed the stream long enough to give the officers and firemen a chance to get a good

laugh as onlookers. Every member of the squad at the
police station, detectives included, took a willing
hand at the hose, elated at the chance to hang onto a
line. The firemen were as eager as the police, and it
was almost a continuous contest for the honor of manipulating the nozzle. (San Diego Union, March 11, 1912,
p. 1)

Arrests began in earnest with the passage on February
13th of a traffic ordinance aimed at street speakers.[11] As
the nightly speaking continued, the jails filled. High bail
and deliberate delays caused overcrowding -- on February
19th, Judge Sloan told two prisoners who asked for immediate
trials: "It would take about five days to each case, and
there are 100 ahead of you. Looks like you get a trial the
latter part of next year, doesn't it?"[12] Jail conditions
quickly deteriorated. A February 20th letter from a prisoner stated that seventy-eight prisoners were confined in a
space designed for twenty, the majority passing the nights
on concrete floors with no blankets. Another letter tells
of thirty-six men placed in a 16'x16' room with an open
toilet and little ventilation; of prisoners kicked and
threatened; of meals of 4 ounces of bread and mush in the
morning, and a like amount of stew or beans -- "sometimes
rotten and sour" -- at night.[13]

The San Diego Sun at first took a critical stance.[14]
Its February 15th headline read, "Free Speech Men Receive
Fate of Dogs."

Even those who are most opposed to free "speech" on the
streets are becoming aroused over the methods of the
municipal authorities in dealing with the men now under
arrest. Murderers, highwaymen, cut-throats of the
blackest type, porch-climbers, burglars, wife-beaters

and all kinds of criminals in jail in the past have been treated like royalty in comparison to the manner in which the street speakers are now being handled. (February 15, 1912, p. 1)

The *Sun* indicted the police leadership:

Since the free speech trouble has started, the police department, under Councilman John L. Sehon, has been guilty of inhuman, brutal treatment to free speech prisoners. . . . What Sehon has done or has allowed to be done by his police, has done more to make this fight a nasty one than any other one thing. Do the people want it to continue? (February 15, 1912, p. 1)

But the police evidently believed the harsh treatment had the approval of civic leaders.

The month's delay in enforcing the ordinance had permitted a rationale for suppression and an expectation of violent confrontation to ripen. Newspaper editorials were hate-filled:

For weeks the city has been infested by a gang of irresponsible tramps, thieves, outcasts and anarchistic agitators, calling themselves Industrial Workers of the World; these avowed enemies of society have undertaken to dictate to the citizens of San Diego how they conduct the affairs of the community; they have defied the laws which we have made for our self-government, insulted the officers of the law, and blasphemed the flag which represents the law of our land. They have not yet resorted to violence, but they have imposed themselves on the taxpayers of the community who are compelled to support scores of these worthless derelicts of humanity in the jails to which they are nightly marched by policemen instructed to enforce our laws. It is threatened that hundreds of others of the same class are on their way to San Diego to assist in compelling this city to acknowledge their right to dictate the processes that should govern the community.
Why are the taxpayers of San Diego compelled to endure this imposition? Simply because the law which these lawbreakers flout prevents the citizens of San Diego from taking the impudent outlaws away from the police and hanging them or shooting them. This method of dealing with the evil that has fastened itself on San Diego would end the trouble in half an hour. No more Industrial Workers of the World would come to San

27

Diego and we would thereafter live in peace as far as this disturbing element was concerned. (Evening Tribune March 5, 1912, p. 4)

———————————————————————————————

In San Diego and other communities that clashed with the Wobblies, language reducing them to a stereotype held a power akin to magical spells and curses. A number of labor, civic, and fraternal associations of San Diego formally condemned the Wobblies in words that functioned much the same as incantations in primitive cultures:

Whereas, the increase in anarchists in these United States, their bold defiance and violation of the law, the outrages perpetrated by them in all parts of the country, constantly increasing in number and enormity, their work of demoralization among the youth of the land, their open denunciation of the government and the flag, all of which is a menace to the peace and safety of the law-abiding people and has become a burden upon them, and
Whereas, further submission on the part of the people to these anarchistic outrages is not only a reproach but also a danger to this government; therefore, be it
Resolved, that we, the members of the Heintzelman Post, No. 33, of the Grand Army of the Republic, department of California and Nevada, in regular session assembled this 9th day of April 1912, do, in the name and memory of the hundreds of thousands of our comrades who laid down their lives so that this nation should live, hereby earnestly urge our senators and representatives in Congress to use their best endeavors to rid this land of the greatest growing evil (brought upon it by alien anarchists) by introducing and actively supporting measures in Congress making it a felony to carry or display in any procession or public place the red flag of anarchy, and providing for the deportation of all alien anarchists to the country from which they

28

came; and to establish a penal colony upon some one of our island possessions where citizens of this country who have become anarchists may be transported and detained, together with other such state criminals as may be sentenced thereto by the courts.[15]

In its formality, this denunciation has a quasi-reasonableness, listing grievances long suffered and asking for justice. But most of the complaints against the IWW were in the form of curses, hexes, imprecations, and murderous expressions, similar to the curse of one of the vigilantes, a Mr. John B. Osborne. Osborne first reprimanded the Reverend Dr. Thorp for mollycoddling the IWW -- "this ulcer which with its virulence is fevering our body politic." He then, in effect, pronounced anathema upon the enemies of his city:

If you Mr. Thorp, and a thousand more like you in this city would come out boldly in the open, and fearlessly, in the strength that should be born of the American blood that flows in your veins, and say in no uncertain tone to this foreign horde that is besetting and hampering us, and whose numbers are made up literally of the veritable offscouring of Europe and the dregs of every dissipation -- I repeat, if shoulder to shoulder you would stand up and be a man, since you have injected yourself into this war, and say with every other red-blooded American citizen: "By the grace of God our fathers redeemed this land with a price awful and precious in our sight, and neither you nor any other deluge of anarchy shall overthrow and beslime with unclean body and unholy touch this ark wherein lies our inalienable birth-right. Go, and go quickly from our midst, or else since constituted law and order cannot sufficiently deal with you, the primeval, primordial law of our nature, that God-given instinct within us of self-reliant, self-preservation, will fall upon you with terrible hand. Go, and never return to curse this community and foul the land that stood ever ready to give you honest work for your honest needs." (San Diego Union, May 21, 1912, p. 7)

Such derogations of the IWW, reiterated in community after community as a ritual prelude to action, confirm the view that speech has a dynamic power to affect the nature of things.[16] Enemies, like natural forces, must be classified in order to be controlled, and language, which condenses reality, is essentially a sorting and gathering process. It makes intelligible an inchoate field of sensory impressions, naming with familiar names, singling out and identifying discrete parts of experience, numbering and categorizing types of action and states of being, subduing the terrifying aspects of nature by naming and describing them. Language likewise harnesses the energy of human emotions by giving them names, capturing and making familiar and governable what would otherwise be the pandemonium of dreams. This naming property of language inheres in the primitive magical belief that to know the name of a person or a spirit is to acquire a degree of power over its owner, and there is a parallel motive in the conjuring of forceful epithets to choke off the Wobbly menace.[17]

This signifying function of language can be expressed in another way. In creating word-signs that stand for and name various separable features of reality, language is in effect creating roles for the things it names. One might further say that these are character roles, since words act as a cue, automatically guiding our understanding along familiar pathways, enabling us to gather in the meaning without having to pause to examine the undifferentiated reality which the words represent in a collapsed and stereotypic fashion. The world is thus ordinarily perceived not in its free permutability but through the mediating moiré of language, a filtered figure-ground Gestalt relationship wherein words in their roles as signs and symbols recreate the world -- with the most important result that we are enabled to communicate with others.

Analogously, social intercourse depends upon casting ourselves and others into recognizable roles, as social psychologists commonly observe. Accepting and operating within the metes and bounds of social roles is prerequisite to being able to act in a social setting. In a community such as San Diego -- where a man could be a civic leader, a business associate, an employer, a father, a husband, a church deacon or a libertine, a hunting or card-playing or drinking companion, a Republican or Democrat, a lodge member or Mason, Catholic or Protestant, devout or free-thinking, middle-class or working-class, Scotch or Irish, German or Italian, a Progressive booster or a moss-backed veteran of the Civil War -- social interaction proceeds on a basis of role-playing whereby intimates, friends, acquaintances, business contacts, strangers and rivals deal with one another in complicated and often overlapping roles that are themselves determined by sex, age, social status, occupation, etc.

In addition, roles are often historically determined. For example, to meet the demand for rational behavior required by industrial capitalism, men are required to suppress emotional life. In particular, middle class roles

31

complied with the demands of modern society for self-control, self-denial, and dedicated, orderly activity. The less that real emotional life entered into these roles, the more stereotypic they became, lacking flexibility, tolerance, and receptivity. This was less the case for women, who were encouraged to learn nurturant, affective roles; but for men in public life -- which most of the San Diego vigilantes were -- foreshortened, stereotypic views of themselves and others were unexceptional. Under intense pressure, such as was generated in the clash with the IWW, tolerance and communication were stymied in part because of the stereotyped responses of males.[18] It is useful to keep in mind that these contests with the IWW were primarily encounters between men who were beneficiaries of the economic system and men who were not. (This is not to say that women did not take part in the free-speech fights on both sides,[19] or did not share and help create the major beliefs and attitudes that underlay social life before the First World War.)

Under ordinary everyday circumstances the roles a man enters into are a convenient social shorthand, easing communication by tacit acceptance of the formulas and conventions that accompany a particular role (much as we "understand" the role of a man in a Santa Claus suit at a Christmas party). But fundamentally such roles are protective devices, projecting images of ourselves as we wish others to see us, and sparing us the anxiety engendered by the demands

32

for rationalized behavior.[20] In essence, role-playing
amounts to a defensive organization of the personality,
sheltering emotional life. We rarely reveal our secret view
of our own worth even to intimates, and the less intimate
our associations are, the more fixed and unelaborated are
the roles that we present to them.[21]

Thus role-playing is first and foremost a function of
language: the sundry mental images that we have of ourselves
and others are made substantive and transformed through
language into the roles we play or assign to others. The
extreme vilification of the IWW is a consequence of the
necessity to gain power over one's enemies. One must create
an image of the enemy that inspires fear (to motivate action) and contempt (to facilitate continued persecution),
but has no sympathetic human qualities. Such a perception
of the Wobblies projects hostile impulses onto the character
of others, an analogue of the scapegoat who is blamed for
the sins of others.[22]

Editors and others who spoke for the collective anxiety
of San Diego's business class thus anathematized the IWW.
The threatening behavior and impudence of the IWW evoked a
psychological response that transformed the Wobbly into an
evil destroyer.[23] Reducing a human being to a fixed, one
dimensional category serves a triple purpose. First, it
denies him his humanity and thus any sympathy for whatever
suffering he might endure:

If there was the slightest possibility of inflicting

33

upon these worthless creatures the full penalty provided for treason there would be no objection to giving
them the benefit of the rope. Hanging is none too good
for them, and they would be much better dead; for they
are absolutely useless in the human economy; they are
the waste material of creation and should be drained
off into the sewer of oblivion there to rot in cold
obstruction like any other excrement. (Editorial, San
Diego Evening Tribune, March 4, 1912, p. 4)

Second, it attributes a single-minded malevolence to him,

justifying ruthless suppression:

[S]eeing the motly [sic] procession of organized anarchists and vagabonds, carrying red flags, marching
through our cities, hearing as we do their wild curses
of our government, to hear these emissaries of hell
declaring that their purpose is to overthrow and destroy it, that its people shall become as they are, like
the aborigines of darkest Africa, without law or any
sense of justice or human rights, as are the beasts
which inhabit its jungles. (Former representative W.
W. Bowers in a speech to the G.A.R., San Diego Union,
March 30, 1912. p. 12.)

Finally, it robs him of his individuality, seeing him only

as an interchangeable part of a larger mass:

"There are still many of these fellows in the city,"
said Captain [Joseph] Meyers of the detective department this morning, "but the public can rest assured
that just as fast as we find them they will be taken
in; the work shall continue night and day and just as
fast as lawbreakers get into the city we will get them
out. It makes no difference how many come or for how
long they keep coming. San Diego is going to thoroughly rid itself of these vermin." (San Diego Evening Tribune, May 3, 1912, p. 1.)

Verbal abuse dehumanized Wobblies in preparation for physically abusing them. But why did the people of San Diego feel so threatened by the Wobblies? What menace required divesting them of human qualities? Their utterances reveal some of the ideas, often hidden in a cloud of outrage, that prompted a fearful response to the IWW.

The leading figure among those who wished to drive out the Wobblies was the Chief of Police, J. Keno Wilson. Because he was the official most often quoted, he helped legitimize extra-legal activity. He ordered arrests and determined the jail conditions, issued the nightsticks and rifles used in roundups and forced marches, turned a blind eye to the midnight removal of prisoners and to the use of truncheons on street speakers, deputized the vigilantes and supervised the use of tar-and-sagebrush at the county line. With the arrests on February 13th, Chief Wilson entered into his role as spokesman. After receiving Superintendent of Police Sehon's orders to "round up all male vagrants and hoboes," the Chief announced:

> We are going to rid the city of beggars and crooks and the idle who don't want to work. The many petty crimes and too-frequent holdups in San Diego . . . have got to end, if we have to arrest every vagrant in the city and drive them beyond the city's gates.[24]

Two themes in Wilson's declaration appear again and again in controversies involving the IWW. In the first, Wobblies are seen as a threat to the community, as invaders who will destroy the peace of the city. San Diego was a tranquil city in 1912, but as the anti-IWW rhetoric intensi-

35

fied, this tranquility was depicted as Edenic. In the second theme, the Wobblies -- the "I Won't Work" brigade -- are seen as hoboes and idlers. Their supposed shiftlessness was troubling because it transgressed against an internalized behavior, the work ethic. The IWW did recruit in the hobo jungles and among the migrant "bindlestiffs" -- the "Overall Brigade" and "The Bummery" -- who felled timber, picked fruit and harvested grain. The very nature of the IWW raised fear and hatred.

The first theme in Chief Wilson's warning refers to purifying the city, protecting it from barbaric destroyers. This imagery reflects a great fear of being contaminated by an underclass. As the troubles in San Diego mounted, the image of a beleaguered town appeared often, with the IWW in the role of outlaws and outcasts. The police were going to "keep back the approaching hordes"; it was a "fact that bands of lawless men are headed for San Diego for the avowed purpose of punishing this community"; there were "approaching forces of lawbreakers," and an "advancing army of anarchists"; a speaker at a G.A.R. meeting praised the police for "protecting this city from the assaults of vandals."[25] The San Diego Sun printed a statement sent by the City Council to Governor Hiram Johnson that said in part:

> It is our belief that when a threat is made to disorganize the city or her forces by a band of men marching from without for the purpose of laying siege to her laws, that we have the right to resist the invaders to the utmost. In this fight for her autonomy -- for the preservation of laws and order inside her boundaries, San Diego hopes that she has the good wishes of the

people of the State of California and that the Governor elected by all the people of the State will see to it that no body of men, whether armed or otherwise, will ever be permitted to use the great highways of the State for the unholy purpose to which these people propose to devote them. (April 25, 1912, p. 9)

These utterances, like Chief Wilson's pledge to "drive them beyond the city's gates," have the biblical ring common to much public parlance of the times, and bring to mind walled cities guarded by strong and vigilant townsmen. This picture accords with pre-World War I versions of history that presented the past as a long train of war, seige, and the moral decay of civilizations. Bible stories and history lessons were regarded as moral instruction for the defense of virtue both in the individual and in the state.[26] Combined with living memories and legends of American frontier settlements beset by Indians, history seen as a succession of besieged towns and civilizations predisposed embattled police and vigilantes to think of themselves as driving back invaders. Such phrases as "city gates" or "our fair city" thus became symbolic figures of speech that activated powerful feelings of patriotism and duty.

On another level, invasion and repulsion are such common images in the statements issued by police chiefs and others in towns menaced by Wobblies, that they can be viewed as reflections of a fundamental psychological drama in which there is a constant struggle to contain and redirect libidinal energy. Insofar as the Wobblies were thought of as rapacious barbarians, the ubiquity of this walled-town ima-

37

gery can be explained as a manifestation of the need to defend against aggressive instincts by projecting them onto others. From this point of view, it is difficult to resist the conjecture that such lurid evocation of pillage and rapine has its origin in what classical psychoanalytic theory calls repressed material. Blocked from consciousness and allowed to appear only in disguised form, such material is often projected onto the character and motivations of others.[27] This is an appealing explanation for the universal excoriation of the Wobblies and other radicals, invested by the public's imagination with unrestrained aggression and sexual appetite. It can also account for vigilante excesses, if we agree with Freud that punishment is often vicarious commission of the prohibited offense.[28]

Projections of sexual fantasies are apparent in the frequent ascription of lasciviousness to Wobblies and other left-wing extremists. As the suffragette, temperance, bohemian, and radical movements demonstrated, the pre-war period was one of increasing anxiety over sexual values and the proper role of women. The "free love" of certain radical free-thinkers was regularly condemned and it was often said that radicals, Socialists, Wobblies, anarchists, reds, etc., wanted to communalize women.[29] The fear and anger this provoked suggest that such imagined excesses aroused aggressive libidinal fantasies that social conditioning had made unacceptable. At the core of this concern was a veiled threat to property ownership. Ownership validated one's independence and personal control; radicals and independent-

minded women were dangerous because they threatened not only

social and psychosexual control, but property relations as

well.[30]

The Wobblies posed a second threat to property. Since

property ownership was predicated upon work and its virtues,

the belief that the IWW scorned work and the work ethic

caused great anxiety. Chief Wilson, for example, was upset

by the "idle who don't want to work." He expressed disbe-

lief that anyone could question the idea of work:

> These men are hoboes who are coming in for the purpose
> of filling the jail, hoping that soon we will have no
> place to put them. In this they will be disappointed.
> None of them wants work -- in fact one man I know of
> quit his job in a grading camp to come to Fifth and E
> Streets and be arrested as a street speaker. I went to
> these men in the courtroom, just now, and offered all
> of them work. Not one would accept.[31]

A letter to the editor makes a similar complaint:

> It is a strange thing that men who labor the year round
> for their own and their families' support should coun-
> tenance such wandering tramps and trouble-makers --
> parasites upon the community -- who are the worst ene-
> mies the labor unions have. If the real working men
> will set their faces and close their purse against such
> idle tramps they will be doing a good work. The hun-
> dred or more idle lawbreakers now in jail had rather be
> confined there and supported in idleness than to do any
> honest labor.[32]

The Wobbly, with his flamboyance and his contempt for

the sacred cows of capitalism, soon came to epitomize the lazy tramp. Scores of newspaper and magazine articles, such as a New York Tribune article entitled "Work and the Police: Mortal Foes of the I.W.W.," excoriated the "I Won't Work" gang:

> The thing is simple. The I.W.W. will run every-
> thing -- just how they do not tell. But that is insig-
> nificant, so long as there is little real work for them
> to do and lots of time for play. You see, it is this
> way. Society is all wrong. It needs turning over.
> Ergo, we should permit Mr. Tannenbaum [of the IWW] to
> superintend the flip-flop. When these little matters
> are arranged the I.W.W. will have proved that the old
> philosopher was right who thought that the earth was
> turning into a bun and the sea into lemonade, that
> mankind might be happy without effort. They are rea-
> sonably happy as matters stand at present. Their regu-
> lar job is war, and their religion is the ever present
> prayer that they may eat, drink and land on the front
> page of the capitalistic press, without working. When
> they can do this -- and their batting average has been
> over .300 since the leaves fell -- they go into mysti-
> cal raptures. . . .
> The general public is wise to the fact that an
> idle dog is mangy. It can discriminate between genuine
> distress and the flannel-mouthed howling of cheap sen-
> timent by a group of men whose avowed belief is that
> the world owes them a good time and nothing to do.
> There is plenty to do but there are plenty of others to
> do it. To the credit of the I.W.W leaders it must be
> said that they make no secret of their beliefs and
> determinations. There is nothing vague about their
> demands. As a bunch they are scurrilously candid.[33]

Idleness was the bête noire of the middle class. Nine-teenth century American schoolbooks taught that moral worth was dependent upon the exercise of industry, perserverance and frugality. Those who failed deserved what they got.[34] Pre-war America put great faith in the work ethic. Captains of industry were cited as examples of the self-made man by popular speakers such as Russell Conwell and James Roscoe

Day.[35] Commercial clubs and trade and manufacturing asso-

ciations, which proliferated during the first decade and a

half of the twentieth century in response to union agita-

tion, socialism, and governmental regulation, all stressed

the virtue of work and the vice of idleness:

> [T]he salvation and success of the "dear people" de-
> pends on their own willingness to work, and the fellows
> who won't work at all, or who will work only eight
> hours per day, will not get anywhere! The genius of
> success is work! Supreme effort only achieves supreme
> success. . . . The socialistic, demagogic penalizing
> and punishment of thrift, honesty, industry and all
> that is good in men, is for the benefit of the "I won't
> work" folks and all those who are vile and vicious. . .
> "Opportunity" (so loudly called for) comes to everyone
> who is willing to work and wait, and never has and
> never will come to the "I won't workers," nor will it
> ever come to those who won't work more than eight hours
> a day.[36]

Such a valuation of work, as expressed by this contri-

butor to American Industry, the official organ of the Na-

tional Association of Manufacturers, is a key to understan-

ding the opposition to the Wobblies. As with the function-

ing of roles, this idea of work has both a psychological and

a historical basis. Freud provided an insight into "the

significance of work for the economics of the libido":

> No other technique for the conduct of life attaches the
> individual so firmly to reality as laying emphasis on
> work; for his work at least gives him a secure place in
> a portion of reality, in the human community. The
> possibility it offers of displacing a large amount of
> libidinal components, whether narcissictic, aggressive
> or even erotic, on to professional work and on to the
> human relations connected with it lends it a value by
> no means second to what it enjoys as something indis-
> pensible to the preservation and justification of exis-
> tence in society. . . . And yet, as a path to happi-
> ness, work is not highly prized by men. They do not
> strive after it as they do after other possibi-lities
> of satisfaction. The great majority of people only

work under the stress of necessity, and this natural human aversion to work raises most difficult social problems.[37]

Work under modern conditions, as Freud notes, involves stress as well as reward. The stress stems not only from shunting aggressive or libidinal energies into work, but from the effects of the behavior demanded by industrialized work. Historically, ideas about the work ethic evolved along with capitalism; the utility of rational method and emotional control was advanced by the entrepreneurial middle class, not by the laboring class. That the laboring poor were denied parity in the economic and social system is the fundamental flaw in the moral basis of the free market theory of the late nineteenth and early twentieth centuries.[38] The demand for emotional control and rational effort must be seen as a technique of a dominant class to implement its desire for independence and to escape a traditional culture's passivity.[39] Hence the unshakeable loyalty to the work ethic, and the real anger at those who would ridicule or subvert it. The need to accumulate capital gave great emotional significance to work.

At root, the idea of work represents the possibility of becoming and remaining free. Labor, when conceived of as a commodity, may be exchanged for money, which upon accumulation can be converted into property, assuring power and independence. Thus Benjamin Franklin, Max Weber's capitalist ideal-type, insisted that debt forfeited liberty: his advice was to "be industrious and free; be frugal and free."[40]   That the object was not to suffer but to enjoy life was never lost on those who recommended hard work.[41] Nor was it doubted that illegality, political influence, and chance played their part.[42]   Nevertheless, although what a man does may be the opposite of what he believes he is doing, what he believes is fundamental to his peace of mind, to the ease with which he takes up his roles in life.   Thus these ideas about work came to be revered as an ethical formula, whose observance is seen as an indispensible condition of freedom.   Further, reverence for the formula varies inversely with its success: the more plodding one's progress on the road to riches, the more one believes the signposts along the way.

In effect, belief in the work ethic is a means of social control.   In order to secure and maintain the independence derived from ownership, a regime of emotional control and purposeful, ordered activity is required.   Diligence, thrift, sobriety and prudence permitted accumulation at the expense of inhibited desires.   Thus the wish to be free and autonomous has deep psychosocial roots.   It requires a continuous struggle against the countervailing wish to be nurtured, to remain passive, to give up control, to behave impulsively, to abandon oneself to sensuality. Giving in would result in loss of independence and be judged a moral failing.[43]   To survive and be free under capitalism requires controlled social behavior.   In order to control emotion and specify rational activity, an internalized pattern of behavior must be established; to trespass beyond it occasions great anxiety and loss of self-esteem. Any who violate it are viewed with alarm, provoking inflexible reactions and often violence.

This pattern of behavior thus takes on a life of its own; conformity is demanded by those who control property in the society. Although liberal-democratic theory (as descended from Hobbes and Locke) justified unlimited appropriation and enshrined the right to property as a natural law, a more fundamental basis for ownership lies in the psychological equation between property acquisition and freedom: ownership of property is a criterion of independence and an affirmation of personal control. Failure to accumulate property, on the other hand, is a sign of moral weakness and dependent status. Traditionally, those without property were not equal members of society; women, children, and workers were excluded from full participation.

Thus, the class differentiation that underlay the San Diego conflict had a powerful psychological basis.[44] The challenge to the time-honored work ethic by radicals who appeared to refuse to work was so baffling, their demands so infuriating, that it is small wonder they were regarded as a separate, inferior class. To the Wobbly, being accused of willful idleness showed a poor understanding of working conditions in industrial America. But to the police chief and the vigilantes of San Diego, conduct regulated by the work ethic was the right and proper way of the world. Those who challenged its rightness were to be hated:

> San Diego's house is swept and garnished. Let it
> remain so. All the vermin that has infested the commu-
> nity during the past month or so has been eliminated.
> It is now the function of the police authorities to
> preserve the city in its condition of cleanliness. . .
> Recently, however, there has been an effort by a hybrid
> so-called "labor organization" to change these condi-
> tions [of labor peace and good life]. Gangs of these
> parasites have swarmed in upon us from the overpopu-
> lated outside communities with the avowed purpose of
> compelling the thrifty working men to divide their
> income with the parasites of labor -- with the agita-
> tors and anarchists of what are called the Industrial
> Workers of the World, who propose to blackmail the
> property owner, the working man, and the capitalist
> into yielding a large proportion of what they have
> honestly earned by their ability and industry, for the
> emolument of incompetents, lazy loafers, impudent beg-
> gars, and unnaturalized foreigners who were compelled
> to leave their native country for that country's good
> and have settled here to defy the laws of this country,
> insult the country's flag, and stir dissension among
> industrious, contented people.[45]

CHAPTER 3

VIGILANTE ORDER AND CIVIL LIBERTIES IN THE SAN DIEGO FREE SPEECH FIGHT

It is not possible to make the ordinary mortal
man understand what toleration and liberty really
mean. He will accept them verbally with alacri-
ty, even with enthusiasm, because the word toleration has been moralized by eminent Whigs; but
what he means by toleration is toleration of
doctrines that he considers enlightened, and, by
liberty, liberty to do what he considers right;
that is, he does not mean toleration of liberty
at all; for there is no need to tolerate what
appears enlightened or to claim liberty to do
what most people consider right. Toleration and
liberty have no sense or use except as toleration
of opinions that are considered damnable, and
liberty to do what seems wrong.

-- George Bernard Shaw (Preface to
The Showing Up of Blanco Posnet)

In San Diego, the stage was set for the violence and
vigilante terror that followed the first arrest in February
of 1912. By early March, some 200 men crowded jails in San
Diego and surrounding communities. San Diego County authorized armed mounted patrol of the approaches to the city.
Following the March 10th use of fire-hoses on a large crowd
of demonstrators, vigilante activity began in earnest with
"deportations" and beatings on a near-nightly schedule.

46

March 22nd saw the introduction of midnight raids on the jail and vigilante gauntlets at the outskirts of town. On March 28th, a previously hale 65-year-old Wobbly died, allegedly of injuries suffered in a jail beating. On April 5th, with tempers at a breaking point, 100 IWW's were met at the Orange County line, forced to kiss the flag and run the gauntlet. That same evening, Abram R. Sauer, editor of the San Diego _Herald_, was kidnapped and threatened with death should he persist in his "unpatriotic" support for the free speech fighters.[1] Tension mounted; the vigilance committee publicly proclaimed its mission:

> We, the law-abiding citizens of this commonwealth, think that these anarchists have gone far enough and we propose to keep up the deportation of those undesirable citizens as fast as we can catch them, and that hereafter they will not only be carried to the county line and dumped there, but we intend to leave our mark on them in the shape of tar well rubbed into their hair so that a shave will be necessary to remove it, and this is what these agitators (all of them) may expect from now on, that the outside world may know that they have been to San Diego.
> (signed) THE VIGILANTEES[2]

California Governor Johnson announced he was sending Harris Weinstock, a respected businessman and an influential Democrat, to San Diego as a special commissioner to investigate the disturbances there. Harris' arrival on April 15th and the news of the Titanic's sinking temporarily blunted vigilante activity, but after a week of spirited public discussion and inquiry, it resumed. On the night of April 22nd, dozens of "vagrants" were herded into corrals, stripped, robbed, beaten, and "forced to run the gantlet of 106

47

men, 55 on each side of the [railroad] track, variously armed with pistols, wheel spokes, bull whips and rifles."[3]

On May 4th, the city asked for federal help from the Department of Justice. On May 7th, a fight left two policemen injured and a Wobbly dead. This event inflamed passions on both sides; rifles were issued to the vigilantes, nightly patrols were beefed up, and a general roundup of suspicious itinerants ensued. The emotional peak was reached with the arrival on May 14th of anarchists Emma Goldman and Ben Reitman. Jeering crowds waving small American flags met them, and that evening Reitman was kidnapped by vigilantes who drove him into the desert, tortured him, and left him with a coat of tar and "my underwear for fear I should meet some women."[4] The next night, May 15th, vigilantes broke into the offices of the San Diego Herald and pied the forms; on the 16th a committee visited the editor, Sauer, and told him he could publish only what passed their censorship. On the 18th, Commissioner Weinstock released a report blaming both the IWW and the vigilantes. That night nineteen prisoners were taken from the jail and forced to run 22 miles to Sorrento, flanked by mounted officers wielding horsewhips.[5]

It is difficult to gauge the real impact of these disturbances on San Diego, or to estimate the numbers involved. Various commentators have suggested that as many as 5,000 Wobblies or sympathizers passed through San Diego during the months of the free speech fight; certainly hundreds were jailed and/or subjected to vigilante methods.

The vigilantes claimed to have recruited 1,000 men, but how many participated is impossible to determine.[6] Much of the vigilante activity occurred on Friday or Saturday nights. In a city of some 50,000, the pace of everyday life was hardly affected. Work, school, church and civic activities proceeded uninterruptedly for most of the population.

There were early attempts to head off the confrontation. Several Councilmen endorsed the idea of setting aside a city lot for public meetings. The Free Speech League was formed in hopes of mediating the dispute. At first, The San Diego _Sun_ and a few public figures complained about the brutality,[7] and the _Sun_ took the clergy to task:

> Not a voice was raised from the pulpit in San Diego yesterday for or against the right of free speech, greatly to the surprise of those who are fighting for it, and for that reason the ministers of San Diego were today officially requested to throw themselves into the fight and to use their influence for a peaceful and righteous solution to the problem. (San Diego _Sun_, February 12, 1912, p. 1)

But these voices soon fell silent. The public regarded the Wobblies as nuisances but, with the exception of a few individuals, was silent as vigilante activity became widespread (see Appendix III).

The vigilante committee soon came to intimidate the community they were trying to protect. If the function of law is to sanction punishment without creating conscious guilt, then vigilantes, acting outside the law, must also distribute liability as widely as possible, in imitation of the law. This requires repetition of the reasons why vigi-

49

lante action is necessary; an editorial printed the day
after the kidnapping of the editor of the San Diego _Herald_
is an example:

> There is an unwritten law that permits a citizen to
> avenge his outraged honor. There is an unwritten law
> that permits a community to defend itself by any means
> in its power, lawful or unlawful, against any evil
> which the operation of the written law is inadequate to
> oppose or must oppose by slow, tedious and unnecessar-
> ily expensive processes. The citizens of San Diego are
> prepared to appeal to this unwritten law in the exis-
> ting emergency, menaced as the city is by the threat
> that thousands of avowed lawbreakers are intending to
> invade the city. . . .
>   If there are any citizens of San Diego who sympa-
> thize with these anarchists, they should rid the city
> of their presence. They are not wanted here, and if
> they go so far as to insist upon the "free speech" of
> anarchy and disloyalty, they will not be tolerated.
> This is San Diego's ultimatum: We claim the right to
> defend ourselves against these confessed outlaws, and
> we claim the right to choose our weapons of defense.
> If the sword of our own law is turned against us, we
> claim the right, under the unwritten law, to resort to
> the law of nature. (San Diego _Evening Tribune_, April
> 6, 1912, p. 4)

Investing vigilante activity with legal worth underscores
the likelihood that such activity can turn on the vigilantes
themselves, since without the protection of due process
anyone may become a victim. Any vigilante who does not
repeatedly swear allegiance challenges the moral correctness
of the repression; thus suspicion, secrecy and terror are an
ultimate outcome of vigilantism.[8]

Under such circumstances, appeals for moderation had
little chance, and public dissent went unexpressed. Pressure for patriotic display grew: Councilman Woods sold flag
buttons at ten cents apiece; merchants twice exhausted their
supply of small silk flags; the city substituted American

flags for red flags on street construction projects; a crowd
of 1,000, waving little American flags and singing the "Star
Spangled Banner," gathered at Emma Goldman's hotel.[9] The
San Diego Union urged: "Let every loyal citizen of San Diego
wear the little flag on his lapel. It is the flag of York-
town and Gettysburg. No American citizen need be reluctant
to wear it, and wearing it his neighbors and fellow citizens
will know just where he stands on a question that just now
is of vital importance to San Diego." (May 24, 1912, p. 4).
The Union portrayed the vigilantes as determined patriots:

> Immediately after the signal of five whistles, repeated
> three times, was blown from the electric power plant
> whistles at 9:35 o'clock, determined-looking men, some
> of them armed, commenced arriving at the police sta-
> tion, first in twos and threes, then in tens and twen-
> ties. . . . Few of the men who gathered at the call
> knew what duty would be required of them during the
> hours of the night, but there was a general feeling
> among all that there would be need for strong arms and
> unfaltering courage, backed by a determination to obey
> orders, and the tenor of those orders was known to be
> to rid the city of the I.W.W.[10]

Nativism, as well as patriotism, animated the free
speech fight in San Diego. Among the leaders of the vigilantes were men of Scotch-Irish and German descent: Bierman,
Braly, Brodnax, Burkham, Burnham, Chamberlain, Dodge, Fer-
ris, Fisher, Fishburn, Forbes, Forward, Goodwin, Hall, Jew-

51

ell, Johnson, Julian, Lea, Litzenberg, Ludington, Moore, Parker, Payson, Porter, Sears, Wangenheim and Walsh. The political administration also had "American" names: Mayor Wadham; Councilmen Adams, Dodson, Fay, Sehon, Spaulding, Woods; City Attorney Andrews; District Attorney Utley and the Assistant D.A.s Walton and McKee; Judges Bryan, Guy, Lewis, Putterbaugh, Sloan; the Police Department's Carson, DeLaCour, Haddon, Hathaway, McDuell, Meyers, Moriarty, Sheppard, Stevens, Wilson and Wisler; and State Senator Wright. Others among the business community had names like Bell, Bingham, Bowers, Brooks, Fox, Magee, Marston, Schultz.[11] Ironically, though some of those arrested had names of South and Central European provenance, most of the free speech fighters and their supporters had "American" names: Brooks, Cassidy, Emerson, Evans, Fraser, Hawkins, Kirk, McAvoy, McKay, Morgan, Moore, Pierce, Quinn, Robbins, Stone, Wightman, Whyte, and so on. That they were perceived as foreigners is an example of the stereotypic attribution necessary to reduce the enemy to a manageable image.

Character typing, based on then-popular racist interpretations of physiognomy, provided a sinister but contemptible scapegoat; descriptions of the IWW almost invariably characterized them not only as foreign but as foreign-looking, unkempt, illiterate, near-imbecilic, shifty-eyed:

> The first prisoner arrested was a youth who wore a pair
> of large rimmed spectacles. He walked along with aim-
> less step. . . . Most of the men were foreigners.
> Their clumsy tongues and awkward gait would indicate
> that some Atlantic Liner poured them but a few years

ago from its hold on American shores to spread a new
doctrine of freedom which is strange to American ears.
(San Diego Union, February, 17, 1912, p. 13)
 Eighty-one half-starved, frowsy members of the
I.W.W., most of them illiterate, half of them foreigners, and every one an avowed enemy of all that the
United States government and its flag stands for . . .
started for San Diego. . . . Most of them were brought
from Oakland and about half are foreigners. They were
disheveled and unkempt. The police said that every
face was strange. . . . (San Diego Evening Tribune, May
7, 1912, p. 1; San Diego Sun, May 7, 1912, p. 8)

These patriotic and racial sentiments demonstrate the

role stereotyping that is a necessary prelude to action

against an outgroup. However, although the newspapers put

forth these ideas daily, it is hard to know who in the

community fully accepted them. When such ideas become the

basis for violence, it is likely that they are both believed

and disbelieved by a passive public. This paradox results

from fear of physical violence, and fear of identifying with

the victims. One believes because it is safer to do so; yet

one cannot believe totally in ideas justifying violence

because of the awareness that there is little difference

between oneself and others.

 This is a common phenomenon in wars and police states,

but it is also a response to vigilantism. The result of

such intellectual coercion is that racist ideas degenerate

(like stereotyped roles) into the shorthand of slogans.

When extra-legal violence affects a community, the authority

of slogans derives both from the ongoing violence and its

eventual bureaucratization. Citizens become incapable of

focussing their thinking and withdraw. In San Diego, exaggerated characterization of the IWW was tolerated by non-participants, because most shared well-rooted negative ideas about the IWW.

In 1912, the political elite of San Diego was synonymous with the business elite: leading businessmen served as Councilmen, Commissioners, Supervisors, Superin-tendents and Mayors past and present. A close-knit group, its members nearly all agreed the "invading army" of Wobblies posed a threat. The vigilante committee was drawn from the business community: it included 4 presidents of real estate companies, 2 bankers, the Assistant Superintendent of Streets, a rancher and former Parks Commissioner, a theater owner, a contractor, a County Supervisor, and a former mayor and present foreman of the Grand Jury engaged in handing down indictments of the IWW.[12]

A plausible correlation exists between such homogeneous leadership and the violence of IWW free speech fights. The most sensational confrontations occurred in smaller-sized cities and towns, where a political circle with similar outlooks was unlikely to be checked by internal dissent when the Wobblies challenged them. Without strong opposition, violence escalates; once vigilante action is decided upon, civic pride is invoked, energies are released, roles are set and occupied, stances are taken, lines are crossed, and no one can quite explain how things happened so fast. (If the materials were available, it would be interesting to review free speech confrontations in terms of game theory. In San

Diego, for example, there were covert limits to the behavior
of the contestants: the IWW remained non-violent, and the
vigilantes, though displaying firearms, preferred clubs,
fists and feet; the rhetoric on either side followed predic-
table formulae; truces occurred regularly, and activity
peaked on weekends. Care was taken on both sides to restrict confrontation to certain symbolic locations, and to
limit the involvement of the rest of the population.)

The attitude of the police in San Diego, as elsewhere,
was crucial. The chief of police shared the property-
owners' disgust with the "idleness" of the Wobblies, and
fostered the belief that the city was besieged by a murderous gang of anarchists. The rest of the police force, with
the exception of four who resigned in protest, apparently
accepted their duty to curb the Wobblies.[13] (This does not
mean that police in San Diego or elsewhere were merely tools
of the business class. Instances where local police forces
supported labor in industrial conflicts -- deputizing strikers and arresting strike breakers, etc. -- demonstrate that
police response varies with the political and cultural context. State police or private police, however, were ordinarily under the control of business elites.[14])

55

Generally the police administration, as in San Diego in 1912,[15] was tied to the political machine. Ward politics, often based on the working class, were the most accessible avenues to power for rising immigrant groups. Although there is no available demographic analysis of the San Diego police force in 1912, the presence of Police Superintendent (and political boss) John Sehon, Police Chief Wilson, Detective Moriarty, and others on the force with Irish patronyms supports the popular image of the Irish cop,[16] and suggests that police work in San Diego was part of a patronage system.[17] The non-meritocratic nature of patronage and the non-democratic form of police organization conflicted with the democratic values police were expected to support. Because police work tends to attract insecure, control-oriented personalities, local police were not only tied to the political machine, they were likely to be predisposed to use violence in subduing protesters. The political ties of local police were reinforced by the low degree, or non-existence, of professionalism -- police work, though generally well-paid, was not a career, and often only a type of migratory employment.[18]

Thus although police almost always identified with property-owners in clashes with the IWW, the reasons were complex. Among police rank and file, it was not so much class division as class competition that spurred antagonism towards the Wobblies. The IWW was not only a rival working class group; it challenged traditional values. Policemen recruited from the working class were all too familiar with the lives of the migratory workers and unemployed roustabouts that the IWW courted, and many tried to distance themselves from the IWW. In addition, police recruited from a rising immigrant group had an economic motive to identify with business interests.

In San Diego the police cooperated with the vigilantes, in spite of occasional denials by the chief. Such collusion was revealed in nearly every newspaper story about the disturbances. For example, a story about the removal of prisoners from the jail for a rendezvous with waiting vigilantes leaves no doubt about the police role:

> Fifteen pale, lean-jawed men, strung together with clanking handcuffs, filed slowly down the side stairway of the police station and grimly climbed into a big auto truck of the fire department that waited in the courtway between the station and the jail, at 9:30 last night. There was no light, all the jail electrics were switched off, the street lights were out, and clouds obscured the moon. Coated, slouch-hatted gunmen sat silent in the truck, silhouetted in the darkness, their rifles pointed upward. No one spoke. The prisoners, each of whom had denounced the flag of the United States, and sullenly, with words of hatred, professed himself a follower of the I.W.W. horde, reluctantly mounted the steps of the truck for the ride north -- destination not announced.
> They heard Chief Wilson say, "Take these men to the lower camp and tell the guards to start them walking away from San Diego in the morning." Policemen assembled in the arena smiled with grim understanding of the order. They would obey the order if they could, but if a thousand maddened, angry citizens of San Diego should appear upon the road and overpower the handful of gunmen guarding the prisoners, they could not be held to answer for the consequences.
> More than a dozen automobiles left just before or after the prison van. Citizens grouped about the darkened station conversed in subdued tones. Five minutes later the lights flashed up, the crowd was gone, and the night routine of the police department was once

more under way. (San Diego _Union_, April 5, 1912, p. 10)

In all the violent free-speech incidents surveyed, the police were centrally involved. That the police leadership determined the course of events is pointed up by the refusal of the San Diego County Sheriff, Fred Jennings, to assist the city authorities and the vigilantes. In a newspaper interview (preceded by the paper's comment deploring his lack of support) Sheriff Jennings stated his position:

> When the grand jury in the last previous session asked me to establish a guard at the county line, I refused, believing I had no authority to turn back any persons coming into the county. I remain convinced that I have no authority to do so. Even if an armed body of 500 men invaded the county and peacefully walked along the highways, I believe I would have no authority to turn them back. Unless some overt violation of the law is committed, I have no authority to make arrests. If this is done, this office will be "Johnnie-on-the-spot." But even if I had authority to make arrests, I would have to bring the men here and lock them up. In no case would I have authority to drive them back. Indeed, should I see persons being driven back and beaten, it would be my duty to arrest the men doing the driving . . . . The district attorney has ordered me to patrol the county line and I have made no move to do so because I believe to follow his instructions would be to exceed my authority. Perhaps I will be indicted by the grand jury. In fact, I rather expect to be. (San Diego _Evening Tribune_, April 26, 1912, p. 3)

Sheriff Jennings was not indicted (nor were any vigilantes), but his example was ignored. The probability that things might have been different had Jennings been in charge underscores the crucial role of the police leadership.

One of the few attitude surveys on this subject was conducted in the late fall of 1920 by the fledgling American Civil Liberties Union. Sent to cities of over 10,000 population, eighty-eight chiefs of police responded to questions

58

regarding police attitudes towards free speech and assembly

for radicals. In 74 of these cities, police required per-

mits for street meetings (the Salvation Army, very active in

these years, rarely fell under this requirement). Of the 88

cities, "only 11 recognized the unrestricted right to meet

upon the public streets," and although 56 required no permit

for meetings in private halls, "21 stated that meetings on

private property are not allowed without a police permit."

Several chiefs replied that such powers, usually assumed

without legal authorization, were informally applied to

private halls, as in the instance of the Police Superinten-

dent at Lowell, Mass., "who says that in the past he 'has

spoken to parties,' and suggested that they refuse to rent

their premises 'and they have always complied.'"[19]

This casual assumption of the power to regulate speech

and assembly illustrates the important role of the police

leadership. Chiefs were hired not for their knowledge of

the law or the criminal justice system, but for their poli-

tical savvy, their leadership, and their connections. Of-

ten, they enforced their personal conception of the law,

which usually reflected property-owners' notions of proprie-

ty and good behavior. Among the general conclusions the

A.C.L.U. drew from its survey was a finding that "the police

act against radicals in response to what they conceive to be

their 'patriotic duty' regardless of the authority of ordi-

nance or state laws."[20]

When San Diego stepped outside the law, its justification was the "unwritten law":

> Whatever may be the ultimate outcome of the conditions
> now existing in this city, it is certain that they
> would have been infinitely worse if the citizens had
> not taken the law which they have themselves made into
> the hand that created the law, and by the firm adminis-
> tration of the law above all other law -- the law of
> self-preservation -- have saved the community from riot
> and bloodshed.[21]

Such intolerance of hateful expression ironically reveals

the power that language exerts on perceptions of reality.

The necessity to anathematize and stereotype antagonists

gives rise to the belief that words are deeds. This idea

was so commonly assumed that it was rarely articulated.[22]

In the 1920 A.C.L.U. survey of police chiefs, the inability

to distinguish between speech and action was apparent in the

responses to two questions that probed the reasons police

interfered with street meetings:

> One question inquired whether the police are instructed
> to interfere if they believe that dangerous speeches
> are being made, and the other whether they are instruc-
> ted not to interfere until some act in violation of law
> is committed. It will be noted that these two ques-
> tions contain an opposition in ideas. You cannot in-
> terfere when dangerous speeches are being made and at
> the same time wait for a overt act in violation of law.
> In spite of this contradiction, 34 police chiefs out of
> 68 answered "yes" to both questions! . . . Of the 34
> answers from the chiefs who got the point of these two
> questions, 16 replied that they would wait for some act
> of violation of law before interfering while 18 said
> they would interfere without waiting for an act.[23]

Some responses indicated a familiarity with the consti-

tutional guarantee of free speech, but some, like the reply

of the Police Commissioner of Montgomery, Ala., were con-

fused:

So long as any citizen, in speaking his sentiments,

conducts himself in an orderly manner, does not violate
any of our laws against obscene conduct, does not make
a nuisance out of himself, does not violate the Espionage Act when the United States is at war, he would be
protected in the exercise of his constitu-tional right
of free speech. Of course we would not permit any
speeches advocating the overthrow of the United States
Government, or preaching anarchy or sedition.[24]

Although this survey was made in the aftermath of the Red

Scare, when attitudes towards radicals had hardened, it

echos sentiments of a decade earlier.

A sampling of attitudes about the 1912 San Diego free-

speech fight shows a similar willingness to deny speech to

radicals. The Stockton Independent, in an editorial commen-

ding "the armed citizens of San Diego who gathered the 100

anarchists in a circle at dawn and made them kneel and kiss

the folds of the flag," warned that

too little attention is paid the soap box gentry who
shout treason day and night from the street curbs.
Tolerating treasonable utterance and the recognition of
free speech are in no sense akin. The mouthings of
harmless individuals can well be suffered smilingly,
but when groups of men make actual invasions under a
banner of anarchy, it is high time that they be held to
strict accountability for their utterances and their
acts. (Reprinted in the San Diego Union, April 10,
1912, p. 4)

The San Diego Evening Tribune explained: "If Emma Gold-

man had been allowed to speak in San Diego on any subject,

however innocuous, however 'philosophical,' however mildly

anarchistic, others of her cult would have been encouraged

to follow her, preaching doctrines that are absolutely dis-

tasteful to the citizens of this city." Without such prior

restraint, the editorial continued, "it is more than proba-

ble that even William D. Haywood, the chief of the I.W.W.'s, would have hastened to San Diego to reorganize the scattered and discomfited battalions of his tatterdemalion, tripe-visaged crew."[25]

A sermon by the Reverend R.D. Hollington, of the First Methodist Church, apparently took exception to the means of curtailing speech but not the ends: "The time is coming when the government must repress license of speech, but it is not necessary that anarchy be suppressed by methods as lawless as its own."[26] The Reverend Willard B. Thorp maintained that "there is no room in this country for those who do not believe in the nation as such, and who are agitating for its destruction as a nation." He conceded that the agitators were "rather a source of petty irritation than a menace. But at any moment, when the matter seems to be of sufficient importance, it would be entirely within the rights of our nation to deprive them of citizenship and deport them from its borders."[27] Discussing the Sauer kidnapping, Council-man H.E. Fay said:

> As a city official and a law-abiding citizen, I cannot
> approve of the kidnapping of Sauer. However, there is
> one way of lookingat it. Sauer has printed articles
> urging violation of law and bitterly and vindictively
> denouncing the authorities of this city. Consequently
> he should not complain if he is made a victim of the
> very thing he has been advocating -- violation of the
> law. (San Diego Evening Tribune, April 6, 1912, p. 8)

His colleague, Councilman A.E. Dodson, observed: "There seldom is excuse for this sort of mob rule, but there are occasions when it seems it is the only way to get re-sults."[28]

62

During and prior to the Progressive years, the concept of civil liberties was simply not a category of thought for most Americans, much less a public issue.[29] "Free speech" did not carry the emotional weight of other patriotic catchwords; to the people of San Diego and elsewhere, it meant noisy agitators and a carnival atmosphere. In short, free speech was considered a license, not a liberty. The free-speech campaigns, expressing long-held grievances, were boisterous and disruptive. Prisoners sang day and night, and turned the jails into noisy "battleships." Not only were the radicals' ideas unpopular; so was their manner of expressing them.

Liberty to speak was thus tied to good behavior. It was a privilege to be earned, reserved for those who respected the work ethic and property.[30] The propertyless were thought morally weak, with no claim to civil liberties. In San Diego, the legal system reflected this attitude. The San Diego _Sun_, reporting on the jury selection process, noted that:

> Bartholomew Moriarty, the silent man of the police
> force, had gone about the city, or part of it, and had
> summoned the jury, and it was easy to see that he had
> not gone among the laboring classes to any great ex-
> tent. It was one of the most prosperous-looking jury
> venires ever seen in [Judge] Puterbaugh's court. Many
> of its members were business men. The sons of toil
> were greatly in the minority.[31]

Against such odds, the IWW had little defense save in the speech they had fought for -- speech such as that of an obscure Wobbly named Jack Whyte who, upon his conviction for violating the ordinance against free speech, addressed the

following to the court:

> The prosecuting attorney accused me of saying at a
> public meeting: "To hell with the courts -- we know
> what justice is." He told a great truth when he lied,
> for if he had searched the innermost recesses of my
> mind he could have found that thought, never expressed
> by me before, but which I express now. "To hell with
> your courts--I know what justice is," for I have sat in
> your courtroom day after day and have seen members of
> my class pass before this, the so-called bar of jus-
> tice. I have seen you, Judge Sloane, and others of
> your kind, send them to prison because they dare to
> infringe upon the sacred right of property. You have
> become blind and deaf to the rights of men to pursue
> life and happiness, and you have crushed those rights
> so that the sacred rights of property should be preser-
> ved. Then you tell me to respect the law. I don't. I
> did violate the law, and I will violate every one of
> your laws and still come before you and say: "To hell
> with the courts," because I believe that my right to
> live is far more sacred than the sacred right of pro-
> perty that you and your kind so ably defend. I don't
> tell you this with the expectation of getting justice,
> but to show my contempt for the whole machinery of law
> and justice as represented by this and every other
> court. The prosecutor lied, but I will accept it as a
> truth and say again, so that you, Judge Sloane, may not
> be mistaken as to my attitude: "To hell with your
> courts -- I know what justice is."[32]

PART TWO

THE BROTHERHOOD OF BUSINESSMEN

How sweet an emotion is possession! What charm is inherent in ownership! What a foundation for vanity, even for the greater quality of self-respect, lies in a little property!

> -- David Grayson (pseudonym
> of Ray Stannard Baker),
> Adventures in Contentment
> (1907)

They must respect that property of which they cannot partake. They must labor to obtain what by labor can be obtained; and when they find, as they commonly do, the success disproportioned to the endeavour, they must be taught their consolation in the final proportions of eternal justice.

> -- Edmund Burke

CHAPTER 4

WOBBLIES INVADE SPOKANE, EVERETT, LAWRENCE
SELF-MADE MEN DRAW BATTLE LINES

Ione, Oregon
January 7th, 1910

Fellow Worker,

A demonstration meeting was just held in Sheep
Camp No. 1, there being three present, a herder
and two dogs. The following resolutions were
adopted: Resolved, that we send $10.00 for the
free speech fight in Spokane.

Yours for liberty,
THOMAS J. ANDERSON

P.S. Stay with it. I'm coming.

Seattle
Jan. 14, 1910

To the Editor
The Workingman's Paper
Seattle, Wash.

Comrade,
I have just returned from the Spokane Free Speech
fight, leaving there Monday, Jan. 10. Upon arriving in
Seattle and meeting with Floyd Hyde, I have been asked
to say something for the benefit of the Paper's readers.
I was arrested on Nov. 2 for speaking on the
street, and was one of the first to be thrown into the
Spokane sweatbox, well-named "The Black Hole of Calcut-
ta," along with Organizer Thompson, Filigno, Wilson,
and about 28 others, the jailer coming to the door and
saying: "Ha! Ha! So you fellows have come in as mar-

67

tyrs for free speech, have you? Well, we will give you a warm reception!" And a warm reception he did give us, immediately closing the air-tight steel door on us and turning on the heat. It was with difficulty that we could breathe and we could not sit down. We were so crowded that we could not conform to the ordinary decencies of human beings, and were compelled to stand in our own offal. One fellow-worker who, when the door was opened, asked that he be given medical attention, was immediately jerked out by the collar and beaten in the face with a club, breaking his jaw in two places, they giving the excuse that he was making too much noise. About an hour after, I was taken sick and fell to the floor, unable to rise again on account of the crowded condition of the sweat-box. They shoved the fellow-worker, whose name has slipped my mind, back into the dungeon, where he laid six hours, unable to move or talk. In the meantime the fellow-workers kept up a hue and cry of "Take them out of here or they will die," until the sweat-box door was thrown open by Jailer Nelson, and we were told that no doctor would be sent for; and that if we did not keep quiet we would all get the same dose. I remember no more that night, being very sick and hoarse and almost deaf from the excessive heat. Next day at 10 o'clock we were taken out and put in a cold steel cell with 20 others, not being even given a drink of water or anything to eat, having been in the sweat-box 29 hours without food.

At 2 o'clock we were taken in to see Judge Mann (Mann in name, but not by nature), in the Police Court, where we were tried on charges of "Disorderly Conduct." On our attorney, Moore, trying to converse with us on our case, it was found that the greater number of us could not talk or even hear what he said, whereupon Mr. Moore arose and stated that this practice must stop of putting his clients in the sweat-box, or there would be criminal and civil suits. Judge Mann arose and said, "I have nothing to do with that; it is up to Chief Sullivan to decide that," and declared that no action would be taken at that time by him (Judge Mann). The writer was the first to be tried. On the prosecutor reading the charge to me and attempting to get a plea from me, I fell fainting out of my chair and remember nothing for about three hours after. I was told afterward that when I was in that condition I was discharged by Mann. It was about two weeks before I could hear or even try to speak aloud.

I was arrested three times afterward and I put in 23 days on bread and water at the Franklin Schoolhouse, and also was one of the 28 men turned out of the hospital because some of us had scurvy and were expected to die. We were laid out on the cold pavement to shift for ourselves, until some fellow-workers from the hall

68

came to our rescue and picked us up and carried us to the hall. Words will never be able to express the horrors we went through; Dante's picture of the Inferno will never describe it.

Yours for the Industrial Commonwealth,

JOSEPH D. GORDON
Local 222, Spokane, Wash.[1]

As this account of the Spokane free-speech fight attests, harsh treatment of Wobblies was not unique to San Diego. Many of the towns that experienced free-speech fights and strikes gave the IWW similar treatment and used language so similar as to be interchangeable.

A transportation center for the logging territory known as the Inland Empire, Spokane was more of a frontier town than San Diego. Richard Brazier, a long-time Wobbly, recalled Spokane circa 1907:

> [I]t was one of the few wide-open towns once so common in the North-west. Everything went there, vice was rampant, prostitution and gambling were legalized. The Red Light district was the showpiece of the town. Saloons were abundant, some of which put on smutty burlesques shows to draw in more customers. Other saloons always had on tap those "knockout cocktails" -- called Mickey Finns -- to serve to patrons who flashed their "stakes" too openly. Graft was rife, and drunkenness was epidemic.[2]

The first of the IWW's major free speech fights occured in Spokane during the fall and winter of 1909-1910. Spokane was the shipping-out point for thousands of migratory workers, many of whom were victimized by the sharp practices of employment agents, logging and railroad employers. In street meetings, IWW organizers warned workers about unscrupulous agents who

> caused hundreds of men to be shipped miles away into
> all parts of the country after taking their money for a
> job. But when these men reached their destination they
> found they had been sent on a wild goose chase, as
> there were no jobs awaiting them. They were stranded
> without money or friends and without work and were
> obliged to ride the 'bumpers,' as they call it, or walk
> back.[3]

The employment agencies complained that the street-
speaking was hurting their business. The city passed an
ordinance against street speaking, and soon numbers of Wobblies and sympathizers came to Spokane. In the course of
the fight, hundreds were arrested, and many others were
rounded up, beaten, and escorted to the county line.[4]

Although Spokane was a rough-and-ready boom-town, it
was not lacking a middle class thoroughly offended by the
Wobblies. Its response was virtually identical to San Diego's in 1912, revealing attitudes fully developed as early
as 1909. For instance, the IWW transgressed against the
work ethic, and were thought deranged by idleness and anarchy:

> Men who have learned to despise all human authority
> have become worse than worthless units of society --
> they will not take the work at good wages that is
> offered in abundance, for that would subject them, in
> some measure, to the authority of their employers or of
> foreman or superintendent. As they are also lacking in
> the virtues of industry, self-denial and thrift, and in
> the necessary mental ability to get on the pleasant
> road to success, they have become totally unfitted for
> any position of usefulness, and now that their minds
> are poisoned by the vicious doctrines of anarchistic
> agitators, they are ripe for any demonstration that
> will give vent to their bitterness and envy. (Spokane
> Spokesman-Review, Nov. 6, 1909, p. 4.)

To many in Spokane, the Wobblies threatened property owner-

70

ship:

> These contentious, ignorant or deluded men are doing
> all they can to injure every Spokane wage earner who
> has property or a home or employment. Their avowed
> purpose is to create disorder, force the employment of
> additional policemen, cumber the courts with trumped-up
> cases and throw upon the working citizens of Spokane
> the burden of supporting a lot of rovers who will not
> work, but lead lives of mischievous idleness while
> respectable and law-abiding wage earners are supporting
> families, acquiring homes and other property, paying
> taxes and obeying the laws. (Spokane Spokesman-Review,
> Nov. 18, 1909, p. 4.)

Conversion of the IWW into scapegoats rested on fami-

liar stereotypes. The Wobblies were foreigners, said the

State's Governor, M.E. Hay: "The I.W.W.'s do not seem to be

able to understand the idea of our form of government. A

large percentage of them are nonresidents, many of them

foreigners, and no small percentage absolutely illite-

rate."[5] In a letter to the Chamber of Commerce, Spokane

Mayor N.S. Pratt called the Wobblies "a horde of alien

vagabonds"; the Chamber of Commerce passed a resolution

condemning the IWW "as un-American, unpatriotic and undesi-

rable, and a menace to the peace, prosperity and happiness

of the community."[6] Following an unsuccessful attempt to

conduct Sunday services at the jail, a Salvation Army worker

reported that,

> in all my experiences with prisoners, I have never seen
> such a hard-looking lot of men as those now in the jail
> for street-speaking. Their actions this afternoon in
> trying to break up our services plainly showed them to
> be a most desperate class. Not even the hardest crimi-
> nals would have done what they did this afternoon.
> Never before have I seen men confined in the jail who
> would not show reverence by quietness at a religious
> service. I am at a loss to find a name which would
> apply to them. They are not men. (Spokane Spokesman-

Review, Nov. 29, 1909, p. 7)

The city authorities -- largely of Irish descent, as in San
Diego -- were openly prejudiced against the IWW. Bailiff
Smith remarked: "I have seen some crude specimens of humanity in my time, but this bunch today is absolutely the worst
from every standpoint that ever was brought into this court.
In all my 15 years' experience as jailer I never saw such
disreputable-looking human beings."[7] Police Judge Mann, in
charge of the judicial proceedings during the free-speech
fight, condemned the Wobblies with unconscious irony:

> "The authorities realized that this was an attempt to
> override the law, create chaos and disorder within the
> city by a lot of malcontents, who by their own state-
> ments, have no aim in life and no responsibility -- men
> who have not even enough interest in the welfare of
> this country to stay in one place a sufficient length
> of time to qualify themselves as voters."[8]

Such statements masked the economic basis of the troubles, and cut off sympathy for the men who were cheated.
The IWW portrayed things differently:

> Over three thousand men were hired through employment
> sharks for one camp of the Somers Lumber Co. (Great
> Northern) last winter to maintain a force of fifty men.
> As soon as a man had worked long enough to pay the
> shark's fee, the hospital dollar, poll tax, and a few
> other grafts, he was discharged to make room for more
> slaves, so that the fleecing process could continue.
> These different fees are split, or cut up with the
> bosses. In most cases these fees consumed the time of
> several days' labor, when the men were then discharged
> and paid off with checks ranging from 5 cents and
> upwards. The victim of the shark in the most cases
> gets the check cashed at the first saloon, and takes a
> little stimulation. Why not? What is life to these
> men? What is there in life for them? The strong,
> barbed-wire whiskey makes things look bright for
> awhile. Then the weary tramp goes to town with his bed
> on his back. Back to Spokane, the slave market for the
> Inland Empire. He hears the I.W.W. speakers on the

street. The glad tidings of a great revolutionary
union. An injury to one is an injury to all. Workers
of the world, unite, you have nothing to lose but your
bed on your back. You have a world to gain. Labor
produces all wealth, and those who produce it are
tramps and hoboes. This gets to him. A new life for
him. He will go through hell for such a union with
such principles. He has gone through hell in Spokane,
and has given his last cent. He is soon coming back,
and then again and again if necessary, until the truth
can be told on the streets.[9]

In 1909, the IWW was not yet widely known. Until 1908,

the organization had been preoccupied with factionalism;

1909 marked its first widespread press notice. Yet their

opponents' ideas and vocabulary were as developed in 1909 as

they were in San Diego in 1912, suggesting the Wobblies were

not the first labor group to challenge middle class values.

––––––––––––––––––––––––––––––––––––––

These same themes were similarly expressed during the

Everett Massacre, seven years after the Spokane free-speech

fight. On November 5, 1916 -- "Bloody Sunday" -- one of the

worst episodes of anti-Wobbly violence occurred in the small

timbermill community of Everett, Washington, 30 miles north

of Seattle.[10] The IWW were supporting the local shingle

weavers' strike, and for several months had carried on a

high-spirited free-speech fight in the face of increasingly

violent reaction.

On Sunday, November 5th, 250 Wobblies left Seattle for

Everett on the passenger steamer _Verona_. They were met at
the Everett dock by an equal number of armed citizen-depu-
ties commanded by Sheriff Don McRae. When the steamer tied
up, someone fired a shot and a fusillade raked both sides of
the _Verona_ for ten minutes. Deputies hidden in warehouses
fired at already-injured men on the top deck of the ship;
many on the dock, including the sheriff, were wounded in
their own crossfire; Wobblies slid off the deck only to be
picked off in the water; one deputy, running from the dock,
shouted, "They've gone crazy in there! They're shootin'
every which way! They shot me in the ear!"[11] The bodies of
five Wobblies were recovered, perhaps a dozen washed out to
sea, two deputies lay dead on the dock, and scores were
wounded. 74 Wobblies were indicted for the murder of one of
the deputies. The first months of 1917 were given over to
the trial, which the IWW used as a forum for propaganda.
They were acquitted, but the victory could not be fully
enjoyed, for America's entry into the World War pushed the
Wobblies off the front page before the verdict was in.

Everett's political life was dominated by several self-
made men who, in association with Frederick Weyerhauser and
James J. Hill, controlled a good part of the timber industry. These men, having risen through adversity, "believed
that their enterprises were the solid extensions of their
own characters, and they would allow no one to dictate to
them in any way."[12] Their power had been recently challenged in Everett and other towns by coalitions of merchants,

74

professional men, ministers and labor leaders strong enough to have elected a Progressive mayor in Everett in 1912, municipalized the Everett water system, and instituted other reforms of benefit to the middle class.[13] The Wobblies support for the shingle weavers struck a sensitive nerve in men like David M. Clough, a former governor of Minnesota with Social Darwinist beliefs. Clough, speaking for the lumber interests, said: "We propose to clean Everett of all members of the I.W.W. and to forcibly prevent the incursion of any more of their ilk."[14]

Clough's statement was part of the standard pattern of dehumanizing Wobblies prior to assaulting them. The local press, controlled by the lumber interests, had a major role in shaping community attitudes towards the IWW. Throughout September and October 1916, The Everett Daily Herald reported on the police harassment of Wobblies, which was supervised by the mayor. The Wobblies were consistently stereotyped as worthless tramps: "All available patrolmen and detectives were detailed to run down the undesirables and round them up in jail. Every portion of the city where an I.W.W. might wander was searched, but the police found nothing of that brand of humanity."[15] Another story, relating a round-up of supposed Wobblies, touched on nativist fears:

> This generous collection of trouble makers was plucked from a freight train on the Great Northern line as it came through Lowell last night. [The] Delta has become known as the happy hunting ground of civilian deputies, police and sheriff's deputies in search of that common

75

bird-of-ill- omen, [known] as "I Won't Work." Last
night's raid on boxcar tourists -- stowaways on the
Great Northern train -- was the largest gathered at one
time in Everett. As the men were booked last night in
the city hall, it was interesting to note their nation-
alities. There were Greek, Dutch, Swede, German, Rou-
manian, Irish and American representatives, the Greeks
and Germans predominating. Each night the police visit
Lowell in time to take from passing freight trains
their supply of I.W.W.'s. Mayor Merrill and police
officers made a haul of 16 early Sunday morning, but
last night's activities of the police surpass any catch
ever before landed in the police net.[16]

Physical aggression against others required denying

their human qualities. The Commercial Club of Everett (ori-

ginally formed by Progressives but purged of its more mode-

rate members in the current crisis), illustrated this kind

of thinking in a statement issued in October as the crisis

was growing.

We wish further to emphasize our determined opposition
to violence so often indulged in by closed-shop advocates in contests with employers, and the Everett Commercial Club pledges its active efforts to prevent such
violence. We ask the active support of the citizens of
Everett to the end that this city may become a place
where law rules; where labor is free and well paid,
where capital is encouraged and protected and where
enterprise is looked on as a virtue, where crimes, if
committed, are punished and where vicious vagrants are
not tolerated.[17]

Deceptively rational and non-violent in tone, except where

"vicious vagrants" are mentioned, this declaration shows the

deep-seated fears that had been built up in Everett about

the Wobblies.

The townspeople were caught between the power of the

mill interests and the threat of alien IWW destroyers.

Innocent citizens were clubbed along with Wobblies during

the many forays that preceded the shooting on the docks.

76

Some merchants put signs in their windows disavowing association with the Commercial Club, but many sided with the Commercial Club. The original causes for the shingle weavers' strike faded into the background as the tension built and the community vacillated over how to handle the situation. Many were outraged after the tragedy on the dock, but by then it was too late.[18]

As elsewhere, the attitude of the Everett police authorities was critical. The sheriff, Donald McRae, elected on the Progressive ticket in 1912, might have been expected to sympathize with the strikers, since he had once been secretary of the shingle weavers' local and editor of the union paper. But McRae shocked his union friends by taking the mill-owners' side and organizing a force of special deputies to patrol for troublemakers and protect strikebreakers.[19] Testimony at the trial made it clear that McRae was responsible for the beatings inflicted on hundreds of men since the beginning of the strike in May; he showed no remorse in his own testimony.[20] McRae's failure was complex: he was perhaps too beholden to the mill interests; he was perhaps retaliating for the threats, vandalism, and anonymous phone calls directed at him and his family.[21]

Economic vicissitude and social change brought unrest to small towns like Everett, where the frontier was still part of the memory of many of the residents. Figuratively and literally, Everett was a step away from the wilderness.[22] Men like Clough and McRae had taken part in the

77

construction of the logging roads, sawmills and finishing mills that put Everett on the map. Many citizens held on to romantic notions about industrialism, railroads, captains of industry and the like, and conducted their business in a rough, personal style. But the depressions of the 1890's, 1907-1908, and 1914 shook this faith. Electrification was making the old steam-operated plants obsolete, and corporate conglomerations were changing business competition. The World War would have an even more profound effect: after the depression of 1921-22, the timber industry would be rationalized by the giant corporations -- Weyerhauser, Crown-Zellerbach, Scott Paper[23] -- and the days of two-fisted entrepreneurs like David Clough would be over. But in 1916, Sherriff McRae was seen by many as a hero who would preserve the town.

The response of McRae and Clough to industrial change, like businessmen of Spokane, San Diego and other towns, was to reject the evidence of bread lines, hard winters for the unemployed, strikes, and Wobbly propaganda about lice-ridden bunks, sour food, dangerous working conditions, long hours, low pay, graft and collusion, free-speech, anarchy, and syndicalism. Because their way of life was increasingly disturbed by outside influences, it was a simple matter to blame the most visible outsider, the Wobbly: David Clough, with McRae at his side, was described striding down the picket lines outside the mills, "with imperious warnings that he would respect an Everett man's right to demonstrate but would not tolerate the intrusion of outsiders."[24] The Wobblies were seen as intruders, and the familiar process of scapegoat formation was at work in Everett in 1916.

H.D. Cooley, one of the prosecutors in the IWW murder case, illustrated the process whereby Wobblies were dehumanized and made ready for vigilante action. In his concluding plea, he not only pictured them as aliens, but saw them as inferiors addicted to idleness, without moral worth. Cooley claimed that the IWW naturally attracted two classes of people. The first was born without ambition, "a class that has been recognized in this country ever since the country existed, a class that don't want to work, that would not work if you gave them an opportunity and . . . I say that every one of these people are members of the I.W.W. organization or should be." The second class was born with a natural criminal instinct,

> men who are habitual, natural and instinctive criminals. Now I don't say that because a man is a member of the I.W.W. he is necessarily and instinctively a criminal, but I do say that every habitual, instinctive criminal, who knows that he intends to violate the law upon every opportunity to satisfy his own criminal desire, has every inducement to become a member of that organization.[25]

Cooley contrasted the people of Everett with the IWW: "Upon the one side were the people who were living in the city of Everett, who had made their homes there, who had come there for the purpose of carrying out their future destiny in that city. It was their home. Their interests were there. Their families were there."[26] Cooley, a mem-

79

ber of the Commercial Club and a deputy on the dock on
November 5th,[27] wanted the jury to see Everett as a story-
book city, a placid and secure island of contentment. In
biblical style, he described Wobblies as invaders come to
violate that tranquility:

> And upon the other side were a class of people who did
> not claim Everett as their home, who did not come there
> for the purpose of amalgamating with the citizenship of
> the city of Everett. They were not coming there be-
> cause they had work there, nor because they were see-
> king work there; they were not citizens of Everett, nor
> were they seeking to become citizens of Everett, and
> there arose a controversy between the citizens of Eve-
> rett on the one hand and these people from the four
> corners of the earth upon the other.[28]

For Cooley, and for those he spoke for, it was important to see the Wobblies as alien to the community, in spite
of the fact that many of them were neighbors who lived and
worked in Everett. Despite repeated economic depressions,
growing unemployment and relief problems, labor strikes and
unrest for the past twenty years, the idea that industrial
growth, rugged individualism, and unrestrained competition
might not lead to success was very hard to accept. What
these men needed was mutual support and reassurance that
their values, under attack by Wobblies, Socialists, muck-
rakers and reformers, were still sound. The irony is that
the more they stressed the individual and competetive entrepreneur, the greater was the need for positive group identi-
fication, stressing conformity and conservatism. When two
hundred and fifty men arm themselves to drive out the evil
they believe is responsible for the disruption of their

community, there likely is a connection between such exorcism and a primal need for community. They had as strong a need for a scapegoat as any group or culture threatened by forces beyond their control.

The fact that anti-IWW rhetoric was so well-developed and uniform from the earliest encounters onwards is a clear indication that the Wobblies had touched a sore spot of long standing. The Progressive years, after all, attempted to alleviate social turmoil that had been growing since the Civil War. Progressive leaders were aware that stability could be restored only by an increase in social responsibility. But this view was intensely resisted by many Americans who felt themselves squeezed in the competition for power and influence. Behind the hatred of Wobblies was a profound anti-union sentiment, a belief in the sanctity of laissez-faire individualism, a deep-seated prejudice against the poor, a fear of immigrants, and a contempt for anyone who suggested that society or government had a responsibility to alleviate the ills of the industrial system.

These sentiments were the outgrowth of the faith Americans had in the unlimited opportunities available to the hard-working individual. The success of the small entrepreneur was held up as a model long after changed economic conditions made such success less likely. By 1900, 40 percent of the population was urban, providing a new market for industrial products and a concentrated labor supply. The traditional agricultural basis of the nation's economy -- supplying the farm population and providing a market for its products -- had been reversed. For the most part however, businessmen, especially those most opposed to the IWW, did not see the social implications of the economic changes they themselves were helping to bring about. By 1910, American industry was considerably changed compared to 25 or even 15 years earlier, but many businessmen were unable to see that factory production, the specialization of labor tasks, the introduction of large- scale mechanization and the speed-up, were alienating the worker from his work and the employer from his employee. Few felt any responsibility for the lot of an increasing number of transient workers, and few acknowledged that the growth of corporations had diminished the opportunities for rising to the top.

Rather, many businessmen subscribed to the popular notion of the self-made man.[29] Despite growing misgivings about financial manipulation, speculation, and monopoly restrictions on competition, they believed, like Andrew Carnegie, that millionaires were "the bees that make the most honey, and contribute most to the hive even after they have gorged themselves full."[30] Russell Conwell stirred audiences with his popular lecture, "Acres of Diamonds": "I say that you ought to get rich, and it is your duty to get rich."[31] Conwell was a Protestant clergyman; most of America's leading businessmen were Protestant, a factor that enhanced group solidarity when the status quo was threatened by labor, radical, or immigrant groups.[32]

Many of the merchants and manufacturers who opposed the IWW considered themselves self-made men or had fathers or grandfathers who were. But there were growing doubts about the existence of opportunities for men of diligence, industry, determination and good manners. Where opportunities for enterprising men once seemed unlimited, by the early 20th century there was so much social unrest and poverty that the effects of industrialism on opportunity were being questioned. In addition, because new techno-logies required engineers and technicians, training and education had become more important. As corporations expanded, young men found that "getting ahead" was limited by corporate bureaucratic structure. The rough style and forceful character of the self-made men who developed mining, timber, oil and other industries were familiar to Americans; but corporate boards of directors increasingly controlled American industry.

While some businessmen turned to Progressivism, joining the National Civic Federation, supporting mild reform measures, and ceding token recognition to unions, many others could not easily reconsider beliefs and values so deeply impressed on their character. They were unable to admit that the industrial society they helped create might be flawed, that a disorderly IWW was a symptom of political, social, and economic inequities. Instead, they reiterated the view that unrestrained individual effort was all that was needed to set things right and keep America as the land of opportunity:

> In this day and age of great prosperity and "book learnin'" we read and hear about new germs and new diseases, their causes and cures. The daily press feeds us on new "isms" of all sorts -- collective bargaining -- arbitration -- recall -- referendum and conservation. Every fad and folly has its cock-sure advocates and sponsors in public and in private, and unless we keep a firm grasp on our horse-sense, our minds become filled with the notion that we are indeed living in a cruel age and that everything is dead wrong. The cry has gone up throughout the land that working hours are too long, tasks too hard and wages too low; that children under eighteen years must not work; that men and women are everywhere abused by their cold-blooded, hard-hearted employers, who exploit the sweat and blood of human lives for sordid gain.
> The man with one horse is made to envy the man who has two horses; the man with a job is made to feel that his employer is a low-down, mean cuss and should be stoned to death.
> The probable reason for all this may be found in the fact that there is a great disproportion in numbers and votes of those who work for wages and those who give employment; this seems to furnish the motive for newspapers and politicans to shriek themselves hoarse in defense of the down-trodden toilers against the cruel and unholy man who provides the jobs. But, be the motive what it may, it is spreading the diseases of idleness and laziness over the land and is breeding a race of pimpled cigarette suckers, sore-heads, incompetent mollycoddles and criminals.

This was written in 1911 by O.H.L. Wernicke, a Grand Rapids, Mich., furniture manufacturer who frequently contributed his ideas to the open-shop, anti-union, anti-radical campaign. He continues with a complaint about the iniquities of organized labor and the lack of backbone in the authorities:

After a generation or two with this sort of twaddle deeply rooted in perverted minds, real men and real women, with red blood in their veins and real bone in their backs, will cease to exist except as curiosities. The good, old-fashioned idea of a fair day's work for a fair day's pay has gone to seed. Nowadays a man must have ten hours' pay for eight hours' work, thirteen eggs for a dozen and patent breakfast foods. Those who still believe in constitutional liberty and that every man is free to sell his time and skill when and how he pleases, are scabs, to be hissed, stoned, slugged and ostracized, while the limbs of the law seem to forget their sacred oaths.

To illustrate by example: Suppose it were known that certain persons were holding others in involuntary servitude; why, the cry of "slavery" would echo throughout the land; the power of governments would be invoked, and, if need be, the army and navy would be called out; the press would make the eagle scream to stamp out this crime -- but when, in the sacred name of organized labor, led by misguided cheap skates, blather-skites and grafters, men who know not honest toil -- thousands of free men, honest citizens who have done no wrong and who desire to do honest work, men who pay taxes and obey the law, are held in slavery -- are forced into involuntary idleness by open threats, intimidation and coercion which does not stop even at murder. Do the citizens, born of noble fathers who fought in the Revolution and the Rebellion, rise up and protect these good citizens in their sacred rights? Not so you could notice it! On the contrary, the bluecoats of the law become blind; the prosecutor finds the evidence insufficient to convict; the mayor advises arbitration; the governor advocates more anti-injunction laws, and the newspapers play the galleries for larger circulation and higher rates for advertising. It is time to place men in office who will enforce all laws, preserve order at any cost, remove from the hearts of honest men who wish to work the fear of their fellow man, make it safe and honorable for man to work as he will -- then the economic problems may well be left to work out their own solution.[34]

In concluding, Wernicke invokes the virtues of self-help and expresses his faith in America as the land of opportunity:

We often hear the remark that a fellow has no chance any more to get up in the world. When I hear a young chap say that, I know his disease. It makes me mad at his folks and sorry for the boy. The world is actually starving for young men who are not diseased with the germ of laziness -- young men who are willing

85

to hustle, study and live within their incomes. There never was a time in the history of the world when energy, knowledge, horse-sense, self-denial and economy held out such large and certain rewards. The hardy pioneers of a generation or two ago struggled a lifetime for results and comforts which we may enjoy almost for the asking. If we do not leave anything more to the next generation, let it be a decent respect for work, and minds free from the disease of idleness. There never was a time or place in the history of the world when and where for so little mental or physical effort man could obtain so much knowledge, so much of life's needs, so much real comfort and real pleasure as in this day in the United States of America.[35]

Messages like this had for years been presented to Chambers of Commerce, school assemblies, G.A.R. veterans, and trade meetings. Yet social unrest, economic dislocation, unethical business practices, and the widening gap between rich and poor raised questions. Although many businessmen profited from recent changes in the industrial order, others, particularly farmers, small merchants, and workers were losing economic and political power. Confronted by these facts, many explained failure simply as a weakness of character.

This idea contrasted with an older, fatalistic view that the lot of the poor was ordered by a wise God, to be tempered only by Christian charity. An 1825 reader entitled, A Pleasing Companion For Little Girls and Boys, insisted "it is the duty of poor folks to labour hard, take what we can get, and thank the great and wise God, that our condition is no worse."[36] But by the turn of the century those promoting the gospel of success and the self-made man had logically concluded that if the rich were morally virtuous, then the poor were depraved and deserving of their lot. Russell Conwell advanced this argument in "Acres of Diamonds":

> Some men say, "Don't you sympathize with the poor people?" Of course I do, or else I would not have been lecturing these years. I won't give in but what I sympathize with the poor, but the number of poor who are to be sympathized with is very small. To sympathize with a man whom God has punished for his sins, thus to help him when God would still continue a just punishment, is to do wrong, no doubt about it; and we do that more than we help those who are deserving. While we should sympathize with God's poor -- that is, those who cannot help themselves -- let us remember there is not a poor person in the United States who was not made poor by his own shortcomings, or by the short-comings of some one else.[37]

Conwell equated worldly success with inner virtue, and vice-versa, claiming that "ninety-eight out of one hundred of the rich men of America are honest. That is why they are rich."[38] (He was willing to concede that "there are some things higher and grander than gold. Love is the grandest thing on God's earth, but fortunate the lover who has plenty of money.")[39]

Thus, for many, the poor were no longer to be treated with charity because their condition was self-willed. For example, The Open Shop Review, published by the National Founders' Association for its members' employees, printed a series of articles on living conditions in American cities that were intended

> to show the workman how really small is the class that has to live among squalor and filth and unsanitary conditions; that the great majority of the class which so lives is there because it wants to be; that these conditions are not due to industrial conditions, but to vice, intemperance, foreign customs and methods of

living, and that the only relief for them is education along the lines of right living.[40]

Employers were quick to furnish examples of the intractability of workers, their apparent preference for squalid conditions, and their ineducability. This was particularly so when foreign workers were the subject of discussion. One employer, an executive for the Northwestern Pacific Railroad Co., complained about the hopelessness of improving camp conditions for construction crews:

> What is the use of providing expensive toilet facilities for men who never have and never will use them? If they did use them, the transmission of disease would probably be so great that our hospitals would be full and the health officers would be quarantining our camps. I am not referring to the intestinal diseases against which the commission very rightly tells us we must guard, but to the venereal diseases that more than 60 per cent of the laborers are afflicted with. It must be remembered that these men come from the lowest classes of the least civilized countries; that they do not bring their women folks with them, and that there is very little incentive for them to keep up a semblance of respectability. When I speak of the inability of the employer to make the employee use the facilities provided, I am merely stating the solution of a problem that all of us have tried to solve time and time again with a negative result. This does not, of course, apply to all camp labor; but the men who try to keep themselves clean and observe the decencies in camp are outnumbered ten to one. You will always find men in camp who will change their underwear once a week and insist upon sufficient time to keep themselves clean; but the majority do not care to do so, and would consider that their personal liberties were being violated if they were made to do so. . . . I know of another case where a contractor put in showers and tried to get the men to use them, and in the several months that his camp was in existence -- the shower was furnished with warm water from the kitchen range so that there could be no objection to the temperature of the water -- and during the entire existence of that camp the timekeeper was the only man who used the shower. And I have heard numberless stories to the same effect. And, as I said before, we must take into consideration the home characteristics and the social plane from which we draw

our men. It certainly is our duty to try to raise them
socially, but it seems like a hopeless task.[41]

As discontent increased and malcontents like the Wobblies agitated, there was little sympathy from employers:

> We have recently been hearing much maudlin sympathy
> expressed for the "downtrodden denizens of the sweat-
> shop" and the "homeless wanderer searching for honest
> employment," and with it all often go many hard words
> for the men in power. Nothing is said about the emplo-
> yer who grows old before his time in a vain attempt to
> get frowsy ne'er-do-wells to do intelligent work; and
> his long, patient striving after "help" that does no-
> thing but loaf when his back is turned.[42]

This disgust and aggravation was voiced in 1899 by Elbert
Hubbard in an influential pamphlet entitled <u>A Message to
Garcia</u>. Moralizing from a parable about an uncomplaining,
hard-working employee, Hubbard reflected the attitude of
many employers; such exasperation with the laboring classes
insulated employers from fellow-feeling and compassion for
hardships of the poor. And although the vogue for Social
Darwinism did not dominate the thinking of most employers,[43] it often appeared in the revised theory of the self-
made man, which now held that since only the rich could be
worthy, it was self-evident that the poor were unworthy.
Elbert Hubbard saw "a constant weeding-out process going
on":

> No matter how good times are, this sorting continues;
> only, if times are hard and work is scarce, the sorting
> is done finer -- but out and forever out, the incompe-
> tent and unworthy go. It is the survival of the fit-
> test. Self-interest prompts every employer to keep the
> best -- those who can carry a message to Garcia.[44]

By the time the IWW began its agitation, it was a
matter of habit for many employers to dismiss complaints

about wages or working conditions as the carping of those who, if they couldn't better their own condition by hard work, sobriety and saving, deserved what they got.

The reaction to the great IWW-led textile strike of 1912 at Lawrence, Massachusetts, illustrated the thinking of much of the American business community. At its height, some 25,000 workers speaking 45 languages were on strike against the mills of Lawrence; the IWW's effective organization of polyglot immigrants refuted trade unionism's complaint that immigrants and unskilled were unorganizable. But the strike, coming on the heels of the Los Angeles Times dynamiting, raised the spectre of class war in the minds of many.

For a number of businessmen who rose from the working class to become self-made men, the achievement was a source of pride -- and an obstacle to understanding. They resented the IWW's attempt to improve the lot of the class they, as individuals, had risen above -- why should anyone get anything that wasn't earned? The Lawrence strike focused national attention on the poverty of the mill-workers, much to the annoyance of those leading citizens who had once been in the mills, but who regarded it as a character-building experience.

One of these, Mr. C.F. Lynch, a former mayor of Lawrence and now Commissioner of Public Safety, appeared as a witness before the U.S. House of Representatives Subcommittee investigating the violence during the strike. Lynch took the stand after dozens of immigrant workers, labor organizers, social workers, ministers, mothers and children had testified about the violence during the well-publicized evacuation of the strikers' children. Understandably concerned about the image of the city fathers, Lynch was anxious to show that he and other officials had the interests of the "working-man" at heart. "I think it is only right to say to you men in as few words as possible," began Lynch,

> to give you an idea of the make-up of the government of only five men, that the mayor of our city is a son of an immigrant who located in Lawrence, was an ordinary laboring man, honest and industrious, and the young man himself, I believe, had a mill experience. Another member of our board is, or was, the secretary, I believe, of the International Typographical Union - Mr. Maloney, by name, Robert S. Maloney -- and a very strong labor advocate, and a thoroughly honest fellow. Another member of our government worked in the mills, or went to work in the mills as a son of a widowed mother, at the age of 9 years. He is now somewhere around 60, and has labored hard. And by the way, he was twice elected for a two-year term as superintendent of streets of the city of Lawrence, and is now preferred as one of the commission. Another member is a young lawyer whose father was a helper in a foundry there, and who was handicapped in his early life. He worked his way through college, was ambitious, has made good in his profession, and from all appearances will do good work for the city that he serves.[45]

Lynch depicted for the Committee his own rise from obscure origins:

The last, referring to myself, gentlemen -- I was left

91

fatherless at the age of 3 with a widowed mother who had five children, born in Lawrence of poor parents. I went to work in the print works of the Pacific Mill at the age of 10 years. You can very well imagine that my sympathies were aroused and my thoughts went back 38 years when I saw those young boys [on the witness stand] who were dressed and looked, perhaps, as I did at that time, as my circumstances were almost exactly similar so far as living went.

I had an ambition, gentlemen, even at that time. It was an honorable one. It may seem strange, but it was there -- that was to be the mayor of my native city. I worked in the mill, gentlemen, until I was 16 years of age -- or I had seen six years of service. By the way, my wages were 50 cents a day, and I was glad to get it. Our hours of labor at that time were, I think, as I recollect it -- we went to work at 10 minutes past 6 in the morning, and we worked -- in the department that I worked in -- the noon hour. We had no hour for dinner, and we got our meals as we could with our machines running, and we came out at 24 minutes past 5. We worked Saturday afternoon, I think, at that time until 4 o'clock. However, as I said, I had some ambition. At 16 years of age I came out and worked for 50 cents a day to learn the plumbing business. I served my apprenticeship there, and at the age of 21, I was elected clerk of the board of health. I served in the department for three years. I was then elected a member of the board of health, and served as its chairman for two years -- the term of my office. . . . 46

Lynch finally realized his ambition to be mayor of

Lawrence in 1904. The humble origins of men like Lynch did

not enable them to see that the plight of the immigrant

strikers was created by an economic system that increasingly

denied blue-collar workers opportunities such as Lynch had

had in 1875. Another leading citizen, William Wood, son of

an Azores fisherman, had worked his way up through the mills

to become the most influential mill owner in Lawrence; yet

Wood was completely unsympathetic to the grievances of his

workers, and his unalterable opposition to the strikers was

largely responsible for the violence in Lawrence.[47] Lynch

and Wood held attitudes widespread among employers. They believed in equality of opportunity, and that self-reliance was a safeguard against poverty; and nothing could convince them that labor unions were anything but a handcuff on individual freedom, initiative, and the character-building aspects of work.

It appeared that neither the businessmen of Lawrence, nor the city officials and police, nor the militia -- Harvard sons of the middle class -- nor the middle class itself, could understand what was happening to their city. In a few years' time, immigration from southern and eastern Europe had inundated their city. New national and international markets controlled the city's economy. Urbanization and ghettoization had changed a city still half-rural. All this created an explosive situation for which no one in Lawrence was prepared.[48] By 1911, 74,000 of the 86,000 population were first- or second-generation immigrants; the city had the highest death rate and highest infant mortality rate in the nation.[49] In 1912, the lid blew off this melting-pot, the workers shut down the mills, and the IWW stepped in. Many respectable citizens were shocked, outraged and frightened.

Their distress was revealed in a statement issued by the Citizens' Association during the height of the strike. The title, "LAWRENCE AS IT REALLY IS -- NOT AS SYNDICALISTS, ANARCHISTS, SOCIALISTS, SUFFRAGISTS, PSEUDO-PHILANTHROPISTS, AND MUCK-RAKING YELLOW JOURNALISTS HAVE PAINTED IT," is a catalogue of the chief offenders of business sensibilities, sparing only professors, legislators, and a few others who had no idea of how to run a business. The Association first complains of "that form of newspaper that caters to the neurasthenic or hysterical which sees only the unusual, the extraordinary, and where the unusual and the extraordinary do not exist proceeds straightway to invent them."[50] However, the Citizens' Association's richest sarcasm was reserved for the decadents from the city:

> The fellow feeling that makes us wondrous kind was in evidence in Lawrence constantly as soon as the strike had become a full-blown and sensational one of the violently syndicalist type. Shoals of the theorizing Socialists from the pseudo-philanthropic societies of New York, those under salary especially; writers of modern studies of the unclean, absinthe-drinking frequenters of the imitation cabarets of New York; those Bohemian writers, whose fate it is according to Brunetiere to foolishly idle away their youth and wake up to find that they have an old age of poverty and ill health before them; paid investigators for faddist-hunting rich men of New York came on, looked over the ground for half an hour, and declared that the syndicalists were everlastingly right and everyone else everlastingly wrong in their ideas of the proper way in which to run a society.[51]

But these city types were harmless compared to the Industrial Workers of the World and their leaders, the "direct actionists" Haywood, Ettor, and Giovanitti. According to the Citizens' Association, the IWW was responsible for all the adverse publicity Lawrence received; it was they who orchestrated

> the widespread, persistent, and diabolically clever way in which the Lawrence strike was kept before the public all over the country and in a manner calculated to prejudice the public, not only against the mill owners and city authorities of Lawrence but against our State

94

and National Governments, and against any government or any regularly constituted authority.[52]

The melodramatic tone was sincere: the IWW was seen as conspiratorial, villainous and foreign, justifying the repressive measures of the Lawrence authorities:

> Terrorism was the strongest weapon that the Industrial Workers of the World used in Lawrence. When it was partially taken from their grasp and the reign of ordered liberty restored, their strength waned rapidly. And only as that terror survived, nursed, and cultivated by the methods of the black hand and the mafia did any of the strength of the syndicalist strike survive.[53]

Descriptions of Wobbly activities commonly linked them with European terrorist methods. Although IWW propaganda about syndicalism, sabotage and the general strike encouraged this belief, the public perception of radicals had long been that of foreign bomb-throwing anarchists. The Wobblies, who spouted "this devil's creed that is to supplant our old-time reverence for the altar, the hearth-fire, the family, the graves of kindred, and the flag,"[54] were plainly un-American. To see the IWW as sinister foreign terrorists not only dehumanized an enemy; it provided a target for the dislike of immigrants.

Southern and eastern European immigrants -- Italian, Slavic, Jewish, Balkan, Greek, Portuguese, Syrian -- were thought very different from the Teutonic, Scandinavian, or English-speaking immigrant who understood democracy and would make a contribution to American society. Rather, they were seen as birds of passage, here only to make money, unskilled, unwashed, "the driftwood and sediment of centuries of brigandage, piracy and tyrannical government," who would never learn American ways."[55] Patriotic societies like the D.A.R. were formed in response to these new immigrants.

> Our founders [of the D.A.R.] realized that with the steady immigration of foreigners to our country something must be done to foster patriotism and love of our country and our flag and to make Americans of them, or there was danger of our being absorbed by the different nationalities among us.[56]

The Wobbly was often portrayed as one of those "foreign born rotten banana sellers, thieving rag dealers, Italian organ grinders, Chinese washmen and Bohemian coal miners, whose aspirations would make a dog vomit."[57] Worse, the IWW recruited such foreigners. A post-Lawrence analysis of the IWW appearing in the open-shop publication, The Square Deal, explained that "their membership is chiefly a foreign membership and that is really the secret of their success so far."[58] Pointing out that the A.F. of L. considered foreign unskilled labor unorganizable, the writer, Hezekiah Duff, portrays the IWW agitator as an unscrupulous demagogue and the immigrant as abysmally ignorant.

> But the Industrial Workers of the World will take them. It has done so and will do so again. Through its organizers, speaking almost every tongue, it has fed them the doctrine of social discontent, the same feed which they were given in their European homes. The lower continental class these days is brought up to believe that the very name of government is synonomous with everything that is bad and works to their destruction. Landing in this country, the famous land of the free, they are met at the pier with the same talk they have heard at home. They know what the rich and the royal have done to others of their kind at home and what is more natural than that they should follow the agitator who immediately tells them that the same class

struggle is in existence in America? They know what
the fight of the poor against the rich means. They are
poor and when they learn that the same fight is on in
the land of their adoption, they of course can enlist
on but one side. They get a job and then they strike.
Out comes the militia and it is worse than the prover-
bial shaking of a red rag at a bull. They have been
taught almost from infancy to abhor the man in the
uniform. To them he represents the force of royalty.
They have seen him before in the service of the Czar,
or the Emperor, or the King, and they know that to
cross his will and let him shoot or bayonet, is merely
a true sign of the martyr. Rioting, except as a show
of their displeasure, is furthest from their thoughts.
The old idea gets into their heads, they hear the
honeyed words of the I.W.W. agitator telling them to go
ahead, and bloodshed is the inevitable result.[59]

This stereotype of the ignorant foreigner open to sini-

ster influences was very common during this period and makes

the hostile reaction to the Wobblies more understandable.

Racial prejudice had already made the foreigner into a

caricature. The Wobblies, who tried to organize foreigners,

were seen as aliens and anarchists. Their sinister image,

current among employers and the general public, was not a

result of cynical manipulation, but a logical extension of

beliefs already formed by existing class- and race-preju-

dice.

Immigrants often ranked themselves in a heirarchy based

on national origins. This ironic application of nativist

stereotypes occured in Lawrence and other New England tex-

tile towns where social and occupational structures echoed

national groupings. Americans of English stock were social

and cultural leaders; English-speaking 1st and 2nd genera-

tion immigrants, mostly Irish, occupied leading commercial

and professional positions and dominated politics; then came

French-Canadians, who were shop-foremen and supervisors and merchants; and then the "foreigners" -- Italians, Portuguese, Poles, Lithuanians, Syrians -- who worked in the mills. Selig Perlman, investigating the New England textile industry for the Commission on Industrial Relations shortly after the Lawrence strike, related a pertinent anecdote:

> To what extent class lines coincide with national lines is quaintly illustrated by a story which I heard from a school teacher in Nashua, N.H., about a little Polish girl who, speaking of her cousin, also Polish, who was going to high school, said: "She is now real swell, she is French now."[60]

In Lawrence, the strike provoked division among immigrant groups along these lines. Earlier immigrants who were assimilated into the community opposed the strike. These included the French-Canadians, who attempted to import labor scabs from Quebec,[61] and the Irish, many of whom were integrated politically, economically, and socially. Following a typical pattern of assimilation, sons of Irishmen now supported the mill owners, where a generation earlier their fathers had opposed them. A historian of Lawrence has noted that,

> the Irish had no representative on the strike committee and none of their organizations paraded with the IWW on Memorial Day. There were many Irishmen among the city officials, most of whom were out of sympathy with the strikers. Judge Mahoney in the city court handed out stiff sentences to strikers; Assistant Marshal John H. Sullivan detained children at the railroad station; School Committee member John Breen hid dynamite; Mayor Scanlon supposedly brought in Sherman Agency detectives, many of them Irish. Father O'Reilly's parish calendar condemned the IWW for misleading the newly arrived foreigners.[62]

When the strike in Lawrence was over, the IWW member-

98

ship evaporated. This was not only because the IWW failed to consolidate their gains in Lawrence; it was also because the newly arrived immigrant Italians and Slavs were just as anxious to assimilate as had been their Irish and German predecessors. Although the Italians "felt that they were absolutely on the outside of the community life, that they did not count at all, that the police could do whatever it pleased with them and that they had no rights and nobody to protect them," yet, as Selig Perlman pointed out, "the Italian small businessmen maintained strict neutrality during the strike, but after it was settled, they began an anti-I.W.W. crusade."[63] As well as wanting relief from oppressive conditions, immigrants wanted what the land of opportunity promised, and many preferred to become Americanized rather than radicalized.

The strike prompted city fathers to take indoctrination in "American principles" more seriously. Lawrence produced a manual, "The American Plan for Education in Citizenship," which became nationally known.

> Its aim was to help the schools "keep the republic safe" and to "permeate every course of study with loyalty to American ideals." History was to teach "love and loyalty for America," civics to inculcate "devotion to the Community," and literature to arouse enthusiasm for the things "which the American spirit holds dear." The principles of the plan were first, "sacrifice for country"; second, belief in America as the "land of opportunity"; third, patriotism; fourth, faith in American democracy; fifth, obedience to law; and last, love of country.[64]

The Industrial Workers of the World derided these ideas; Lawrence turned its wrath upon the IWW. Reverend

99

E.M. Lake summed up the community's fears, suggesting the
IWW be treated as traitors:

> If Industrial Socialism, which is destructive to the
> family life and a menace to the civic life is to conti-
> nue in this country, then we shall need a new interpre-
> tation of the meaning of freedom of speech and the
> significance of the word treason. To deride our civil
> authorities, vilify our courts, and influence an igno-
> rant foreign people to riot is nothing less than trea-
> sonable to the best interests of society.[65]

In all, the Lawrence strike was a warning of what was
in store for the IWW. Intolerance of their ideas, prejudice
against them as foreigners, indifference to the industrial
conditions they sought to rectify, and fear of change would
ultimately destroy the IWW. In 1912, with San Diego and
Lawrence in the headlines coast-to-coast, the nation was
thoroughly alarmed by the IWW, and many were determined to
resist them. On a chilly February day in 1912, two groups
of Americans stood across from each other on the streets of
Lawrence. On the one side was a crowd of strikers and
"anarchists," carrying a banner that read:

ARISE!!! SLAVES OF THE WORLD!!!
NO GOD! NO MASTER!
ONE FOR ALL AND ALL FOR ONE!

On the other side of the street, a group of Lawrence citizens held up another sign:

FOR GOD AND COUNTRY
THE STARS AND STRIPES FOREVER,
THE RED FLAG NEVER.
A PROTEST AGAINST THE I.W.W.
ITS PRINCIPLES AND METHODS.[66]

CHAPTER 5

UNIONS BE DAMNED: "WE WILL FIGHT YOU.
WE HAVE A RIGHT TO DO IT. WE HAVE GOT THE POWER."

My observation leads me to believe that while
there are many . . . contributing causes to
unrest, that there is one cause which is
fundamental, and it is the necessary conflict
between . . . our political liberty and the
industrial absolutism.

> -- Louis Brandeis (Commission
> on Industrial Relations
> testimony, 1914)

The emotions aroused by the strike at Lawrence, in
which hatred of Wobblies and fear of immigrants fortified an
already cold view of the laboring classes, originated in a
distrust of the labor movement long held by the majority of
Americans. Historically regarded as a conspiracy to deny
property rights and restrain trade, attempts to organize
labor in the United States were resisted at every turn,
obstructed by class prejudice and the popular conception of
laissez-faire.

Those who opposed the Wobblies were anti-union from
life-long habit: anti-IWW sentiment drew upon anti-union
attitudes that had roots in 19th century education. Studies

of 19th century American schoolbooks, such as Ruth Miller
Elson's _Guardians of Tradition_, show that "in no [school]
book published before the 1870's is labor organization mentioned."[1] Elson notes that even when the great railroad
strikes of the 1870's made the "labor question" unavoidable,

> with one exception, the professional historian McMas-
> ter, there is absolute unanimity among schoolbook au-
> thors on the evil results of labor unions. . . . In all
> other books labor organization is equated with vio-
> lence. No attempt is made to define "union," "strike,"
> or other related terms used in the texts, let alone
> explain why labor organizations increased in the post-
> Civil War period. Very often the words "strike" and
> "riot" are used interchangeably to describe the rail-
> road strikes of 1877: "In the summer of 1877 a riot
> broke out among the employés of some of the great
> railroads upon a general reduction of wages. A large
> amount of property was destroyed by the rioters in
> Pittsburgh, Baltimore, Chicago and other railroad ci-
> ties." Property destruction is always carefully de-
> tailed while grievances of workmen are not.[2]

Elson points out that since such schoolbooks had to be
approved by school boards made up of leading citizens, a
conservative, non-controversial text was most likely to be
adopted. In addition, "nineteenth-century schoolbooks were
designed to train the child's character rather than his
powers of critical thought."[3] As for the labor movement,

> there is no doubt that the nineteenth-century child who
> was influenced by his schoolbooks would identify labor
> organization with irresponsible violence and probably
> with doctrines subversive of American institutions. He
> would know nothing of the background of the growth of
> labor unions, and he would probably assume collective
> bargaining to be a device designed by unscrupulous men
> in search of personal gain. The laborer who accepted
> American labor conditions and worked hard would get
> ahead. To question American labor conditions was un-
> American.[4]

In short, anti-unionism was a normal state of mind for

most Americans of the late nineteenth and early twentieth centuries. Most employers insisted upon the open shop -- by which they invariably meant the non-union shop. The open shop was an expression of the individualism they believed made the American character. They were unable to see any parallel in employers' organizing manufacturers' associations to combat unionism, or big business consolidations to cut industry competition, or lobbying efforts for tariff and other federal regulation.

Union activity simply violated a sense of what was right. A contemporary observer, the economist Carleton Parker, described this anti-union attitude:

> To the American employer the breaking of a strike satisfies a curious medley of desires. It appeals to his strong primitive sporting instinct; it is demanded by his highly cultured American individualism; and it satisfies whatever ideas of legal rights he has imbibed from the loose traditions of laissez faire. Taking all the environmental influences which focus on industrial management and property ownership in this country, strike-breaking is a very normal managerial activity.[5]

Another writer on social issues, John Fitch, like Parker a first-hand observer, commented in 1924 that

> there exists among certain employers much good will towards the unions. Nevertheless, it is clearly apparent that this sympathy seldom goes so far as to indicate a desire to have union influence and strength further extended. Under the most favorable conditions the sympathetic employer refrains from doing anything to weaken the unions. At the other extreme there are unsympathetic and hostile employers whose opposition is keen and persistent, and who would destroy unionism root and branch if they had the opportunity to do so. It is probable, on the whole, that the majority of employers in America tend toward the latter rather than toward the former view.[6]

The turn of the century saw unprecedented growth in

union activity and membership. After the reverses of the 1890's, it appeared that the A.F.of L.'s conservative bread-and-butter unionism was at last gaining headway. Union membership mushroomed from 900,000 in 1900 to over 2,000,000 in 1904, largely due to a boom in the economy and a strong demand for skilled labor.[7] But the recession of 1903-04 stopped union growth and gave employers an opportunity to deal organized labor a blow from which it would not recover until the First World War gave broad concessions to labor. Steel, meatpacking, construction, shoes, textiles, metal work and other industries and employers flexed their muscles and shook the union off their backs.[8]

1903, two years before the IWW first met in convention, marked an increased belligerence of employers' associations. The National Association of Manufacturers, the Citizens' Industrial Alliance, and various trade associations were determined to crush unionism.[9] An aggressive propaganda campaign was begun denouncing unionism and radicalism. C.W. Post, the cereal king, addressed the first meeting of the Citizens' Industrial Alliance in October of 1903:

> Do you hear the murmur and the mutterings and see the lightning flashes of the storm of public indignation rolling up in mighty grandeur? It is coming and coming fast. The 14,980,000 decent, upright, peaceful voters who love work and demand liberty are now arising in their might, and the text on the wall, writ by the hand of Almighty God, writ in letters of glistening steel, proclaims that the slimy red fingers of anarchy shall be crushed by the mailed hand of the common people and their law.[10]

David M. Parry, John Kirby, Jr., and James Van Cleave

led the National Association of Manufacturers in a militantly anti-union course. Parry, in his presidential address to
the 1903 NAM convention, declared that union practices were
"un-American," that unions knew only "one law, and that is
the law of physical force -- the law of the Huns and the
Vandals, the law of the savage."[11] Parry, owner of an
Indianapolis car factory, also helped form the Citizens'
Industrial Alliance. As its president, he told the 1904
convention that "the labor question is a conflict between
two antagonistic and opposing systems of political economics. In reality on the one side of this contest is the
American system of government, while on the other side is a
mixture of socialism and despotism."[12]

John Kirby, Jr. attacked unionism, and the A.F.of L. in
particular, in apocalyptic style. To Kirby, organized labor
was a "beast with the seven heads and ten horns, that was
stalking up and down the earth, demanding that no man should
work, buy, or sell, save that he had the name or the mark of
the beast upon his right hand or in his forehead."[13] As
president of the NAM, Kirby told the 1912 convention that he
held Samuel Gompers and the A.F.of L. morally responsible
for the depredations of the McNamara brothers, whose recent
confessions to the Los Angeles Times and other bombings had
stunned organized labor. Echoing Lincoln, Kirby warned the
delegates that "no country can exist half-free and half-
throttled by criminal unionism."[14]

Kirby's successor to the NAM presidency, the bicycle

manufacturer George Pope, also borrowed from Lincoln in his
1913 message to the membership: "To the breeders and exploi-
ters of industrial and social distress, I say: I believe it
is impossible for this nation permanently to endure if class
is to be pitted against class." Pope also assured the
members that,

> on the issue of criminal unionism my adherence to the
> avowed principles of this organization [the NAM] admits
> of no misinterpretation; to the backs of the betrayers
> of honest labor I would be among the first to apply the
> lash. . . . I am and shall continue in opposition to
> the un-Christian, un-American closed shop.[15]

This campaign against unionism, spearheaded by the NAM
and the CIA, became increasingly strident prior to the First
World War. These smaller employers felt threatened by the
growth of the trades-union movement and the emergence of
giant conglomerations. They separated themselves early on
from the more moderate segments of the business class, who
either had the vision to see the need for amelioration of
social problems, or recognized the twin threats of irrational industrial conditions and federal regulation.

Among those counseling moderation were leaders of the
largest corporations, many of which, like Sears, Roebuck and
Company, the National Cash Register Company, International
Harvester, and the most successful union-buster, U. S.
Steel,[16] had the resources to experiment with corporate
welfare schemes, company unions and the like. These corporate leaders supported Ralph Easley's and Mark Hanna's National Civic Federation, which hoped to reconcile the social

and labor "questions." The thought of these big business leaders meeting amicably with prominent labor leaders like Sam Gompers of the A.F.of L., or John Mitchell of the U.M.W., caused considerable resentment among the NAM and CIA, whose members did not have the same resources to withstand labor strikes and boycotts.

The NCF and the NAM were at swords' points almost immediately. The NCF's Easley deprecatingly pointed out that the newly-founded employers' associations included "none of the great employers of labor representing the basic industries, such as coal, iron and steel, building trades and railroads."[17] Kirby, during his tenure as president of the NAM, railed at the National Civic Federation:

> It has been charged, and it is here charged, that the National Civic Federation, through the cunning manipulation of its "inner circle," has been, and is now used, as an annex to the American Federation of Labor; that its affiliation with the latter is one of thorough sympathy and specious insidious co-operation, and that the "core" of the National Civic Federation, and the executive bone of the American Federation of Labor, are so near akin as to amount to but little -- if anything -- less than a distinction without a difference so far as the labor policies of the two organizations are concerned.[18]

The defiance of these employers' associations towards unions, reformers, and big business alike, had broad appeal across the country. The NAM had branches in every major city in the U.S., and the CIA and like-minded Merchants and Manufacturers Associations and Commercial Clubs soon appeared in cities and towns everywhere.[19] Their appeal was due to their uncompromising militancy, insistence on the old

virtues of hard work, reverence, and patriotism, and determination to defend a civilization hard-won from the wilderness by rugged individuals.

The contemporary labor historian, Robert Hoxie, catalogued the "underlying assumptions, theories, and attitudes of
employers' associations" as they appeared to him just after
World War I. Hoxie's list holds the mirror up to the lais-
sez-fairciom of a hundred years earlier, unchanged in its
veneration of natural law and natural rights, or in its
belief in the inviolability of property, the rational calcu-
lation of interests, and the natural social harmony and
social order that follow. As expressed by Hoxie, employers'
associations' anti-union beliefs were:

1) that a natural harmony of interests prevails in
society and therefore the unions are to be restrained
when they use coercive methods;

2) that the employers' interests are always identical
with the interests of society and therefore unionism is
to be condemned whenever it interferes with their
interests;

3) that the interests of the worker and employer are
harmonious, and therefore when the unions oppose the
employer they are misled by unscrupulous leaders and
are to be condemned;

4) that the employer gives work to the laborers and
therefore they are ungrateful and immoral and to be
condemned when they combine to oppose him;

5) that the employer has an absolute right to manage
his own business to suit himself as against his workers, and therefore the unions are to be condemned when
they interfere in any way with that right;

6) that the business is his, an absolute property
right, and to compel him to bargain with the men
collectively, with men not in his employ, with an
irresponsible committee, and to assert a voice in the

108

matters of hiring and discharge, the conditions of
employment, and a right to the job and the trade;

7) that the employer has an absolute right to manage
his own business as against workers <u>not</u> in his employ,
and therefore outside workers are to be condemned when
they act in sympathy with his workers;

8) that every worker has an absolute right to work
when, where, and for whom he pleases and therefore the
unions are to be condemned when they restrict this
right and freedom;

9) that free competition of the workers is always in
the interest of society and therefore that any interference by the unions in this is to be condemned;

10) that the greatest possible production is always in
the interest of society and therefore the union is to
be condemned whenever it interferes with this;

11) that the law, the courts, and the police represent
absolute and impartial rights and justice, and therefore the unions are to be condemned whenever they
violate the law or oppose the police.[20]

In this scheme of things, there was simply no place for
unions. Workers' demands for a say in determining industrial conditions were rejected as preposterous. Democracy
meant political equality -- and that only when voters were
properly qualified by sex, race, length of residence, lite-
racy, property, and general good citizenship. It definitely
did not mean industrial democracy. Robert Bruere, a newspaper correspondent and writer of social commentary, encountered this attitude while reporting on the Bisbee deportation (in which hundreds of IWW strikers were shipped by
boxcar into the Arizona desert.)

When I had my first interview with an Arizona mine
manager and told him that what I wanted was to make a
dispassionate and impartial report of the facts behind
the strikes and deportations, he was magnanimous enough
to say that he was convinced that I would be impartial.

"But," he proceeded, "however impartial you may
be, your decision is bound to go against us."
"Why?" I asked in surprise.
"Because," he concluded, "you believe in democracy
and we don't run our mines on a democratic basis."[21]

Bruere outlined this problem from the mine operator's point

of view:

As a citizen he was committed to political democracy.
But to speak of the democratic principle as if it were
applicable to the government of industry seemed to him
fantastic, unreasonable, absurd. If you played with
democracy, how would you ever get out the ore? That
was not a problem of democracy or autocracy, either --
it was a problem in precise mechanical engineering.
His dream was of a mine from which the ore might be
taken by automatic machinery as it is now crushed, and
concentrated and smelted by machinery. Until then, the
utilization of men -- stupid, intractable, inefficient
men -- was a necessary evil, the best one could do was
to make them sychronize with the machines as closely as
possible. Democracy implied intelligence, initiative;
and these were precisely the most undesirable qualities
in a mucker, the man who shovels the ore deep down in
the stopes and drifts, the man who feeds the
machines.[22]

As for unionism, even the most conservative bread-and-

butter unionism that fully accepted the capitalist order, it

was just plain wrong. There was an intense psychological

investment in property ownership because property was the

tangible evidence that a man had attained independence,

power and control. To say, "I own this," was to say, "This

is a part of me"; the things a man owned completed his

identity. For unions of any description to affect the

control of property was tantamount to a violation of the

personality of the owner, and a threat to his identity.

This was especially true of the merchant or manufacturer who

had daily contact with the physical plant he owned; unlike

110

corporate owners of far-flung enterprises for whom salaried executives stood in as managers, smaller employers had no such buffer between them and the threat any union demand posed.

Thus, employers' propaganda about the "open shop" was generally just a sugar coating to disguise their adamant opposition to unionism. Employers could claim that they weren't opposed to their men belonging to unions, that they hired union and non-union workers alike, and that they were opposed to the "closed-shop" because it denied employment to non-union workmen. What they really meant was that they intended to run non-union shops, and would brook no interference of any kind. Such employers so strongly considered their property an extension of themselves that they felt they owned their workers' labor as well. This often resulted in a curious denial that there was a strike at their plant at all; instead, their employees had been misled or coerced by insidious union agitators who were selfishly fomenting trouble only to gain some obscure advantages for themselves. Rather than define their employees as disloyal, a definition that would raise the psychologically dangerous spectre of loss of control, they preferred to blame the hypnotic powers of evil union trouble-makers.

This attitude applied to all unions, and the continual portrayal of union leadership and organizers as "outsiders" whose aims were detrimental to the common good, set the tone and created the atmosphere in which it became possible to repress the IWW. Examples of this presumed separation of the union from the workers are numerous, such as the following excerpt from a 1914 interview with an employer conducted by an investigator for the Commission on Industrial Relations. A Mr. J.B. Rider, who was General Manager of the Pressed Steel Car Company and Western Steel Car and Foundry Company of McKees Rocks, Pa., was asked for his comments about the hard-fought and bloody strike the IWW had organized there in 1909. Rider acknowledges no grievance at the root of the strike. Rather, the cause of the strike is a puzzling mystery, except as a result of "agitation."

> As far as I know they [the employees] were not organized at that time, but they did organize during the progress of the strike, forming an industrial union known as the Industrial Workers of the World. They were all in the one union comprising metal workers, machinists, molders, patternmakers, blacksmiths, carpenters and others. The cause of that strike, as we learned later, was agitation on account of imaginary grievances which was carried on in the works by agitators who were socialists and members of the I.W.W. The strike at the end of the eighth week was called off. The Company made no concessions whatever. Much disorder was witnessed during the strike, including riots and loss of life, which we do not attribute to our employees, but to labor agitators who made their appearance shortly after the strike took place, under the guise of labor leaders offering their assistance for the purpose of forcing this Company to recognize their union.
>
> Speaking personally, I wish to say that if I found I had to do business with such an aggregation as the I.W.W., I would go out of business, as I might just as well do it at first as they would sooner or later force me to do so. I am of the opinion that the government should suppress organizations of that character for the reason that they are a detriment to wage-earners and employers. We treat our employees with the greatest consideration. It is true that they are almost all foreigners. The Company has established social and welfare work among them and is doing everything possible to improve their conditions, and they seem to be

well-satisfied with the treatment we are according
them.[23]

Unionism deeply offended businessmen like Rider. It is
hardly surprising that socialism and "IWW-ism" were thought
pernicious. What was said about the evils of unionism doub-
ly applied to socialism and syndicalism. A July 1913 editorial in The Century Magazine attacked socialism as the work
of the devil:

> Simon-pure Socialism is so ugly, so red in tooth and
> claw, that to be hated it needs but to be seen and
> understood. . . . It is time that the men and women of
> this country awoke to an understanding of the true
> nature of Socialism, of what it is, of what it aims to
> do, and how it seeks to achieve its ends. Socialism is
> revolution, it is blood, it is overthrow, spoliation,
> and a surrender of the priceless conquests of civili-
> zation, an extinction of the noble impulses that have
> raised mankind out of the condition of savagery.[24]

Industrial unionism, as advocated by the IWW, was regarded
as the quintessence of radicalism. A. Parker Nevin, in 1914
the General Counsel of the National Association of Manufacturers, warned:

> But now we see a new menace completely alien to our
> history, traditions, laws and institutions. The so-
> called "new unionism" is within our gates and evokes
> our grave concern. By the term "new unionism" is meant
> the recent conception of a world-wide labor movement,
> which finds its expression in that erratic mass called
> the Industrial Workers of the World. . . . Denying the
> right of any established national authority, it quite
> consistently denied the emblem of a nation, its flag,
> and even more consistent in its gospel, denied God.
> The movement, therefore, represents a denial -- gene-
> ral, comprehensive, dynamic. Its quality of liberty is
> the liberty from which all limitations are removed. It
> is therefore completely revisionary. It is an angry
> sea surging against established bulkheads of society.
> It is utterly repugnant to Americanism; sneers at so-
> cialism and smiles at anarchy with bene-volent appro-
> val. Lawlessness is its law. So far we have not
> excluded these alien hosts. But they must be taught

that when their fantastic and impossible philosophy of
industrialism collides with our Anglo-Saxon laws, that
the latter will always be enforced, rigidly, justly,
fearlessly -- mawkish sentimentality of misguided emo-
tionalism to the contrary notwithstanding.[25]

Thus at the peak of IWW activity, many employers were
militantly anti-union and anti-socialist. There is perhaps
no better available evidence of this sentiment than the
testimony collected between 1912 and 1915 by the United
States Commission on Industrial Relations. Chaired by Missouri liberal Frank P. Walsh, the Commission included Professor John R. Commons of Wisconsin, Florence J. Harriman,
wife of the New York railroad magnate, three representatives
of labor, and three businessmen, including Harris Weinstock
of California.[26] Under the direction of Walsh, the Commission focused national attention on the state of American
labor by means of regional hearings that took testimony from
hundreds of witnesses: employers, managers, foremen, attorneys, efficiency engineers, employment agents, bankers,
corporation directors, trades-union officials, workers,
Wobblies, Socialists, agricultura-lists, public officials,
educators, economists, sociolo-gists, editors, clergy.[27]
The hearings held in Seattle and Portland in 1914 were the
most representative of employers' anti-union, anti-IWW atti-

tudes, for the Pacific Northwest had long been native ground
for the Wobblies. All of the testimony carries the flavor
of life in America as it was before the World War.

The testimony of M.C. Banfield, a long-time Portland
businessman and vice president of the Employers' Association
of the Pacific Coast, demonstrated his laissez-faire individualism and adamant anti-unionism. Banfield told the Commissioners that he divided society into three classes: the
employer, the employee, and "the barnacle on the body public
-- that is, the man who is a leech." He conceded, after a
bit of sparring with members of the Commission, that besides
politicians, thieves, pickpockets and burglars, he meant
business agents and officials of trade unions.[28] To him,
work was a blessing, a molder of character, a guarantor of
liberty, and unions interfered with these beneficial effects:

> Give the men individual liberty, the same as I had when
> I was a boy myself. Don't tie him down to eight hours.
> If you want to make a law for women and children all
> right, God bless them, let them get along with as
> little work as possible. But keep the men at work;
> idle hands find mischief still for men who are out of
> work. I did not quote it exactly, but you know what I
> mean. The man who is out of work is in a bad way, and
> is liable to do things he should not do. That is what
> I wanted to get at. (5:4650; references to the CIR
> Final Report are abbreviated by volume and page num-
> bers.)

Banfield illustrated what he meant with a story of his
own disillusionment with unions. Having endured several
strikes by teamsters while head of the Banfield Fuel Co. in
Portland, he settled with the union; but not for long:

115

We went along for a little while. Two months later,
though, I met a man coming up on Sixth Street with one
of our valuable teams. The team cost six or seven
hundred dollars. He was driving down Sixth Street and
on a heavy trot. They were too large horses to trot,
and should not have been trotted. I whirled my buggy
around and followed, for fear they might get away from
him; went to the corner at the depot. I drove down and
went around to the depot, and at one place I saw my
team standing there without a driver and the lines
without being tied, and I stood by the side of the
team; they were all excited. Finally the driver came
out and got on the wagon. I didn't say anything to
him. I turned my buggy around and drove back to the
office; phoned down to the yard, "When Jack comes in
take his team from him and give him his time check";
that I didn't want him any more. So that was done.
The next morning about 8 o'clock six of my teamsters
came into the office. I said, "Well, boys, what's the
matter?" They said, "We came to see you on a little
matter." I said, "Where are your teams?" They said,
"They are in the barn." I said, "What do you want to
see me about?" "Well," he said, "we came up to see if
you won't give Jack another chance -- put him back to
work again." I said, "Is it going to cost me $30?"
which I figured my time was worth -- $5 apiece. I
said, "Is it going to cost me $30 to know, or tell you
whether I will put a man back or whether I have a right
to discharge a man?" They said, "Well, this is orders
from the union, Mr. Banfield -- that we are to come to
see you this morning to give Jack another chance." I
said to my bookkeeper, "You give those men their time."
I said, "Boys, I don't need you any more." I went into
my private office and one came in and he said, "Mr.
Banfield, this is all right with us, but I suppose you
know what will happen in the morning?" I said, "I
don't know." I said, "If I can't live without you, I
can't live with you; that's a cinch." So I said, "I am
ready, if needs be, to walk out of Portland on the ties
along with you, barefooted, before I will ever, under
any circumstances, deal with the labor organization
again in any shape or form."
    This was only one or two of the conditions that
came about. They drew the line while I was working
under those union arrangements on making four loads of
wood a day's work. Sometimes four loads would be a
day's work. Some places we have to go 20 blocks with
deliveries, and other places only 4. But they had made
up their mind there in the union that four loads was a
day's work, and that no more should be done. So one
afternoon we found them out in the yard -- four men
sitting in a wagon playing cards -- about half past 3
or 4 o'clock. We wanted to know what was the matter

and they said they had done their day's work; that the
union decided four loads a day was a day's work; that
they had hauled their four loads. So I suppose you
gentlemen know -- any man who is in business would know
-- what happened to those fellows right then; that is,
you can surmise what happened to the men, with a man of
my temperament, can't you? (5:4652)

There was nothing so irritating to a self-made man like

Banfield as featherbedding by the unions. Banfield's tale

was typical of dozens like it told to the Commission justi-

fying an anti-union stance; most businessmen could not see

beyond these demonstrations of union shiftlessness to any

historical appreciation of working conditions or economic

fluctuations. To them, anything that interfered with indi-

vidual liberty -- including meddlesome Commissions -- was a

failure, pure and simple. This was especially true for

businessmen who had been laborers themselves, such as the

Gray's Harbor, Wash., lumberman, Neil Cooney, who told the

Commission "I came to this country from Canada right off of

the farm 34 years ago a common laborer, built myself up to

the position I have, and had no education" (5:4278). Cooney

would not acknowledge that opportunity was in any way li-

mited, that not every drawer of water and hewer of wood

could become a manager of industry, and that there was thus

any need for protection or organization for the average

worker.

This insistence on unfettered individualism and its

corollary assumption that the poor were worthless and deser-

ved their fate sometimes led employers into awkward moral

cul-de-sacs. In Portland, during the winter of 1913-1914,

117

unemployment was severe, with thousands of men out of work
and destitute. Their plight was taken seriously by the
Oregon Civic League, whose executive secretary, a lawyer
named Isaac Swett, related the circumstances to the Commission:

> We sent out committees to discover as to whether or not
> there was a large number of people that were utterly
> destitute, no shelter, and without food. This commit-
> tee reported that it found a very large number of
> people that were sleeping, in one instance, in a store,
> all over the floor, in the basement, without blankets,
> that those people were eating one meal a day, many of
> them, and some one meal in two days, and that many of
> the lodging houses were packed with people; that the
> hallways, the stairways were littered with men sleeping
> there at night. A serious condition was there, and it
> presented itself in a rather alarming way, and action
> was immediately taken to find whether we could not
> place them in one house. We found we had a building
> here in the city called the Gypsy Smith Tabernacle, a
> very large building, that could hold very many people,
> probably all we needed; that this, I say, was the
> city's property, it was leased by the city. Every
> effort was made to induce the city authorities to open
> that. The city authorities were very loath to do so.
> There was, I believe, pressure brought to bear upon
> them by certain interests not to do so. But eventually
> the building was opened. (5:4597-4598)

The Commissioners were interested in Mr. Swett's statement
about "certain interests" in opposition, and pressed for a
further explanation. "Generally speaking," he responded,

> it may be said it was the business interests of the
> city of Portland, who were very much afraid of the
> consequence of having these people to be cared for in
> that manner. There seemed to be and there was at that
> time a feeling of financial unrest, and the business
> people seemed to be afraid that this would tend to
> exaggerate that condition, and that this matter must
> not be known throughout the State, that there was a
> condition in the city of Portland demanding assistance
> of the people in general; that there was starvation;
> that there was a large number that wanted shelter.
> They didn't want that phase of it to be distributed to
> the people throughout the country. They wanted the

idea to be that this was a very prosperous city. I
think that was the main reason. There are again a
great many others that are generally opposed to matters
of that kind entirely. They are of the opinion that
this is merely the view of a few people who have exaggerated notions of conditions of that kind; that, as a
matter of fact, there was no property [sic: poverty],
or very little of it.

Indeed, there were a considerable number of people
during the very worst period that claimed very positi-
vely that there was no want in the city; that there was
no starvation; that there was nobody who could not get
work. I have personally phoned a good many people
requesting their assistance in the shape of funds on
account of the need at the tabernacle, and many of them
answered me that there was no need of it, men could
obtain employment; that we were entirely in error in
that we were taking a place in the community that was
harmful in this, that we were presenting a theory that
could not be. (5:4604)

In corroboration, a workingman named Ed Gilbert, who

helped administer the efforts the unemployed made to help

themselves, told of a man who offered tents, supplies, food

and wages to a group of 100 unemployed men for clearing his

land. "They readily accepted the proposition, but then

there was quite a few people in that vicinity in that town

that went to this man and told him that if he employed those

men, those vagrants they called them, they would run him out

of town with the vagrants" (5:4723). In spite of the fact

that the announced object of the Unemployed League was to

seek work and not charity, "there was no charitable organi-

zation, or no church as an organization, in any way rendered

assistance to the unemployed," nor did the state, city, or

county provide any work, thus placing them in the position

of seeking charity (5:4721).

The business interests of Portland preferred to deny

119

there was a problem beyond the power of individual initiative to resolve; M.C. Banfield told the Commissioners his opinion regarding causes of industrial dissatisfaction:

> Now, we don't have to go out of this room for one of
> the causes. I don't know how many people are here, but
> you can see the number as well as I can. Every one of
> us should be doing something instead of being here.
> This day and this hearing here caused the greatest
> disturbance, the greatest dissatisfaction in the city
> among certain classes, of anything that has happened.
> Every one of us here, if we were earning something to-
> day, it would be far better than this inquiry going
> back to the Government. If we could only get away and
> work and stop the agitation instead of having one
> organization bucking the other -- in short, I will say
> that the old adage, "Prepare for war in time of peace,"
> is a failure, an absolute failure, and has never been
> so exemplified before the world as it is to-day in the
> old country, and this organization of labor pitted
> against capital is brought about through the influence
> of those who don't care either for labor or capital.
> In many cases they are not taxpayers, and I maintain
> that all of this inquiry interferes with the individual
> liberties of men to get out and do their work as they
> please. It is all wrong -- no good will come from it.
> (5:4649)[29]

Banfield hated unions. The anti-union bias of other employers who testified before the Industrial Relations Commission was only thinly concealed behind the "open shop" facade, as the summarizing report prepared by the Commission makes clear:

> It is very significant that out of 230 representatives
> of the interests of employers, chosen largely on the
> recommendations of their own organizations, less than
> half a dozen have denied the propriety of collective
> action on the part of employees. A considerable number
> of these witnesses have, however, testified that they
> denied in practice what they admitted to be right in
> theory. A majority of such witnesses were employers
> who in the operation of their business maintained what
> they, in accordance with common terminology, called the
> "open shop." The theory of the "open shop," according
> to these witnesses, is that workers are employed with-
> out any reference to their membership or non-membership

in trade unions; while, as a matter of fact, it was
found upon investigation that these employers did not,
as a rule, willingly or knowingly employ union men.
(1:64)

The Commission uncovered many illustrations of this _de facto_

discrimination, though perhaps none as straightforward as

the following letter from a Pacific Coast employers' asso-

ciation to its members:

> SEATTLE, WASH., June 16, 1910.
> To the members of the Washington district:
>   GENTLEMEN: At the regular monthly meeting held
> last night in this office, the following resolution was
> unanimously adopted:
>   "Resolved, That this association forthwith adopt
> the absolute nonunion shop. And the inclosed notice
> was ordered sent to all members of the association,
> with the request that they post in their shops on
> receipt of same. For the benefit of members of the
> association who were not present last night we will say
> that the association has taken this stand after giving
> the open shop a good trial and has found that the
> minute union men get into the shop they immediately
> start to organize and interfere with the nonunion men
> and create discord, and the meeting was unanimous in
> its declaration for an absolutely nonunion condition in
> their shops hereafter."
>   Yours, very truly,
>   UNITED METAL TRADES ASSOCIATION,
>   A.H. Garrison, Secretary.
>   (5:4338)

Another witness before the Commission was Hiram C.

Gill, the Progressive mayor of Seattle. Gill had a reputa-

tion for being outspoken: in the aftermath of the Everett

Massacre, he would declare the men who fired on the Verona

to be cowards and murderers.[30] Testifying in an exchange

with Commission Counsel William O. Thompson, Mayor Gill

described the intransigence of Seattle employers during a

1914 teamsters' strike in his city:

    MR. GILL: Why, I think the fact that I refused to

maintain 50 men on the city's payroll as special policemen here last spring had considerable to do in
inducing people to get together in this little teamsters' strike. It wasn't, as a matter of fact, the
team owners we had our difficulty with, it is what is
known as the employers' association here, mostly big
men who are absolutely non-union, maintaining this
employers' association. It was through them that my
predecessor put these men in as special policemen. As
long as they can have all the special policemen they
want and the taxpayers and the city care for them, they
don't care much about settling things. And as soon as
they can't, why they begin to feel conciliatory immediately. That is my experience.
     MR. THOMPSON: What theory did the employer have
of the use of the police?
     MR GILL: Why he had the theory that if you let
him, he will have his employees for policemen paid by
the city.
     MR. THOMPSON: Well, then, what would these po-
licemen do, would they make attacks on strikers, would
they protect property from destruction?
     MR GILL: I think that is the assumption. I think
back East they would probably go out and shoot a lot of
men. (5:4112)

Much of the violence that occurred in Western labor

disputes was justified by a peculiar notion of the innocent

boisterousness of the West. In addition, there was an

admiration, or at least a perverse respect, tendered the IWW

by some of the rough-hewn employers of the West. One of

these, a Mr. J.V. Paterson, a small town banker, farmer,

lumberman and shipbuilder, and a stubborn individualist,

revealed his attitude both towards the East and the Wobblies

in a 1918 interview:

Say, the cocky attitude of the East toward the West
makes me laugh. The people in the East have got the
idea that the men out West are a lot of damned nuts,
pigs, wild men. But we have never produced any Harry
Thaws [mad slayer of N.Y. architect Stanford White,
1906]. Sometimes I think we have too much freedom. It
gets 'em off their feet. But we are fighting our fight
here in the West in the open. Take this I.W.W. strike,
now. Why, this I.W.W. strike is an expression of the

122

real Western democratic disobedience, and rebellion against things that a decent man won't stand for.[31]

This was the same Paterson who was one of the most outspoken and instructive employers to testify before the Commission on Industrial Relations during its sessions in Seattle, and was undoubtedly one of those "big men who are absolutely non-union" that Mayor Gill criticized. Paterson began with a heated attack on labor unions, calling them "an absolute abomination" and a "cancer" (5:4314,4519). He denigrated reform-minded Congressmen as "half-made utter failures of lawyers" and "infernal cowards" (5:4321,4322); with equal vehemence he condemned liberal professors, the clergy, Woodrow Wilson, and the Clayton Bill. Disregarding the surprised exclamations from the hearing's spectators, Paterson hectored the Commission:

> I don't see the good in passing Clayton bills or any other kind of bills. That won't help us a bit, because, gentlemen, you will force us, the people, to the point where we will fight you. We will rise with a counter revolution. We will fight you. We have a right to do it. We have got the power. We certainly have the power. We will destroy you if it comes to that. And that is the end. That is what it is coming to. It is coming to a civil war, gentlemen, and we will fight. Don't be the least surprised about that. We will fight. That is what it is coming to. I am ready. (5:4322)

In this context, least surprising was Paterson's admiration for the Wobblies: "the contrast between the I.W.W. and the unions is tremendous to me," he expounded; "the I.W.W. appreciates the individual. He has got something to offer above the sordid, rotten existence. He has got ideals. And he is nearer to Almighty God than many other political

123

propagandists that I know of." (5:4317)

But the similarity between fed-up Wobblies at the bottom and self-made businessmen at the top did not make much of a practical difference to Paterson. For despite his preference for the IWW over the trade union, Paterson was adamantly opposed to both. The effect of his attitudes was concisely summarized by a union business agent, J.A. Taylor, who followed Paterson as a witness before the Commission. Remarking that it would not be very healthy for a business agent to go poking around Paterson's shipyard, Taylor added, "I might say, perhaps, he is one of the causes of industrial unrest in this part of the country." (5:4336)

Indeed, there was irony in Paterson's uncommon praise of the IWW spirit, for he spoke from a long experience of opposing them. In a 1911 free-speech fight in Aberdeen, Washington, Paterson had organized a vigilante committee of 500 to drive the Wobblies out of town.[32] When Robert Bruere interviewed him in 1918 for the New York _Post_'s series on the IWW, Paterson revealed a very human motive for the vigilantes' actions: "Guided by a simple physical reaction, by the vague fear that seizes men in the presence of other men the springs of whose actions they do not understand, we organized that night a vigilante committee -- a Citizen's Committee, I think we called it -- to put down the strike by intimidation and force."[33] This comment suggests the complexity of emotion that was involved in local contests with the Wobblies and hints at the kind of guilt that

All of the businessmen that the Commission on Industrial Relations interviewed in Seattle expressed much the same beliefs as Paterson. Some, like lumberman W.J. Rucker, were reluctant witnesses: "I don't believe that this Commission can aid very materially the man that won't aid himself or do for himself." As for the Commission's usefulness, Rucker left no doubt, "I don't think I would want a commission to dictate to me, though, how I shall run my business, if I have got to pay the bills" (5:4307). Rucker had nothing to recommend in regards to the conditions of labor, beyond admonishing the Commission to mind its own business:

> Well, I think that this commission will have to let labor hoe its own row. You go to taking care of labor -- put a man in the shade and fan him, and he will never develop, he will never create. I don't believe the time will ever come when another man can look after the interests of his neighbor. He is liable to make pretty short grazing in the other fellow's pasture. (5:4305)

The extent to which a man like Rucker felt he could do as he pleased where his business was concerned may be gauged by his testimony regarding his activity as a banker. At the prodding of the Commissioners, Rucker described the operation of his bank:

> MR. RUCKER: . . . . We don't pay our men in money, we give them a deposit slip.
> COMMISSIONER O'CONNELL: Well, are you interested in the bank in any way?
> MR. RUCKER: Yes, we own the bank.
> COMMISSIONER O'CONNELL: You own the bank?
> MR. RUCKER: Yes.
> COMMISSIONER O'CONNELL: You don't want the money to get away at all, do you? Now we are getting acquainted. . . . It is simply a deposit credit you give them in lieu?
> MR. RUCKER: Yes; and then they have a check and

125

check it out as they please. . . .

COMMISSIONER O'CONNELL: Do you pay them interest on their deposits?

MR. RUCKER: We do if they leave it there for a number of months, and we encourage them to make investments, and we endeavor to get them securities, if they save their money -- warrants or any securities that they want. We want to see the men become prosperous and become taxpayers, we need help.

COMMISSIONER O'CONNELL: Are your employees fairly good depositors?

MR. RUCKER: Yes; very good, most of them.

COMMISSIONER O'CONNELL: What is the capitalization of your bank?

MR. RUCKER: There ain't no capital.

COMMISSIONER O'CONNELL: A private bank?

MR. RUCKER: Just a private bank -- my brother and I.

COMMISSIONER O'CONNELL: What is the last statement published by your bank?

MR. RUCKER: We don't publish a statement.

COMMISSIONER O'CONNELL: If you didn't do anything of that kind, you ought to make money.

MR. RUCKER: What's the use?

COMMISSIONER O'CONNELL: Well, what are the resources of the bank?

MR.RUCKER: Well, the resources of the bank are whatever Rucker Bros. have; it is a private partnership.

ACTING CHAIRMAN COMMONS: Unlimited liability as far as the bank is concerned?

MR. RUCKER: Yes.

COMMISSIONER GARRETSON: Any system of State bank examination in this state?

MR. RUCKER: Oh yes; there is under incorporated banks.

COMMISSIONER GARRETSON: Private banks?

MR. RUCKER: This bank doesn't come under that.

COMMISSIONER GARRETSON: A private bank can be run here without any inspection?

MR. RUCKER: Yes, sir. . . .

(5:4310-4311)

Businessmen like Rucker made little connection between their own activities and the growth of labor discontent. Instead, employers the nation over, particularly those in daily contact with "the labor problem," took a tenacious hold on nineteenth century small-town values, and blamed the turmoil on their neglect. The picture that emerges of the local businessman who was most often involved in conflicts with the IWW is of a staunch believer in laissez-faire and the Constitutional right to make money. Committed to the work ethic, he was deeply offended by those he perceived as idlers, and his education had trained him to think of the poor as moral failures who deserved little sympathy. Unions threatened his independence with their unpardonable interference in his affairs. He treasured his family, took pride in his city and its progress, and resented outsiders, be they corporate intruders into the city's business, or ignorant foreigners threatening the homogeneity of the community. He was uncompromisingly patriotic, and disrespect for the flag inflamed him, threatening his sense of identity as an American, and calling the fundamental social order into question. Like men of Lawrence or the Pacific Northwest, the anti-Wobbly employer was most likely a provincial man at heart, cherishing his own rise from the bottom of the heap, protective of his individual liberty, and resentful of any interference with his property rights.

The modern turn taken by industrialism, which had made his success possible, frustrated him because it was changing the quality of his life. Rapid urbanization, the increase in seasonally unemployed and migrant workers, and the immigration of unfamiliar national types was destroying his sense of community. The big merger movements had produced a bureaucracy to administer new national market structures,

shifting political and industrial control away from the
local level. These developments challenged his idea that
success was the reward of virtue and created a sense of
disorder.

Such businessmen saw who was provoking the disorder --
the Wobbly agitator, the anarchist bomb-thrower, the union
organizer, the radical, the syndicalist, the socialist, the
foreigner, the immigrant, the tramp. In these confrontations with the Wobblies, employers often could not fathom
the reasons for discontent. Since they had risen above
adverse conditions, they could not understand why other men
could not or would not do the same. Lazy grumblers were
bottom-of-the-barrel sediment who deserved a less-than-equal
place in the social order. Few businessmen had the means,
or the time, or the insight to make any other analysis.

For most businessmen confronted by the IWW, trade
unionism had been bad enough. But when the Wobblies came,
they saw their communities invaded, their laws flaunted,
heard themselves vilified, their values mocked, their businesses tasked as evil. Their newspapers and weekly magazines informed them that the Wobblies were ruthless saboteurs and agents of the black hand, fomenting violent
strikes and lawlessness and bent on pulling the capitalist
order to the ground. It was small wonder that curtailment
of civil liberties and other drastic measures were quickly
adopted. "Any means, legal or illegal, to get rid of the
I.W.W. leaders," was the way a Paterson, N.J., construction

128

engineer and contractor put it to the Industrial Relations

Commission:

> CHAIRMAN WALSH: In other words, did you think
> that they would be justified, if a man was a known
> agitator and had caused trouble, as you understood it,
> at other places, to arrest him as he got off the train
> and not give him a chance to be heard?
> MR. FERGUSON: Not give him a chance; simply say,
> "When the next train goes out you go out on it."
> (3:2581)

PART THREE

"THE WEST IS DEAD"

O masters, lords and rulers in all lands,
How will the Future reckon with this Man?
How answer his brute question in that hour
When whirlwinds of rebellion shake the world?
How will it be with kingdoms and with kings -
With those who shaped him to be the thing he is -
When this dumb Terror shall reply to God,
After the silence of the centuries?

                    -- Edward Markham, "The Man
                        With the Hoe" (1902)

    While there is a lower class, I am of it,
    While there is a criminal class, I am of it,
While there is a soul in prison, I am not free.

                    -- Eugene Victor Debs

CHAPTER 6

THE BINDLESTIFF'S DAYS ARE NUMBERED

By trying we can easily learn to endure adversity.
Another man's, I mean.

-- Mark Twain, "Pudd'nhead
Wilson's New Calendar" (1897)

Before the Civil War, in the 1855 Preface to Leaves
of Grass, Walt Whitman spoke of "the noble character of the
young mechanics and of all free American workmen and workwomen."[1] He addressed a paean to this spirited American
workforce in a poem first published in 1860:

I HEAR America singing, the varied carols I hear,
Those of mechanics, each one singing his as it should be
    blithe and strong,
The carpenter singing his as he measures his plank or
    beam,
The mason singing his as he makes ready for work, or
    leaves off work,
The boatman singing what belongs to him in his boat, the
    deckhand singing on the steamboat deck,
The shoemaker singing as he sits on his bench, the
    hatter singing as he stands,
The wood-cutter's song, the ploughboy's on his way in
    the morning, or at noon intermission or at sundown,
The delicious singing of the mother, or of the young
    wife at work, or of the girl sewing or washing,
Each singing what belongs to him or her and to none
    else,
The day what belongs to the day -- at night the party of
    young fellows, robust, friendly,
Singing with open mouths their strong melodious songs.[2]

Some twenty years later, in February of 1879, Whitman recorded in his journal: "I saw to-day a sight I had never seen before -- and it amazed, and made me serious; three quite good-looking American men, of respectable personal presence, two of them young, carrying chiffonier-bags on their shoulders, and the usual long iron hooks in their hands, plodding along, their eyes cast down, spying for scraps, rags, bones, &c." Whitman found this phenomenon disturbing:

> If the United States, like the countries of the Old World, are also to grow vast crops of poor, desperate, dissatisfied, nomadic, miserably-waged populations, such as we see looming upon us of late years -- steadily, even if slowly, eating into them like a cancer of lungs or stomach -- then our republican experiment, notwithstanding all its surface-successes, is at heart an unhealthy failure.[3]

By 1905, when a portion of the "poor, desperate, dissatisfied, nomadic, miserably-waged" met in Chicago to organize the Industrial Workers of the World, life in America for the working man was far from ennobled: for millions of industrial workers there was little to sing about. The progress of industrialism since the Civil War had altered the nature and conditions of work in the factories and the fields. By the turn of the century, it was clear to many that the benefits and great wealth of industrial development had been generated at the expense of the working classes. Although electric power, railroads, the auto, and other inventions were destined to raise the general standard of living, there were too many who fell victim to poverty,

134

sickness, industrial accident, and crushed spirit.

Of a population of some 90 million, contemporary researchers estimated that up to 10 million were living in poverty; the U.S. Census of 1900 reported 6 million illiterates; and observers like Jacob Riis painted unforgettable pictures of poverty in New York and other city slums.[4] Work all too often meant not the fulfillment of personality or the reward of a job well done, but grinding toil in sweatshops, factories and mills. Children, women, and unskilled laborers who performed exhausting work at low wages constituted a demoralized underclass of workers. "I am a worker in the Goodrich 'pit,'" wrote a striker during the IWW strike of Akron rubber plants in 1913,

> We work thirteen hours on the night shift and eleven hours on the day shift, with no noon hour to rest and eat. We are allowed to eat any time between 10 a.m. and 2 p.m. if the work permits. If the work comes out so that we are not able to eat our lunch during those hours, we are not permitted to finish the meal at any time during the rest of the day. If we are caught eating we are liable to be discharged, even though we may be idle at the time. We would not be eating on the company's time for we work piece work.
> The cores upon which the tires are built are solid iron and a great many are so heavy they are all one man can lift. The cores are so hot that the men are compelled to wear two pairs of canvas gloves, one over the other in order to handle them at all. Some men have been there two years; some have to be changed because they are worn out in eight months. Some come down, look and say, "I don't want that job" and leave.
> During the night shift when the men get a few minutes to sit down, you will see their heads nod and they will fall asleep, utterly exhausted and unable to keep awake. I have seen men stand at their tables dazed for the want of sleep. I have seen these men walk over to the water cooler and hold their head under the faucet and let water run on their heads so as to revive them and I was one of them. One night I saw a "stripper" walk over to the night foreman and asked to

be "fired." The foreman told the man that he knew just how he felt, and advised him to go back and try and stick it out until morning.

In conclusion I wish to say that thirteen hours is too long for that kind of work, or any kind of work, for that matter. We are too tired to even get out of bed at all during the day; it wears a man down; he has very little time to spend with his family and his life is a cheerless, endless struggle.[5]

Work under such conditions resulted in substantial turnover and instability in the work force. In addition, high unemployment resulted from economic fluctuations as well as from seasonal layoffs in agriculture and extractive industries. Table 1 gives some indication of how severe unemployment could be, especially for non-agricultural em- ployees who by 1916 were 2 1/2 times as numerous as farmwor- kers.[6] With the exceptions of the brief period preceding the Panic of 1907 and the war years of 1918-19, unemployment was chronic, unstable and subject to wide fluctuations over this thirty-year period. And as the figures from 1900 on show, non-farm wage-earners shouldered the brunt of unem- ployment.

But even for the majority of those workers who had relatively stable year-round employment (at best, about 288 working days per year[7]), income from wages was inadequate for a minimum standard of living. Contemporaries' estimates of adequate income drew less on the scanty statistics avai- lable than on their own educated perceptions. But although the statistical basis for these cost-of-living estimates was often inadequate or dubious, they were so conservatively formulated that at the least they were a measure of reasona-

TABLE 1

Unemployment, 1890-1920

Year	Total Unemployed[a]	Percent of Civilian Labor Force Unemployed	Percent of Non-farm Workers Unemployed
1890	904,000	4.0	---
1891	1,265,000	5.4	---
1892	728,000	3.0	---
1893	2,860,000	11.7	---
1894	4,612,000	18.4	---
1895	3,510,000	13.7	---
1896	3,782,000	14.4	---
1897	3,890,000	14.5	---
1898	3,351,000	12.4	---
1899	1,819,000	6.5	---
1900	1,420,000	5.0	12.6
1901	1,205,000	4.0	10.1
1902	1,097,000	3.7	8.6
1903	1,204,000	3.9	9.0
1904	1,691,000	5.4	12.0
1905	1,381,000	4.3	9.5
1906	574,000	1.7	3.9
1907	945,000	2.8	6.0
1908	2,780,000	8.0	16.4
1909	1,824,000	5.1	10.3
1910	2,150,000	5.9	11.6
1911	2,518,000	6.7	13.0
1912	1,759,000	4.6	9.0
1913	1,671,000	4.3	8.2
1914	3,120,000	7.9	14.7
1915	3,377,000	8.5	15.6
1916	2,043,000	5.1	9.1
1917	1,848,000	4.6	8.2
1918	536,000	1.4	2.4
1919	546,000	1.4	2.4
1920	2,132,000	5.2	8.6

Source: US Census Bur., Hist Stat. of the U.S., Colonial Times to 1970, Bicentennial Ed., Pt. 1 (Wash., D.C., 1975), Ser. D 1-10, D 85-86, pp. 126, 135.

[a]Persons 14 years old and over. Annual averages.

bly adequate income. For example, John A. Fitch, a noted labor economist, acknowledged that standard-of-living figures "merely represent the opinion or guess of some individual as to the amount necessary to maintain a family in accordance with standards which, in his opinion, are 'proper' or 'necessary,' or 'decent.'" But, Fitch noted,

> compilers of budgetary standards have been far more apt to err on the side of moderation than on the side of over-generosity. Even a cursory examination of the quantities enumerated in the typical budget reveals ample evidence of a studied conservatism. In the budget worked out by the U.S. Bureau of Labor Statis-tics, for example, a man is allowed one-third of a suit each winter. That is, one winter suit every three years. A woman is allowed one-half of a winter hat. She is allowed eight pairs of cotton stockings a year. When one comes to examine the details of these budgets he is inclined to wonder, not whether the investigator was over-enthusiastic, but whether it is possible for any family to scale down its consumption sufficiently to keep within the limits indicated.[8]

Table 2 summarizes a sample of contemporary estimates of the minimum cost of living for various years between 1900 and the World War. Though the statistical bases of these estimates are too different from one another to permit useful correlation, there is sufficient broad agreement to warrant accepting them as an approximation of a minimum standard of living.

Their unweighted, unadjusted average (for a family of five) is $675. That this figure indicates the general range may be illustrated by a few comments on the studies. For example, the figure for the 1901 U.S. Bureau of Labor study, $618 (line 2), was an estimate of the cost of living based on an average of consumption expenditures for a large sample

TABLE 2

Various Selected Estimates of Annual
Minimum Cost of Living, Pre-World War I
(in current dollars)

Year	Family Size	Estimated Minimum$	Survey Locale	Source of Estimate
1901	5	754	Massachusetts	Mass Bureau of Labor Statistics[a]
1901	4	618	32 States/D.C.	US Bureau of Labor[bc]
1902	?	520	NYC	NY Bureau of Labor Statistics[a]
1903	6-7	600	All US Cities	Ryan, A Living Wage[d]
1903	4-5	600	Anthracite Coal	Mitchell, Organized Labor[e]
1903	5	624	NYC	NY Charity Official[a]
1904	5	460	New England, NY PA IN OH IL	Hunter, Poverty[a]
1907	5	825	NYC	NY State Conference of Charities[b]
1909	5	900	NYC	Chapin, Standard of Living[f]
1909	5 3/5	700	All US	US Immigration Commission[g]
1910	4-5	800	All US	Numerous studies[h]
1911	5	650	US Cities	Streightoff, Standard of Living[f]
1913	5	750	Northern Cities	Nearing, Financing[j]

[a]Robert Hunter, Poverty (New York, 1917 [1904]), pp. 51-52.
[b]John A. Fitch, The Causes of Industrial Unrest (New York, 1924), pp. 41-44.
[c]US Census Bur., Hist. Stat. of the U.S., Colonial Times to 1970, Bicentennial Ed., Pt. 1 (Wash.D.C., 1975), Ser. G 554-563, pp. 309, 321.
[d]John A. Ryan, A Living Wage (New York, 1912 [1906]), p. 150.
[e]John Mitchell, Organized Labor (Phila., 1903), p. 118.
[f]Robert C. Chapin, The Standard of Living Among Workingmen's Families in New York (New York, 1909), p. 245.
[g]US Commission on Industrial Relations, Final Report, 1:22.
[h]Carleton Parker, "The I.W.W.," Atlantic Monthly, 120 (Nov. 1917), 660.
[i]Frank H. Streightoff, The Standard of Living Among the Industrial People of America (Boston, 1911), p. 162.
[j]Scott Nearing, Financing the Wage Earner's Family (New York, 1913), p. 97.

of the population. This budget study examined expenses for rent, fuel, lighting, food, clothing and sundries of 11,156 "normal" families in thirty-two states and the District of Columbia, and included wage and salaried occupations. "Normal" was defined as families with a working husband, a wife at home, no more than 5 children (none over 14 years of age), with no dependents, boarders, lodgers, or servants. The average income of these fathers was $651, which, as shall be shown, was more than the average annual income of most workers, thus raising the question as to whether "normal" is an appropriate description of these families. In fact, some 6,000 families in the survey had incomes lower the average $651, and consequently had less to spend than the $618 average expenditure. But granting that the compilers of the budget survey used the word "normal" in an ordinary sense, it is safe to infer that they would have considered $618 a reasonable expense to maintain a minimum standard of living.[9]

What is excluded by this definition and hence missing in the 1901 survey is a comparable study of the income and expenses of families who needed the earnings of other family members and/or income from outside sources, such as boarders and lodgers, to maintain a minimum standard of living. The 1909 study by the U.S. Immigration Commission (line 11) found that 30 per cent of its 15,726 families depended on income from board and room, and 79 per cent of the fathers of these families earned less than the $700 per year judged to be a minimum for "anything approaching decency."[10] In

1905, the Census of Manufactures similarly found that 62 per

cent of some 2,600,000 male workers studied earned less than

$12 per week,[11] or less than $576 per year if they worked

full time. (Based on a 288-day year and a 6-day week: 288/6

= 48x$12 = $576. See n. 7.)

However, whatever the bias or inadequacy of minimum

cost-of-living estimates, many contemporary economists were

agreed that income for a great many wage-earners consistent-

ly fell below even these approximations. Figures for the

total number who did not earn these minimum incomes were

difficult to garner then, but various surveys indicated the

ubiquity of low wages. The researchers used a variety of

statistics to illustrate their impressions, such as that 51

per cent of unskilled workers in shoe-making (as reported by

the U.S. Census for 1900) earned less than $300 annually;

testimony before the 1901 Industrial Commission showed that

some 350,000 railroad shopmen and trackhands earned less

than $375 per year in the North (less than $150 in the

South), 60 per cent of the miners in the anthracite coal

districts earned less than $450, and workers in a Georgia

cotton mill received an average of only $234 per year.[12]

The U.S. Census for 1910 was quoted, reporting the average

annual wage for workers in manufacturing plants in New York

City as $584, and $592 in Pittsburgh;[13] the Federal Immi-

gration Commission report of 1910 was cited to the effect

that 8 of 12 basic industries failed to pay the family

breadwinner $550 per year.[14] Frank Streightoff, using the
1904 Census of Manufactures, and counting factory workers,
coal miners, railroad hands, domestics, clerks and other
urban workers, reckoned "it would be conservative to estimate the number of adult males usually classed as industrial
workers and persons engaged in personal service, who receive
less than $600 a year for their labor, at five million"; and
in 1915, Scott Nearing concluded that the wages for 4/5 of
the men and 9/10 of the women employed in industry fell
below $750 annually.[15]

More recent attempts to measure the annual income of
workers are indicated in Table 3. Though none of these
directly assess the situation of the unskilled and migratory
workers to whom the IWW made its appeal, it is reasonable to
assume that their earning power fell below the average
incomes represented by these studies. Columns (1) and (2),
for example, reflect a higher average than the average
worker was likely to receive since they summarize the earnings for employees in all occupations, including salaried
executives' compensation and income from high-paying profes-
sions such as finance, insurance and real estate.[16] The
income differential shown in Column (2), derived by adjus-
ting full-time earnings by the relevant unemployment percen-
tages (as shown in Table 1),[17] is probably a closer estimate of the average worker's earnings.

Employees in manufacturing made up a large part of the
total work force, and included great numbers of unskilled

TABLE 3

Average Annual Earnings of All Employees, 1900-1920;
Comparative Estimates for Employees in Manufacturing
(in current dollars)

Year	All Fulltime Employees Lebergott[a] (1)	Adjusted for Unemployment Lebergott[a] (2)	Full-Time Wage Earners In Manufacturing		
			Lebergott[b] (3)	Rees[c] (4)	Douglas[d] (5)
1900	418	375	487	432	435
1901	438	401	511	446	456
1902	472	437	537	474	473
1903	477	441	548	481	486
1904	482	432	538	471	477
1905	490	451	561	487	494
1906	504	488	577	526	506
1907	529	502	598	538	522
1908	519	446	548	482	475
1909	545	496	599	512	518
1910	575	517	651	538	558
1911	587	520	632	545	537
1912	601	554	651	564	550
1913	633	587	689	585	578
1914	639	555	696	574	580
1915	635	547	661	---	568
1916	705	647	751	---	651
1917	807	748	883	---	774
1918	994	972	1,107	---	980
1919	1,142	1,117	1,293	---	1,158
1920	1,342	1,236	1,532	---	1,358

[a]Stanley Lebergott, Manpower in Economic Growth: The American Record Since 1800 (New York, 1964), Table A-16, pp. 479-480.

[b]Lebergott, Table A-18, p. 480.

[c]Albert Rees, Real Wages In Manufacturing, 1980-1914 (Princeton, 1961), Table 10.

[d]Paul H. Douglas, Real Wages in the United States, 1890-1926 (Boston, 1930), Table 147.

factory workers, often immigrants, who occupied the bottom
ranks in pay. In 1910, for instance, there were some
7,828,000 workers in manufacturing.[18] Since average income
is the quotient of total wages divided by the total number
of wage-earners, considerably more than half of these, over
four million, earned less than the $651 of Lebergott's
estimate of average income in manufacturing for that year
(3). This low-paid group was probably larger in actuality,
since Lebergott's figures in Column (3) also include salaried employees and are unadjusted for unemployment. Both
Lebergott (3) and Rees (4) utilized the fundamental research
of Paul H. Douglas (5). The differences among them are
accountable, in brief, by various corrections. Douglas, in
some cases, used union wage scales to compute his series,
standards often not met in practice. Rees corrected his
figures for this, but used a smaller sample; Lebergott
restored Douglas' sample size.[19]

In any case, the differences among them are slight.
What they confirm, as shown by a comparison with Table 2, is
the judgment of contemporary observers like John A. Fitch,
who found that "it is difficult to avoid the conclusion that
in the leading industries of the country the average wage-
earner of this period was in receipt of an annual income
that was somewhat below the most competent estimates as to
the amount necessary for the decent support of a family of
average size."[20]

What this meant for such a family was an increasing

144

dependence on the labor of women and children for supplemental income, and reliance on charity. It meant decreased educational opportunity. Above all, it meant malnourishment, which in turn shortened life expectancy, increased susceptibility to illness and disease, and led to higher infant mortality rates. The Federal Children's Bureau reported infant death rates up to three times as high for the poor as for the fairly well-off: in one such study the rates were 256 per 1,000 for families earning less than $10 per week (less than $520 annually), and only 84 per 1,000 for families earning at least $25 per week.[21] As one economist remarked about these rates, "we might call certain low earnings a dying wage instead of a living wage."[22]

But by far the most injurious by-product of inadequate incomes was the creation of a vast number of underemployed and migratory laborers, whose unstable life deprived them of family ties, education, the franchise, and dignity. Unskilled laborers, cast upon their own resources, contended with the vicissitudes of the economy and the cupidity of their fellow man. The numbers of this floating labor population -- migratories, casual laborers, drifters, hobos, tramps, bums, vagrants, rounders, blanket-stiffs, snow-birds, knights of the road -- were estimated by students of the subject (all of whom lamented the lack of accurate statistics) at anywhere from two million to five million. The 1910 Census, for instance, listed some 12 million unskilled and semi-skilled laborers, nearly 1/3 of the total labor force.[23] Of these, Carleton Parker estimated that 10,400,000 were unskilled male workers, of whom "some 3,500,000 moved, by discharge or quitting, so regularly from one work town to another that they could be called migratory labor."[24] A report by Paul Brissenden for the National Bureau of Economic Research estimated that more than 15 per cent, or some 3-1/2 million urban wage-earners, were under-employed in 1915.[25]

A Commission on Industrial Relations staff report on the labor market focused on the high rate of seasonal unemployment in all industries.

> At least 800,000 wage earners who are employed by the manufacturing industries of our country in the fall of the year are laid off every winter. The railroads drop about 200,000 working people, mostly track workers, for part of every year. The grain belt of the middle west calls for 100,000 men during harvest time and then turns them adrift. Our coal mines work ordinarily only about two-thirds of the year, and lay off close to 100,000 men during the slackest month. Every kind of industry, agriculture, mining, trade, transportation, employs its people irregularly and drops from the payroll a large portion of its workers for part of every year.[26]

The same report pointed out the great turnover in all industries, a pattern that called into question the usual business explanation of this constant shifting as being due to deficiencies in character, work habits, etc.

> A large mail order house which began the year with about 10,500 employees and ended with about the same number, engaged during that year 8,841 people in order to maintain their force. A manufacturing establishment employing an average of 7,200 people in 1913 hired 6,980 during that year. An automobile factory is reported to have hired in 1912 21,000 employees in order to maintain an operating force of 10,000. A large steel plant employing about 15,000 men normally hires

146

an equal number to maintain that force. During the
years when it wanted to increase the force 3-1/2 times
as many were hired as were actually needed to make up
the increase. In some lumber camps and saw mills on
the Pacific Coast all men are discharged twice a year,
in July and December, and complete new forces are
hired, when work is resumed. In the logging camps it
is customary to hire five men in the course of the
season to keep one job filled.[27]

Inadequate wages, hard working conditions, and an irra-

tional labor market helped create this population of floa-

ting laborers. Uneducated, undernourished, often of foreign

birth, they were the propertyless down-and-outs of the lower

classes. The middle class employed them for fixing a roof

or cutting firewood, for harvesting wheat or laying track,

provided they stayed out of sight in labor camps or moved on

when the job was done. This was the class of labor the IWW

was determined to organize and raise from the depths. As

the IWW voiced their grievances and disillusion and the

injustice and indignities they had experienced, attitudes

towards this underclass of migratory labor hardened. The

middle class blamed the trouble on the moral weakness of the

individual, the low intelligence of the "dregs of Europe,"

the insidiousness of the agitator. The more visible the

"Tramp Question" became, the more prejudice was evoked; soon

any itinerant laborer was suspected of being a Wobbly.

147

This class prejudice was ubiquitous, affecting even educated professionals. It appears, for example, in a U.S. Department of Labor bulletin entitled "Industrial Relations in the West Coast Lumber Industry." Cloice R. Howd, an authority on West Coast labor relations, describes the jobs, working conditions, and the strike history of the industry. In a chapter on "The Workers," Howd classifies lumber workers according to their ambitions. There are five types: those for whom the job is a means to another end (e.g. "stump ranchers," who, in their spare time, clear land they hope to farm); ambitious workers who hope to rise to better positions within the industry; typical lumberjacks, who see the job as a means to maintain a normal existence; migratory workers who "seek in the job merely the means to live a self-supporting but essentially unstable life"; and "hobos," men "who have lost all touch with society and who work just enough to secure a stake to provide only for a mere animal existence."[28]

For Howd, these were moral categories. The belief that hard work is the key to success informs his description of the "ambitious worker." This group "contains those men whom we are pleased to think of as having the typical American attitude toward industry. When he enters the industry the boy hopes some day to own the plant in which he works, and he endeavors to make his dream come true." Howd maintains that "a great many of the employers in the industry have risen from the ranks, and the way is still open for a man of intelligence, energy, and ambition to rise from laborer to foreman or higher," although he concedes that "such opportunities are relatively less numerous now than formerly."[29]

Most of the fourth type, migratory workers, were "industrial misfits or failures" (a category that also included "the artist, the pioneer, the genius"). Referring to an application of the Stanford revision of the Binet-Simon intelligence scale to casual laborers, in which 19 per cent of them ranked as morons (compared to prisoners and street-car men), Howd cites a lack of mental ability as a primary reason for the existence of migratory workers.[30] Even though Howd was an economist familiar with working conditions in the competitive lumber industry, his explanation for the migrant's situation did not touch on economics or industrial psychology. Instead, he blamed the moral qualities of the man:

> The man without interest in his work is usually a poor workman, and so is the first to be let go in times of slack work. Unemployment forces him to move and the first move makes the second easier and more necessary, the steps downward become more rapid and certain. Soon the worker has lost all connection with a settled life, his family is abandoned or disintegrated, and he becomes entirely foot-loose.[31]

Why certain industries had a high proportion of migrant workers, or whether these industries created, maintained and exploited this type of labor for their own ends, are questions Howd does not consider.

When Howd describes the "hobo," his language reflects disdain. Hobos are "the lowest type of worker"; he sees them as having "sunk down through the ranks of the true migratories." The hobo works "only when he is compelled to by hunger," and does not hesitate to beg or steal. He is blamed for the immigration problem: the hobo "is the most unreliable and unsatisfactory of workers, and it is usually to avoid dependence upon such men that south European and Asiatic laborers have been favorably received." The hobo is identified with the IWW: "it is the hobo workers who present the really dangerous element in the labor problem. They are foot-loose rebels who no longer recognize the ordinary conventions of modern society but challenge the whole industrial system."[32] Howd's explanation of the causes of this challenge showed where his sympathies lay:

> That challenge may be but the dumb resentment of the failure and outcast against the man who has succeeded, or it may be the very much more dangerous challenge of the I.W.W., which has a very positive philosophy to take the place of laissez faire and respect for private property. With such a group there can be no common ground. The I.W.W. refuses to accept any of the assumptions of the employer or of society, and declares eternal and uncompromising war against the whole system in which the employer finds a place. It should be frankly recognized that the members of the I.W.W., and to a lesser degree all the migratories, stand on this platform: "The working class and the employing class have nothing in common. . . . Between these two classes a struggle must go on until the workers of the world organize as a class, take possession of the earth and the machinery of production, and abolish the wage system."[33]

Howd was not the only educated investigator who disliked the Wobblies and lacked sympathy for migratory workers. The IWW also offended Daniel O'Regan, an investigator for the Commission on Industrial Relations. Reporting on

150

the free-speech fights, he could not conceal his shock. In his report, O'Regan reveals his distress at the Wobblies' irreverence for business, government, the Army and Navy, the flag, and religious sentiment. "In fact, everything we have been taught to respect from our earliest days is the subject of abuse by the members of this organization. I have had hundreds of conversations with different members of the I.W.W. and have yet to find one who believes in any of our institutions and who has any regard whatever for the property rights of others."[34]

After describing the tactics of a typical free-speech fight -- provoking arrests, insisting on jury trials, raising a din in the jails, provoking violence by the jailers, capitalizing on publicity -- O'Regan comments, "some of these I.W.W.'s, the 'Ammunition,' they are called, will suffer a terrible lot for 'The Cause.' If they'd do as much for wages as they do for The Cause they'd get a good job and quit the I.W.W.'s."[35] O'Regan described the "water cure" administered by fire-department hoses during the Fresno free-speech fight, where "every bit of clothes was torn off the prisoners by this stream and there were very few who were not black and blue."[36] O'Regan evidently felt the treatment was deserved:

> Of course this was a very extreme punishment, but if we remember that it is a policy of the I.W.W.'s in jail to force a demonstration, that they insult everyone, women, and children, who come near the jail during their incarceration, it will be evident that some such treatment must be given them. In their newspapers they make a big fuss about this kind of punishment but they

151

respect it nevertheless and it's hard to get any of
them to return to a city where they are treated like
this.[37]

Like Howd and O'Regan, it was difficult for most Americans of the middle class to understand the phenomenon of
migrating labor. Part of this difficulty was a widely
accepted belief that self-help and self-reliance were sufficient for success, and that failure was evidence of a flawed
character. Few Americans were able to pose the problem in
other terms. That the industrial system depended upon large
numbers of casual laborers; or that technological displacement, seasonal unemployment, disorganized and dangerous
transport of workers, or market fluctuations contributed to
the increase of floating workers, were not easy notions to
accomodate for minds trained in 19th century schools. Such
appraisals sounded too much like excuses for failure.

The growing number of drifters, casual laborers and
Wobblies was much on the minds of men of affairs during the
Progressive period, but their concern did not often focus on
the underlying industrial structure or the reform of bad
conditions. In large measure this was because the middle
class put a psychological distance between themselves and
the squalid life of hobo workers. Instead, remedies either

152

proposed a return to moral uplift -- a popular 19th century theme -- or promoted various social engineering schemes to control the problem.

Among the former of these remedies was a strong faith in the ameliorating effects of agricultural life. Industrial Relations Commission witness J.V. Paterson pointed to "the broad acres that are waiting"[38]; another Commission witness lamented, "we have had these unemployed men walking the railroad tracks back and forth through this land for years, and they haven't done anything with it."[39] These businessmen were among a great many Americans who still idealized the tiller of the soil and believed in the rehabilitative powers of farming. Professor John R. Commons, one of the Commissioners, was later to incorporate the "safety-valve" of Western land into his explanation of the development of American labor: "As long as the poor and industrious can escape from the conditions which render them subject to other classes," he would write, "so long do they refrain from that aggression on the property rights or political power of others, which is the symptom of a 'labor movement.'"[40]

But it was not easy to become a landowner. The Commission on Industrial Relations examined this issue on several occasions. For example, Washington State Labor Commissioner Edward W. Olson was asked:

> COMMISSIONER LENNON: What opportunities are there now in the State of Washington for securing homesteads -- getting land either under the homestead laws or for

very small compensation?

MR. OLSON: As far as I know there is very little opportunity, and where there is opportunity for a man to secure land, to secure a homestead, he would necessarily have to have considerable money in order to carry it through successfully. That has been my observation. Our land problem is a very deep one.

COMMISSIONER LENNON: Not easy to get onto the land unless you have means, then?

MR. OLSON: You must have means, and small means are not sufficient, such as they used to be.[41]

Like belief in the self-made man -- held more firmly as possibility receded -- the less likely homesteading became, the more it was felt to be the common American denominator. Ole Hanson, who succeeded Hiram Gill as mayor of Seattle and became famous as the man who "crushed the bolshevists" during the 1919 Seattle General Strike, bore witness to this faith in farming in the patriot's handbook he subsequently wrote. "The man who raises food," Hanson asserted in Americanism Versus Bolshevism, "is seldom a bolshevist." He lamented the passing of the day when the immigrant "went out on the land and tilled the soil, established a family and took out his citizenship papers, acquired a farm, and became a real American." Hanson, like others, attributed the decline of this practice to the Slavic and South European immigrant, who "does not go out on the land; he does not have a family; he does not establish a home, but herds in congested, foreign colonies in our great cities; and hence does not become Americanized as readily or as rapidly. Ofttimes he becomes an itinerant and wanders from place to place."[42]

For Hanson, "character" determined whether a man got

154

ahead or not. He advocated selective immigration on the
basis of national need and the desire of the prospective
immigrant to become Americanized. He called for population
distribution to areas of "need," because

> the greatest problem of our country is to get people on
> the land and stop, in a measure, the overgrowth our
> cities. We have become a great industrial nation, but
> our farming development is not keeping pace with our
> industrial growth. Why not select men who are farmers,
> preferably men with families, and send them to that
> part of the country in need of farmers?"[43]

As social disorder increased prior to World War One,
others proposed labor colonies. The rationalist view of
labor as a commodity made it seem natural to blame unemployment upon the moral depravity of the unemployed rather than
upon fluctuating economic conditions. Thus British workhouses and European labor colonies under mercantilist policies exacted forced labor and treated the unemployed poor as
degenerates;[44] in the late nineteenth century, detention
colonies were proposed for the moral failures among London's
poor.[45] Likewise, the idea of labor colonies was propoun-
ded in pre-World War I America, stimulated by the jingoism
of the Spanish-American War, by fears generated by McKinley's assassination, and by the appearance of radical labor
groups.[46]

Concern with control and punishment of vagrants stemmed
from the equation of work with virtue. To many, laziness
was criminal. So believed Mr. L.A. Halbert, Superintendent
of the Kansas City Board of Public Welfare, who was called
by the Commission on Industrial Relations as an expert

155

witness. Among the suggestions solicited from Mr. Halbert
was one for labor colonies:

> Until we reach a comparatively ideal state of society,
> any complete scheme for dealing with unemployment needs
> some machinery for dealing with the backward and incom-
> petent people who are really incapable of full self-
> support, especially under competitive conditions, and
> the other class of people who are criminally lazy or
> really unwilling to work, although this class is compa-
> ratively small. For the incompetent and defective
> classes there should be voluntary labor colonies or
> colonies with only a mild degree of restraint and
> supervision, and for the last class of vagrants or
> criminally lazy people there should be compulsory labor
> colonies.[47]

Halbert's proposal was not unique; others developed

elaborate plans. One of these appeared in Western Woman's

Outlook for January 23, 1913 (p. 15). Entitled "A Scheme

For Labor Colonies Under A State Board," the proposal sug-

gests that "each colony should contain four groups or sec-

tions, separately located in one neighborhood, three of the

groups to consist of free laborers, and one group to be made

up of forced laborers." The first two groups would be

composed of able-bodied and non-able-bodied "free" laborers

unable to secure employment. The third group

> consists of vagrants, penniless wanderers; hoboes,
> able-bodied unemployed accustomed to casual labor and
> willing to work only at odd jobs; tramps, traveling
> without funds for personal recreation and willing to
> work temporarily. These make a contract to work for at
> least two months steadily. Their clothing is taken
> from them and they are loaned a sufficient amount of
> apparel for use until the end of the contract. While
> in the colony they wear the clothing of the colony
> which is not observably uniform, although ineradicably
> marked. If they depart with this clothing they are
> arrested for stealing and removed to the fourth group.
> Curative and reformatory methods are followed, and
> instruction is given in manual work. . . . The fourth
> group consists of misdemeanants, sentenced by court for

periods of from two months to three years; and of vagabonds, drunkards, able-bodied persons refusing to work and vagrants refusing to enter one of the other three groups. They are all under police control, may be chained, and are forced to labor.[48]

Romance with bureaucractic control pervaded these reform-tinged years. Even Peter Speek, one of the most clear-sighted field investigators on the Industrial Relations Commission staff, was attracted by the idea of efficient (and altruistic) labor colonies. Speek, whose proposed reforms for improving housing, transportation, farm credit and tenancy laws, education, etc., formed the basis for many of the Commission's conclusions, recommended establishing "labor colonies for those who are vagrants, in order to rehabilitate them by means of proper food, regular habits of living, and regular work that will train them for some particular trade or calling."[49] Speek's motives were perhaps more humane than others; his experiences investigating migratory labor were sobering and powerful. He felt the existing situation might be mitigated by introducing order and humane treatment for a floating labor population that he estimated at one million, "among whom 80 per cent to 90 per cent are unskilled, and no less than 50 per cent of whom are immigrants, the South-European races predominating."[50]

In 1915, The New Republic, in an editorial entitled "Salvaging the Unemployable," linked the current vogue for scientific management with industrial labor colonies. This editorial, presumably written by Herbert Croly, referred to "five hundred thousand tramps, more or less, beating up and

down the lanes and highways of the country, mildly menacing
life and property, seriously menacing morality and the spirit of independence."[51] It offered a "rational program"
that was designed "to collect from the city and country the
hordes of tramps and loafers, to restore as many of them as
possible to independence, and to force the rest to draw
their own weight;" social progress depended upon "disem-
barrassing society of the incubus of the work-shy."[52] No-
ting that "what makes a man unemployable is not, as a rule,
lack of good intentions, but lack of will power to master
the complicated series of operations that make up even the
simplest ordinary task," it proposed the organization of
"great industrial colonies under charge of a corps of expert
scientific managers."

> In such shops there will be hundreds or even thousands
> of tasks, each perfectly definite, simple, quickly
> learned and easily controlled. The tramp just brought
> from the roadside or the loafer committed from the
> slums will be set at the simplest task, taught how to
> perform it, and kept at it until he can earn a good
> day's wages.[53]

Since the work-shy care little about money, and the few
wants they have "are of a devitalizing, stupefying character
-- unrestrained sex indulgence, drugs, alcohol, or even the
mere shifting of scenes," they must be provided not only
with incentives to develop industrial habits but must be
conditioned to build up "a system of normal wants."

> And this would require the presence of experts in
> practical psychology, to devise wholesome enjoyments,
> reduced to advance the subject from the more simple to
> the more complex, until in the end he might be restored
> to society with his full complement of wants to satis-

158

fy, as well as with the industrial habits essential to their satisfaction. . . . It is a matter of common observation that the work-shy frequently suffer from neurasthenia, originating, perhaps, in obscure physical lesions -- latent tuberculosis, hypertrophied organs, obstructed ducts, etc. Competent medical observers would of course be attached to the colonies, and by cooperation with the psychological and industrial experts, should be able to discover and remove many such defects, thus restoring normal efficiency.[54]

The left-overs, the "irredeemables," "could be made to earn at least the cost of their maintenance, and, with due regard to the provision of suitable recreations and enjoyments, might be indefinitely interned without sacrifice of such right to happiness as society can afford to accord to their kind.[55]

Labor colony schemes were essentially designed to control the lower classes; social control was also implicit, and often explicit, in the scientific management movement. Its attitude towards unskilled labor is suggested by the reported remark of Frederick W. Taylor, the founder of scientific management. Having taught a Dutchman to shovel forty-seven tons of pig-iron a day -- by precisely calculating the size and weight of the shovel, the arc and distance of the toss, the number and duration of rest periods, etc. -- Taylor commented, "one of the very first requirements for a man who is fit to handle pig iron as a regular occupation is that he shall be so stupid and so phlegmatic that he more nearly resembles an ox than any other type."[56] To devotees of scientific management, labor was merely one of a number of factors of production, like tools or machinery;

159

when these time-and-motion studies encountered worker opposition, scientific management revealed its willingness to sacrifice workers' welfare to improved costs and profits.[57]

Where the businessman did take an interest in his employee, it was often in one form or another of "corporate efficiency." So-called "welfare work," pensions, and profit-sharing plans were often means of enforcing acceptance of the company's policies, including anti-unionism.[58] The proliferation of company towns, whose failures were punctuated by the Pullman strike of 1894, was a movement to institute controls on what were in effect labor colonies. Such efforts were sometimes motivated by a belief in stewardship, and usually by the need to rationalize large industries. In either case, the results served industry first and only incidentally served the workers.

CHAPTER 7

FLOATING LABOR
AND THE FAILURE OF COMMUNITY

You ask me why the I.W.W. is not patriotic to the
United States. If you were a bum without a blan-
ket; if you had left your wife and kids when you
went West for a job, and had never located them
since; if your job never kept you long enough in
a place to qualify you to vote; if you slept in a
lousy, sour bunk-house, and ate food just as rotten as they could give you and get by with it; if
deputy sheriffs shot your cooking cans full of
holes and spilled your grub on the ground; if
your wages were lowered on you when the bosses
thought they had you down; if there was one law
for Ford, Suhr, and Mooney, and another for Harry
Thaw; if every person who represented law and
order and the nation beat you up, railroaded you
to jail, and the good Christian people cheered
and told them to go to it, how in the hell do you
expect a man to be patriotic? This war is a
business man's war and we don't see why we should
go out and get shot in order to save the lovely
state of affairs that we now enjoy.

-- Big Bill Haywood, 1917

Although there was much talk about the "labor question"

during the pre-war years, few seemed able to grasp its

dimensions, or trace its origins to the industrial system,

or see its human costs. The middle class, eager for auto-

mobiles, aircraft, electric power, telephones and wireless,

did not want to be reminded about the bad luck of a few

161

immigrants or tramps. During the Progressive era, class
consciousness was apparent in the unwillingness to give
harvest, mill, timber, or mine workers a say in determining
industrial conditions.

Unskilled workers made up a traveling population who
worked construction camps, farms, orchards, forests and
mines. They were drawn principally from five sources: 1)
sons of farm hands or tenant farmers with no prospects; 2)
sons of common laborers in the cities; 3) immigrants; 4)
skilled and semi-skilled workmen who were technologically
displaced, disabled by accident or disease, or blacklisted;
5) former members of the middle class who had failed in
business or profession.[1]

The life stories of these workers were occasionally
recorded by field investigators or by the men themselves.
Peter Speek, one of several staff investigators for the
Commission on Industrial Relations, interviewed more than
1,000 itinerant laborers and vagrants.

> Almost all laborers interviewed for life stories who
> had spent their childhood in the country in the family
> of a farm hand, tenant, or settler on new land, stated
> that they could not get any schooling to speak of, nor
> any training in a trade, because the parents were so
> poor that they, in their childhood, as soon as they
> were capable of doing anything useful, had to help
> their parents earn bread.[2]

He selected sixty-four of these case histories as representative of American farm boys who became common laborers.
Speek also prepared a composite description of the life of
such a casual worker that clearly illustrates the human

costs of industrialism; his picture of the demoralization of American workers is rescued from melodrama by its verisimilitude.[3] This composite and several examples from Speek's field notes can be found in Appendix IV.

Others researching the problem of migratory labor drew similar pictures. Carleton Parker, in his appearance before the Industrial Relations Commission, cited statistics from a study of 100 typical life stories of such workers made in 1913-1914 by the Commission of Housing and Immigration of the State of California. Among the figures quoted by Dr. Parker were these:

> 55 per cent had left school before the age of 15, and of 26 per cent we were unable to get figures. It seems probable they had never been at school. Seventy-nine per cent of the total were below the age of 40 years; 54 per cent had been migratory and seasonal laborers for less than 10 years, and we were unable to get data for 16 per cent; 20 per cent had worked on an average less than 7 months in the year; 62 per cent worked less than 10 months. The best daily earnings of 36 per cent had never exceeded $3 a day. As to their occupations: 76 per cent had never been anything except common laborers, even the 24 per cent who were classed as skilled, these had in most parts fallen or been forced out of the trades they professed; 35 per cent were or had been members of labor unions, while 65 per cent were absolutely unorganized, knew nothing of any labor organization; 51 per cent sought what work they wanted or could get through the present system that we have, the haphazard private employment agency system.
> The extent of the social unrest which has been typical of the California agricultural laborer for the past two years was shown by the fact that 42 per cent of these accidental individuals investigated expressed extremely radical political and economic opinions; 30 per cent professed to be seeking steady work and planning to steady down. Practically the remaining 70 per cent gave their occupation as floating laborers; had no ambition, apparently, or at least, had no prospect of getting a steady job. Of nationalities -- American born, 58 per cent; foreign born, 42 per cent; of the foreign born 6 per cent were Swedes, 5 per cent Ita-

lians, 5 per cent English, 1 per cent Austrian, 5 per cent French, 3 per cent Russian, 7 per cent Irish, 4 per cent German, and 1 per cent Finnish, Danish, Mexican, Bohemian, and Portuguese.[4]

Another witness before the Industrial Relations Commission was Dr. A.E. Wood, an instructor in social science at Reed College in Portland, Ore. Dr. Wood submitted brief sketches of personal histories obtained from migratory workers who sought charity relief during the winter of 1913-1914 when unemployment was very high. Among them were several who had once had a trade:

No. 4. An Italian barber who had come to Oregon from Pittsburgh. In different cities all the way to the West he had tried to get work in his line, but was unsuccessful, possibly because he was not a union man. His clothes now were so worn that he could not make a good appearance. Said that he could not work on the rock pile, as the tools were poor and the work was too heavy for him. He said that the last three months he had been able to get only 10 or 15 days of work. He had been begging at the doors for dry bread until the opening of the tabernacle.

No. 5. Man of Irish and German descent about 43 years of age. Lost his wife and three children in the San Francisco earthquake. Lost his paper hanging and painting business. He tried to get his insurance from the insurance company, but did not succeed. This man looked sober and worried. He said that at one time he had made some money on an onion crop in California, but had paid it all out for sickness. Again he had had work in a lumberyard, when his leg was broken by a falling log, and the money he had saved was all gone before he got out of the hospital. He had attempted to start a paper-hanging business in Marshfield, Oreg., but came away from there and wanted to go to Australia. He brooded over his ill luck continually. . . .

No. 7. An Englishman, 27 years old, whose home was in Liverpool. He was a photographer by trade, and had his camera materials in a trunk somewhere. He came to this country with money made in a camera exhibit. Came first to the United States and then went to Canada, where he went broke. Came back into the "States" in the "crow's nest" (cowcatcher). Has no hopes for the future. Used to worry about it, but now takes things as they come. Had worked in the harvest fields in Canada, but had acquired the wandering spirit, and wanted always to move on. At this time he was getting most of his meals by cutting wood and general work. At the rock pile he could not finish his one-half cubic yard in four hours; so he went back the next day. He said that he would go back to Liverpool again if he had the money.[5]

The middle class found it hard to understand or sympathize with such men. The loss of self-esteem, the gradual slide into despair, poverty and alcoholism was an invisible process. What was visible to the middle class -- lazy tramps, noisy agitators -- was the end result. Few considered what such laborers faced daily: deplorable working conditions in factories and labor camps, an exploitive labor market, hazardous travel by foot and freight, uncompensated accident and illness, seasonal employment, child labor, blacklists, etc.

Employers, especially self-made men who had risen above such a background, commonly expressed exasperation at the constant turnover in their work force. Seattle lumberman Paul E. Page explained the problem to the Industrial Relations Commission:

> MR. PAGE: Yes. Well, now, let me explain this rover. We have a vast number of men in this State, swarms of them, as I suppose there is in other States, who work at a low wage. They are men who work at the construction of logging railroads, and they are the men who do the work in the yards of the lumber mills. Now, these men as a class won't work more than three or four days a week. That is all they want to work; and they are the rovers. They keep coming and going all the time. Now, let me illustrate that to you just a minute while we are on that.
> MR. THOMPSON [COMMISSION COUNSEL]: Yes.
> MR. PAGE: To show you how that, what that roving

propensity is. Now, in working a crew of 138 men in
January we worked 186 men, in February 222, in March
224, in April 229, May 234, and June 170. Now, those
figures mean a little bit more than that. Now, the
month of January, 186 men were on the payroll to work
138. That means that their means had been exhausted
for the Christmas holidays, and they went to work for a
stake. In February they commenced to rove; March,
April, and May, and June, before the 4th of July, in
order to accumulate a stake for the 4th of July, we
worked 170 as against 234 in May. That is the --
    ACTING CHAIRMAN COMMONS: Mr. Page, does that mean
so many men hired, new men hired?
    MR. PAGE: Yes; our crew is 138 men. Now, in
order to work that 138 men constantly we have on the
pay roll 234 men; you understand?
    ACTING CHAIRMAN COMMONS: Constituting how many
men that you have to hire during the year to keep up
the force?
    MR. PAGE: That is what I am telling you. We use
138 men. But in order to work 138 men every day there
are 234 men coming and going to take these places. One
man works to-day and he drops out; another man takes
his place to-morrow.[6]

Such complaints were an unwitting condemnation of the low

wages and unregulated labor conditions of unskilled workers,

and underscored the haphazard restless life these marginals

lived.

Year after year, the "roving propensity" asserted it-

self as workers floated from one low-paying job to another

with little hope of something better. For many, such work

was merely a succession of odd jobs. In his report on

floating labor, Peter Speek included copies of the employ-

ment records of several typical casual workers who applied

for work through the State Free Employment office at Milwau-

kee. The record card for one Fred Miller (Table 4) shows a

total of 59 jobs during six months in 1913, or one job every

3-1/5 days.[7]

166

TABLE 4

Employment Record for Fred Miller, Wisconsin, 1913

No.	Occupation	Date Sent	No.	Occupation	Date Sent
1	Handy man	May 28	31	Help move	Sep 9
2	General Labor	Jun 19	32	Roofer helper	Sep 12
3	Load car	Jun 30	33	General labor	Sep 15
4	Unload car	Jul 3	34	Unload car	Sep 17
5	General help	Jul 5	35	"	Sep 17
6	"	Jul 8	36	General labor	Sep 18
7	"	Jul 9	37	Beat rugs	Sep 19
8	Pile Flour	Jul 11	38	General labor	Sep 19
9	Roofer helper	Jul 12	39	Peddle bills	Sep 20
10	General labor	Jul 14	40	Roofer helper	Sep 20
11	General labor	Jul 17	41	Unload car	Sep 20
12	Unload car	Jul 23	42	Wheel brick	Sep 24
13	General labor	Jul 24	43	Farm hand	Sep 24
14	Unload car	Jul 28	44	Farm hand	Sep 27
15	Unload car	Jul 29	45	Beat rugs	Sep 27
16	Wrecker help	Jul 30	46	Unload car	Sep 29
17	General Labor	Aug 2	47	Help move	Sep 30
18	"	Aug 4	48	Help move	Oct 1
19	Help Move	Aug 15	49	General labor	Oct 2
20	Unload car	Aug 18	50	Carry samples	Oct 6
21	" "	Aug 19	51	Unload car	Oct 10
22	" "	Aug 20	52	General labor	Oct 30
23	Help move	Aug 21	53	Help move	Oct 31
24	Help move	Aug 23	54	Unload car	Nov 3
25	Roofer helper	Aug 23	55	Unload car	Nov 4
26	Shovel coal	Aug 23	56	General labor	Nov 5
27	Pack tires	Aug 27	57	Unload car	Nov 29
28	Beat Rugs	Sep 2	58	General help	Dec 1
29	Handle Barrels	Sep 2	59	General help	Dec 5
30	Help move	Sep 8			

This was casual labor in and around an urban center. Other workers followed the harvests, or worked the lumber camps from the Gulf States to the Pacific Northwest, picking up whatever work they could. One such worker, a Wobbly named James Foy, who had been a migratory worker for twenty years, sent to the Industrial Pioneer an account of a typical year's employment.[8]

The following is a year's diary which I have kept and which I believe is typical of the average migratory worker. It is absolutely truthful. I give reasons for leaving jobs, together with location and names of employers.

1. Prosser, Farmer, Blackwell, Okla. Thirteen days, $1 per day and board and room. Quit; wages too low.

2. Bates & Rogers, Contractors; excavating for new railroad at Matfield Green, Kansas. Four and a half days at $3.25 for 10 hours; $1.05 per day for board and room. Fired for not working on Sunday. Balance, $9.37.

3. Roberts brothers, Contractors; laying steel at Eldorado, Kansas. Eight days at $3.25 for 10 hours; 10 days board and room at $1.05 per day. Fired; worked too slow. Balance, $15.50.

4. Powers & Jergens, Contractors. Mucking, team outfit, 10 1/2 days; $4 for 10 hours; 11 days board and room at $1.05 per day. Cassidy, Kans. Laid off. Balance, $26.25.

5. Oklahoma Pipe Line Co., Newkirk, Oklahoma. Twenty-eight days, $4 per 9 hours; 53 days bed and board at $1.50 per day. Finished the job. Balance, $62.50.

6. Roberts Bros., Contractors; track work. Lake Mills, Iowa. Eleven and one-half days; $4.25 per 10 hours; 16 days board and bed at $1.20 per day. Strike; black-balled. Balance, $22.25.

7. Robert Bros., Contractors. Custer, Mont. Relaying steel. $4 per 10 hours; 6 days board and bed. Strike for shorter hours and more pay. Balance, $13.60.

8. Thomas Donlan Lumber Co., Paradise, Mont. One day. $3.80 per 8 hours. Board and bed, $1.25 per day. Quit to keep them from taking $4 for tax.

9. Campbell & McGrines. Ostrander, Wash. Labor, building new logging road. Three days, $4.50 per 8 hours. Four days bed and board at $1.20 per day. Fired for being IWW. Balance, $7.50.

10. C. Lind, Auburn, Wash. Farmer and state senator. Pitching hay. Four and a half days, $4.50 per 9 hours. Board and bed in town. $1.50 per day. Got through. Balance, $12.75.

11. Clarence Dirks, Walla Walla, Wash. Farmer, making hay. Four dollars and board per 10 hours. Three and a half days work. Done. Balance, $13.00

12. Mose Burgman, Walla Walla, Wash. Stacking hay. Five days work; $4 per 10 hours, board and bed. Done. Balance, $20.00.

13. R. E. Burrows, Rulo, Wash. Hauling sacked

wheat; $5 per 10 hours and board and bed. Quit. Wanted me to work more hours per day. 12 days work. Balance, $60.00.

14. John Turnbrow, Palouse, Wash. Threshing two and three-quarter days. $4 sun to sun. Quit. Bad conditions and long hours. Balance, $11.00.

15. John Vic, Harrington, Wash. Working with combination harvester. Nine and one-half days, $6 per 10 hours and board and bed. Finished job. Balance, $57.00.

16. Henry Wetter, Rocklyn, Wash. Harvest field. $5 per 10 hours. Job done. 14 days work. Balance, $15.25.

17. Bonnel and Savage Paving Co., Longview, Wash., five and one-half days, $4.50 per 8 hours. $1.20 board and bed. Insanitary living conditions. Balance, $15.25.

18. Morrison and Knutsen. Contractors. Wetherby, Ore. Labor 3 days $3.82 per 9 hours; $1.20 board and bed. Quit; rotten camp, low pay. Balance $5.47.

19. Ranquist, farmer, Blackfoot, Idaho. Picking spuds, some by sack and by day. This man is in the habit of beating his labor bills. Did not know this until I asked for some cash. Had a hard time getting this money. Balance, $17.55.

20. Leroy Bevard, Idaho Falls, Idaho. Working at the spuds, picking and grading; 17 days. Amount, $54.78 and bed and board. Balance, $54.78.

21. Calipatria, Calif. Cushing, Contractor, Paving streets, driving Fresno 17 days. $4.50 per 8 hours. It costs $1.50 per day to eat in restaurant, poor food at that. $3.50 per week for room, so that makes $2 per day board and bed. 18 days. Balance, $40.00.

I will not get more than 4 days more work at the most this year so you will have a complete diary for this year. I have these jobs all itemized in my day book. I thought it will be sufficient for information.

I have talked with a good many fellow workers and all seem to think this would interest Pioneer readers.

It is raining today and so monotonous here, so to have something to do, got busy on this. I have never written for a paper or magazine in my life so, of course, I did not try to write a story but if I could express myself with the pencil I could, I believe, write a very interesting and truthful story about this.

These figures amount to $539.82. There has been a good deal of argument about what a stiff makes going through the country, so here you have the facts.

I have been of the migratory clan for twenty years and believe a good many fellow workers make moves similar to these.

Calipatria, Calif.

In all, Foy worked less than eight months. Out of twenty-one jobs, he was fired 4 times, once for being IWW; he quit 5 times on account of low pay or bad conditions, and was twice involved in strikes. His total income, although earned in the post-war period of higher wages, was below the minimum annual income thought adequate to support a family a decade earlier.

Foy's travels covered 8 states: Oklahoma, Kansas, Iowa, Montana, Washington, Oregon, Idaho and California. He does not say how he traveled, but it is likely he rode the freight trains like the half-million other transients estimated by the railroads to be stealing rides at any one time.[9] In response to a questionnaire sent by the Industrial Relations Commission in 1914, eighteen railroads responded that nearly 2,500,000 men annually stole rides on their lines, a number of whom suffered death or amputation in railroad accidents.[10] Carleton Parker cited figures of 23,964 trespassers killed and 25,236 injured on rail lines between 1901 and 1905, most of whom were hobos.[11] Often such mishaps were not accidents at all, as Peter Speek pointed out, but were

> a result of fights among the jumpers themselves, or between them and petty criminals who are preying on the men, robbing them of whatever money or property they happen to have with them, or between the men and car-men, railway detectives and the local police. Very often the freighters are "ditched," as a result of continual war between the "jumpers" and the carmen, the latter, getting angry and desperate, ditch the men, for instance, in a desert where no water and shelter is available -- so that heat and thirst may ditch the men forever, or in the winter's cold in mountains, or some

other exposed place where there is no shelter nearby. In many cases the poorly clothed men thus ditched perish from exposure. Not seldom one finds news items in the press that here or there along the railway track was found a body of an unidentified man, supposedly a tramp, who had accidently fallen from a freight train. He may have fallen, as all sorts of accidents to the "jumpers" on a freight train are only too common, but also he may have been "ditched" to death by some angry carman. Not only are jumpers killed in fights with the train crews, but also the carmen themselves. In the harvest season of 1914 in the grain States, several such fatal cases occurred.[12]

Between jobs, the drifter slept in boxcars, stables, missions, police stations, or in cheap lodging houses in the cities; or more often,

with a stake of ten dollars he will retire to a hobo camp beside some stream -- his "jungle," as the road vernacular has it -- and, adding his daily quarter or half a dollar to the "Mulligan fund," he will live on until the stake is gone. If he inclines to live further on the charity of the newcomers he is styled a "jungle buzzard" and cast forth. He then resumes his haphazard search for a job, the only economic plan in his mind being a faint realization that about August he must begin to accumulate his thirty-dollar winter stake. Each year finds him physically in worse disrepair, psychologically more hopeless, morally more bitter and anti-social.[13]

When casual laborers were on the job, living conditions were as bad or worse. Another Commission investigator's report described the accomodations for workers who came to the harvest fields of the Middle West.

For a lodging place, the harvest hand is usually left to find accomodations for himself at the barn, the granary, the straw stack or the grain barge or anywhere he pleases outside ot the house. Usually, but not always, he is given blankets or quilts. Some of the larger farmers provide bunk houses and a few furnish beds for the men in the family dwelling house or set up tents for the men, with cots to sleep on, in the yard. Farmers explain their failure to provide better sleeping quarters for their harvest hands as being due, first, to their fear of taking strange, and often unclean and diseased men, into their homes and second, to their belief that the expense of providing special quarters outside the family dwelling house is not warranted by the use which would be made of these quarters. The men come for a few days only in each year, they say, and they expect to sleep outside the house and therefore "don't mind it."

The fact is, however, that many of the men do mind it. They object to sleeping in granaries full of rats and mice, on the bare ground in tents or in barns where the odor of the stable is strong. They object, even when the physical discomforts are not serious, to the attitude which the farmer assumes when he sends them to the barn or the straw stack to sleep.

When the farmer provides a bunk-house and furnishes beds the sanitary conditions may be such as to repel any man of cleanly habits. Sometimes, the men say, the mattresses and blankets are infested with vermin. At other times the bunk-house may be so crowded that there is great danger of the spread of communicable diseases among the men who sleep there. The necessity of using a common towel is another feature of bunk-house accommodations of which complaint is sometimes made.[14]

This same investigator, William Duffue, was sufficiently distressed by what he saw during the summer and fall of 1914 to offer some strong remarks in his report.

The harvest hand and the prospective harvest hand suffer because they cannot find work. Men and boys who have come in good faith to the grain-growing states in search of the high wages and steady employment advertised broadcast over the country as awaiting the willing harvest hands find themselves stranded in towns full of others like themselves without work, food, shelter, money or friends. And the pity of it is that a considerable proportion of these men and boys have left employment or good opportunities to secure employment and have spent their last cent to get to the harvest fields. . . .

It is difficult to paint the picture of these conditions as it should be painted. To appreciate the conditions the members of this Commission should sit in the office of the secretary of the Commercial Club at Aberdeen, South Dakota, and face with him, as this writer did this summer, a large room packed full of men, honest-looking men, begging for work with no questions as to wages, at a time when the city of Aberdeen was full of men like these and the farmers for miles around in all directions were supplied with all the

harvest hands they could use. Or the Commission should
see, as the writer saw, a long column of 150 or 200 men
being marched around the same city of Aberdeen outside
of the city limits from one railroad crossing to another by the police in order to prevent them from coming
into the city of Aberdeen and adding by their presence
to the apprehensiveness of an already overstrung community -- men, too, against whom no crimes where charged
except that they were suspected of being IWW sympathizers and who were mostly free born American citizens
guilty of nothing worse than being without money or
baggage and of having followed the universal practice
of beating their way into town on a freight train, a
practice which was earnestly advised by the police of
Aberdeen, with the approval of the local railroad officials, as a means for leaving the city. Or, if this is
not sufficient, the Commission should walk up and down
the streets of little cities like Oakley and Colby,
Kansas; Huron and Redfield, South Dakota; and Cassel-
ton, North Dakota, and watch the men who sit along the
curbs in long rows, crowd the side walks, lean against
buildings, and hang around the railroad stations waiting, waiting -- always waiting -- for some farmer to
come into town to hire a hand; and note the hungry,
tired, despondent and sometimes sullen looks on the
faces of these men.

If the farmers of the grain growing states want to
know why it is that their harvest hands lack the interest in them and their work that the old time harvest
hand is said to have had, they can find a good part of
the answer in the conditions described in this report.
How can a harvest hand feel a keen interest in the
welfare of a community which induces him to come to it
with the promise of high wages and then runs him out of
town as a vagrant or an I.W.W. when he comes and is
unable to find the work which was advertised, because
other men in his position have been allowed to flock
hit-or-miss about the state without any pretense at
organized direction? And how can a harvest hand be
expected to feel a keen interest in the welfare of a
farmer who sends him to the barn, the granary or the
back yard to sleep or gives him to understand that he
can sleep anywhere about the place except in the house?

The fact is that the conditions described in this
report and similar conditions prevailing in other industries throughout the country outside the harvest
fields are yearly manufacturing just the kind of men of
whom farmers and other employers so bitterly complain.
One who studies large groups of men gathered for the
work of the harvest fields and investigates the life
history of typical individuals can easily see the process of moral decay in operation and observe just how
conditions such as those here discussed contribute to

that process. The men can be classified into grades, ranging from that of the honest, aggressive, young fellow full of plans for the future to that of the broken derelict whose only hope is for a square meal and a night's shelter, and the downward passage from grade to grade can be traced in the life history of individual after individual. One can see in this way how men of spirit who have to submit to the conditions under discussion pass gradually from bewilderment and astonishment to resentment and then to bitter hostility against those whom they believe to be responsible for these conditions. Similarly one can see how men who start out in life as industrious and conscientious workers gradually become incapable of doing a consistent, honest day's work under any circumstances.[15]

Conditions in labor camps in all parts of the country were no better, and were often worse than those endured by harvest workers. A New York State official charged with inspecting labor camps told the Commission on Industrial Relations of one such place that was home for immigrant labor gangs working on the Erie Railroad:

We found there were 25 or 30 hovels in this particular place. I use the word "hovels" advisedly. They were boards and old pieces of tin and iron, put together by the men themselves. . . . A number of them testified to us under oath that they put up these shacks themselves -- without windows, bad air, and very foul smelling, and very poorly kept. Yet they were charged $1 a month by the Commissary. They had to pay rent for something they put up themselves.[16]

Cheating unskilled and migratory workers was common. The Grays Harbor Commercial Co., of Washington, was in the habit of paying its workers late, and offering them instead coupons "good only for merchandise at the store of Grays Harbor Commercial Co." If a man wanted some cash he could take the coupons to the saloons in Grays Harbor -- rented from the company -- and cash them in at a discount of 20 cents on the dollar.[17] A railroad camp commissary in New

174

York automatically deducted $3 per week from the pay of
illiterate immigrant laborers regardless of whether that
amount was purchased or not.[18] The silk mills of Paterson,
N.J., routinely put the cut mark at 63 or 64 yards instead
of the specified 60 yards and paid the weavers for less than
they had really done; one Paterson mill was particularly
known for its cheating, as the Secretary of the Paterson IWW
testified:

> They hire a girl and get her to sign a contract for a
> year. She is to learn ribbon weaving, and she works
> there a year. In the meantime during that period the
> firm keeps 50 per cent of the wages she makes until the
> year is up. At the end of the year she is supposed to
> get this 50 per cent in a lump sum, but, as I stated
> before, as a rule, very few of them reach the time
> limit of a year. They are discharged for one thing or
> another. Of course, they do not receive the 50 per
> cent that has been held from them.
> They also have a docking system in this particular
> matter. When a girl loses a pair of scissors, which
> she has paid for to the firm, she is docked a quarter.
> If a girl comes in with a torn apron, which is her own
> personal property, which does not interfere with her
> working, she is docked a quarter. If she should happen
> to be away from her loom, and the foreman sees her loom
> running and her not there, or her loom stopped and her
> not there, she is docked a quarter or whatever they
> feel like docking. If she comes in late, probably two
> or three minutes, she is docked an hour's pay. If the
> power should stop during the day for any breakdown or
> any cause from a breakdown, if it is stopped half an
> hour, they work half an hour overtime to make up for it
> but no extra pay for it.[19]

Among other abuses was the nearly universal custom of
charging employees in lumber and construction camps a monthly hospital fee. This was usually $1.00, and given the
high turnover, many workers were charged this fee several
times over. James Rowan, an IWW organizer testifying in the
1918 Wobbly trial in Chicago, described the system in prac-

175

tice in the lumber camps:

> Well, then, sometimes if a man was sick enough he
> could go to the company hospital, or the way they had
> those contracts made out, those hospital contracts, you
> would get a ticket, when you paid the hospital fee, you
> were supposed to get a ticket. You did get it some-
> times and sometimes you didn't get it, and it specified
> on that ticket the diseases that you would get treat-
> ment for and there was a certain number of diseases on
> that that you would get no treatment for, and these
> diseases that you did not get treated for, were practi-
> cally all the diseases that a working man was ever
> liable to have.
> If you got actually hurt on the job, had a tree
> fall on you or something, they would probably take you
> into the hospital, but it would be the worst thing that
> could happen to you to go into that company hospital.
> If I could beg, borrow or steal the money to go to some
> other hospital I would never go to a company hospital,
> because I have seen men that would have comparatively
> trifling injuries such as a broken leg, I have seen
> them crippled for life; the leg would not be set right,
> and decay of the bone would set in, or something, and
> they would have to lose the leg just from want of
> proper medical attention at the right time.
> Another thing about those hospital fees, sometimes
> a man would pay three or four in one month, because if
> you did not get a slip from the time keeper, when you
> got your time and went to another camp to go to work,
> they would take it out of your pay there again. I have
> myself actually paid as many as four hospital fees in
> one month.[20]

Mr. F.M. Andreani, an official of the Italian Immigra-

tion Office, located in San Francisco, related to the Indus-

trial Relations Commission how little the hospital fee bene-

fitted a railroad construction worker in a California camp.

> MR. ANDREANI: Now, under this particular contract
> a man was injured, suffering a fracture of the spine.
> This man was taken to a field hospital. He stayed in
> the field hospital just a few days and found that the
> seriousness of his injury was such that he could not
> possibly dare to remain there and stand that treatment,
> so he had himself taken to a hospital, costing him $40
> for transportation. He paid $130.50 hospital fees in
> the hospital and $90 for the surgeon's fee there. That
> made $220.50, besides the $40 for transportation. Then
> at his own expense he came to San Francisco. We sent

him to the Lane Hospital a little while and then sent
him to the City and County Hospital.
    MR. THOMPSON: He paid his dollar?
    MR. ANDREANI: He had paid his dollar a month.[21]

Andreani added that "I don't blame him a bit for going to

the hospital and putting in his last cent after having seen

the field hospital up there." He described it as rudely

constructed, poorly ventilated, and understaffed; even so,

it was a luxury most camps didn't possess. None of the

lumber camps in Grays Harbor, Washington, the largest lumber

district in the country, had camp hospitals. These camps

employed some 3,000 men, and if the men only paid their

dollar apiece just once a month, there was profit in hospi-

tal fees.[22]

The worst swindling, however, was perpetrated by the

employment agents who controlled the job market. The Indus-

trial Relations Commission, which found that "the business

as a whole reeks with fraud, extortion, and flagrant abuses

of every kind," estimated that some $15,000,000 was paid out

in fees every year "chiefly out of the meager earnings of

domestic servants, clerks, and unskilled laborers."[23] The

commonest abuses of employment agencies were described by

William Leiserson in a report to the Commission:

> Fees are often charged out of all proportion to
> the service rendered. We know of cases where $5, $9,
> $10 and even $16 apiece were paid for jobs at common
> labor. The fees paid by scrubwomen in one city is at
> the rate of $24 a year for their poorly paid work.
> Then there is discrimination in the charges made for
> the same jobs. An employment agent in Chicago told us
> that he charges $1, $2 and $10, to different people for
> the same kind of work, depending on whether he ever
> expected to see those people again. In many cases,

too, fees are paid for no jobs whatever. The employment agent advertizes for a hundred men. He collects
his fee from each and tells them to report in time for
the evening train. When they come, he says the order
has been cancelled and he will send them to work the
next day or the day after. Meanwhile a number fail to
report back to the office and he keeps their fees. The
others are kept coming to the office on the promise of
work for many days and finally the employment agent
returns the fees, but enough have tired of calling so
that a considerable amount of money is left in his
hands. Often, too, men are sent long distances, made
to pay fees and transportation, only to find that no
one ordered men from the employment agent. The distance is too far to return and ask for the fees. If
some do find their way back, the agent is quite willing
to return the small proportion of what he collected in
order to avoid trouble. . . .
    A most pernicious practice is the collusion be-
tween foremen and superintendents by which the employment agent "splits fees" with them. That is, the
foreman agrees to hire men of a certain employment
agent on condition that one-fourth or one-half of every
fee collected from men whom he hires be given to him.
This leads the foreman to discharge men constantly in
order to have more men hired through the agent and more
fees collected. It develops the "three gang" method so
universally complained of by railroad construction
laborers; namely, one gang working, another coming to
work from the employment agent, and a third going back
to the city.
    Finally, there is the most frequent abuse -- mis-
representation of terms and conditions of employ-ment.
Men are told that they will get more wages than are
actually paid or that the work will last longer than it
actually does, or that there is a boarding house when
there really is an insanitary camp, or that the cost of
transportation will be paid and later it is deducted
from wages. They are not told of other deductions that
will be made from wages; they are not informed about
strikes that may be on at the places to which they are
sent or about other important facts which they should
know. Often they are hired for a kind of work that
they want and can do, only to find on arrival at the
place of employment that it is work that they cannot do
or that few people want to do.[24]

Such a life, exploited and without dignity, had des-

troyed any sense of community or family ties for millions of

workers. In 1917, a Commission was created by President

Wilson to investigate the conditions in the Pacific Northwest that had led to the IWW-inspired lumber strike of that
year. The results published in the Mediation Commission's
Report contained the following analysis of the migratory
labor problem:

> Partly the rough pioneer character of the industry, but
> largely the failure to create a healthy social environ-
> ment, has resulted in the migratory, drifting character
> of workers. Ninety per cent of those in the camps are
> described by one of the wisest students of the problem,
> not too inaccurately, as "womanless, voteless, and
> jobless." The fact is that about 90 per cent of them
> are unmarried. Their work is intermit-tent, the annual
> labor turnover reaching the extra-ordinary figure of
> over 600 per cent. There has been a failure to make of
> these camps communities. It is not to be wondered,
> then, that in too many of these workers the instinct of
> workmanship is impaired. They are -- or rather have
> been made -- disintegrating forces in society.[23]

Part of the problem was a result of the changing nature

of the industry; the human interaction that had created a

community of interests in the earlier small-scale enter-

prises of the nineteenth century was impossible to maintain

in the age of corporate industries. The distance that now

separated employers from their workers may be gauged by the

admission of an Arizona mine manager, interviewed in 1917 in

the aftermath of the strike troubles there, that he knew

nothing about the men who had struck his mine, yet had

branded them as Wobblies and traitors. "But how am I to

learn to know them?" he asked,

> I haven't got time for it, I've got to run the mill and
> the mine. My business is to get out copper. The
> people back East judge me by the balance sheet. They
> are fine people, personally speaking, but they put
> their money into this property to make money. We had
> an accident in the mine here a little while ago to one

of our old employees -- a man I happened to know well. It was a horrible accident; one of those tragedies there is no way to prevent. One man was killed outright. Another was terribly injured and his eyesight was permanently impaired. In considering the matter, I decided that this old employee, who had been desperately injured in the course of duty, ought to be generously compensated. I named a figure to the office back East. In reply I got a telegram asking me if I didn't think I might find a way to cut my figure by a few thousand.[26]

Such estrangement was inherent in the push to rationalize industries. But ironically, as the Mediation Commission pointed out, "the greatest difficulty in the [lumber] industry is the tenacity of old habits of individualism."[27] Employers refused to acknowledge the effects of industrialization and social change although they saw evidence of it every day, for they were disinclined to view deplorable working conditions, social unrest, and worker alienation as a result of anything other than the failure of individual character to meet life's challenges. It is ironic that the threat to the cherished sense of community was what so troubled those who hated the Wobblies, since the Wobblies also shared this need for community: the red card and the IWW hall and even the free-speech fights were in some measure attempts to meet this need, however inadequately. The logging camp certainly did not.

Just how great the "failure to make of these camps communities," was illustrated by the testimony of Reverend Oscar McGill, who followed the Seattle lumbermen J.V. Paterson and W.J. Rucker as a witness before the Industrial Relations Commission's hearings in Seattle in 1914. Rev.

180

McGill was a "social-service secretary," a social worker who put in all his time visiting logging, mining, and railroad construction camps. In his testimony, he catalogued the conditions under which large numbers of Americans worked and lived. In the construction camps, for example, workers on different shifts were all crowded into the same windowless bunkhouse, when "at midnight one shift would come in, and here are men trying to sleep, and here these men come in all wet, and they make their fire in the bunk house, say there are 60 or 80 men in the bunk house, and they light a fire and smoke and dry their clothes and talk." The bunkhouses in almost all of the 150 or more camps McGill visited were filthy, and the toilet conditions were "simply inexcusable." "A man said they often threw the mattresses out of the window," McGill told the Commission, and added, "if you could see the mattress, you wouldn't wonder why they did. In this particular bunk house, where I talked the most, the men fight every night to see who will sleep on the table. There is just one table in the bunk house. They have reason to get just as far away from the bunks as they can. It is up in the mountains, and they can't sleep out of doors."28

McGill told the Commission of the exploitation of workers by "job sharks" who, often in collusion with the employer or the foreman, hired two or three times as many men for the job as were necessary, counting on high turnover because of mass discharges or deliberate overworking of the men. "Very many of the men have the impression that conditions are made in the camps just as bad as they can be so that the men will quit. The men do quit; they don't stay." Malnutrition was among the various reasons why this was so, McGill continued;

> A great many of them are out of work -- they don't save any money; nobody could save money on the wages that they get; they live on coffee and 'sinkers,' as they call them, and they are physically not strong. . . . Many of these men can't work more than 4 or 5 or 6 or 10 days until they must lay off. A great many of them are old men, and their physical condition is such that they can't stand it long."[29]

Where the businessman saw the foul conditions of his camp produced by the bad character of the workers, Reverend McGill saw the reverse. He was willing to agree with the employer on one point, however: the "bindlestiff" was a menace to society.

> REV. McGILL: . . . In the first place, you must know that a man who goes around with a bundle on his shoulder, carrying his bed on his shoulder, in the first place loses his self-respect to a large extent, because -- well, just because he does. The men go around with bundles on their shoulders, and they are not like other men.
> COMMISSIONER LENNON: He is a nomad?
> REV. McGILL: All right; he is also a menace to society for this reason: he is likely to carry disease. It is a wonder if he does not. Every one of them is a menace to society.[30]

The man with the bundle on his back, undernourished, often diseased, was despised for his condition and treated with contempt. If he quit an unbearable job he was, in the words of one businessman, a "rover who wants to work three days out of the week and loaf the other four," and if he should complain about his treatment, "he gets just what is coming to him." Reverend McGill indicated the type of

182

treatment migrant workers sometimes got:

> The point that strikes me is that of the constant
> injustice to these men. May I give you an instance in
> this case up here? It is the construction work. The
> men are sent out from the employment office here and
> put on railroad cars, and they can't ride when they go
> out; they can't ride on the ordinary [passenger] cars.
> I rode up with them a short time ago and there was
> twice as many men in the baggage car as there should
> have been in there. They had their beds and stuff
> piled in the seats, and there was not room to sit down
> or scarcely to stand up. . . . In the [passenger] car I
> was in there were seven or eight people. Some of those
> men wanted to go back and sit in there with us, but
> they were not allowed to do so. . . . A number refused
> to go, and the conductor and brakeman forced them out
> and one man they just dragged through and used language
> that was unprintable, in handling them. The men were
> given to understand that they were not to ride with the
> ordinary people, they were to ride in the baggage car.
> It is such treatment as this that makes these men
> bitter.[31]

Reverend McGill's testimony revealed another practice

that was a source of bitterness. He related how the

Y.M.C.A. cooperated with employers in "welfare work."

> REV. McGILL: . . . In the camps there is more or
> less of what is known as welfare work, Y.M.C.A. work,
> and that sort of thing. . . .
> COMMISSIONER O'CONNELL: What does the Y.M.C.A.
> do?
> REV. McGILL: They have a general secretary, Mr.
> Goodall, who had charge of four States, and he goes if
> he is sent for by the owner of the mill company or
> camps and establishes a camp Y.M.C.A. They build a
> building and then they pay the secretary $75 a month.
> They pay the secretary -- Mr. Goodall furnishes the man
> -- and the company pays the secretary, and he comes in
> and often he helps to work on clerical work or scaling
> logs or something like that.
> COMMISSIONER O'CONNELL: The secretary does?
> REV. McGILL: Yes, sir.
> COMMISSIONER O'CONNELL: Is that welfare work?
> REV. McGILL: Well no; that is not welfare work,
> but I know some of them do that.
> COMMISSIONER O'CONNELL: What do they really do?
> What do they do for the people, the people that really
> do scale logs?
> REV. McGILL: They have phonographs and come to

the city and from the public library get a lot of books
and a big number of old magazines and put them in
there, and this place is left open, and they have a
pool room, and the men pay a dollar a month membership.
COMMISSIONER O'CONNELL: For this welfare work?
REV. McGILL: They pay this for welfare work.
COMMISSIONER O'CONNELL: The men have to pay for
everything?
REV. McGILL: The company pays the secretary's
salary, and the secretary is under the direction of the
company.
COMMISSIONER O'CONNELL: Where does this dollar
a month go?
REV. McGILL: To the payment of buying books and
phonograph records and that sort of thing.[32]

As Commissioner O'Connell commented, "That would buy a lot

of phonograph records." McGill then submitted a letter from

a mill owner to the Y.M.C.A. local secretary, stating the

owner's displeasure with the secretary and cutting off his

funds, because the secretary had failed in his duty as a spy

and a strike breaker.

I have been much dissatisfied with the Y.M.C.A. ever
since 74 men walked out from camp No. 1, on the 5th day
of June. This is the most men that have walked out of
any other camp in the country. In our camp No. 2,
where there is no Y.M.C.A., not a man went out. If the
secretary had had the company's interests at heart and
been onto his job he would have been close enough to
the men to have prevented this walkout, or notified us
of the existence of I.W.W. organizers. When the secre-
taries are at the camp and think they must simply toady
to the men and let the company go to hell does not appeal to me, and I have about come to the decision that
we can not make this thing satisfactory to the company
the way it is running. Of course, if the company was
not paying any of the bills it would be none of our
business, but it is a business proposition with us to
see that we get value received for the money we
spend.[33]

Such a man likely supported his local Y.M.C.A. and, perhaps,

like J.V. Paterson, railed against the pulpit of Seattle

because "it has become a business like everything else. It

184

has become a business, a money-making proposition."[34]

Protestant churches usually functioned as a middle class institution, promoting stewardship on the one hand, and the virtues of industry, frugality, sobriety, on the other. Class conflict, property relations, economic injustice, or social conditions were rarely given serious consideration. When churchmen like Reverend McGill did speak out, they met with disapproval. It was probably McGill that Seattle businessman Paterson had in mind, when he referred to meddlesome clergy

> who denounce capital as if capital was a living creature with attributes belonging to a man. The[se] men are so insincere, so rotten to the core, that they can't think straight. They can't see the facts. And these are the people that are teaching our I.W.W's and our unrest people the tenets of the Prince of Peace. It is just -- in plain language, the pulpit of this town is disgusting.[35]

Commissioner Garretson questioned McGill with Paterson's allegation in mind: "We have heard it said that the clergy of this city are utterly undesirable from the standpoint of the man expressing the opinion. Is it on account of opinions like you have expressed here, and the expression of them, as to the attitude of employers toward employees in many instances, that that opinion is held?" After agreeing that he thought that was the case, Reverend McGill was asked to comment on what the church had done or tried to do to ameliorate conditions. His response, which caused the Commissioners to rephrase their query several times, reflected the economic reality behind the conservatism of the church,

and its implicit sanction of a social order based on the
views of its leading church members.

> REV. McGILL: The church is placed in a peculiar
> position. These men themselves are mostly churchmen.
> COMMISSIONER GARRETSON: You mean the master or
> the man?
> REV. McGILL: The men who own the industries.
> COMMISSIONER O'CONNELL: They are churchmen, you
> say?
> REV. McGILL: Yes, sir; largely. Quite largely.
> They largely subscribe to and pay to the support of the
> church.
> COMMISSIONER O'CONNELL: Would you imply by that
> that they are religious men?
> REV. McGILL: Yes, sir.
> COMMISSIONER GARRETSON: Do you mean religious men
> or claim to be?
> REV. McGILL: Well, they are; I think they are
> religious. I think Mr. Paterson is a very religious
> man.[36]

Many American businessmen were autocratic where their

business interests were concerned. They denied any connec-

tion between political democracy and industrial democracy.

To them, the imbalance of power that the IWW attacked was

the normal and proper condition of American industry. But

for unskilled and unorganized labor, there was little relief

from exploitation; as Reverend McGill noted, "what is needed

is more democracy." He condemned the situation that great

numbers of workers faced daily.

> When a man will own, as the owner of these logging
> camps does, a whole community, a whole town, and re-
> fuses to allow discussion, refuses to allow his men to
> organize, to meet together; refuses to allow men to
> come in and address them, and if men come to address
> them they must go out on the public road or go off
> somewhere -- meet out, as they do, in almost all those
> logging camps -- he is wrong.[37]

It is little wonder that many workers were radicalized.

Outcast and without hope, millions of unskilled laborers

endured low wages, a degrading life, and the indifference or hostility of employers and others of the middle class. As a writer who worked as a harvest hand in the Pacific Northwest put it:

> One found one's self working with men whose single hope of rehabilitation and human dignity lay in the revolutionary programme of the I.W.W. Out of the heavy fatigue, the fetid torpor of the bunkhouse, at the end of the day's labor, the only influence that could stir the sullen hulks who lounged in the bunks was the zeal of the agitator tirelessly and astutely instructing the "working stiff" in the strategy of class warfare.[38]

The Industrial Workers of the World were virtually the only ones, aside from a handful of intellectuals and charity workers, who tried to better things for this underclass of men and women -- gandydancers in the railroad camps of New York and Colorado, black longshoremen in Philadelphia, black and white lumberjacks in Louisiana, immigrant men, women and child weavers in New England mills, rubber workers in Ohio, hop pickers in California, Finn and Bohunk miners on the Mesabi Range, long loggers on the western slopes of the Cascades and short loggers of the Inland Empire, steelworkers, copperminers, timber beasts, harvest hands, and others who labored to produce the wealth of the nation.

At heart, the Wobblies spoke up for a simple idea --

187

justice through industrial democracy. Big Bill Haywood, who in 1905 had hailed the delegates to the 1st Convention of the IWW as "the Continental Congress of the working class,"[39] addressed the Commission on Industrial Relations after a decade of struggle on behalf of this idea. Haywood answered Commissioner Harris Weinstock's query as to how the IWW "would direct the affairs, under your proposed system, of 100,000,000 of people as we are in this country today?"

> Well, how are the affairs of the hundred million people conducted at the present time? The workers have no interest, have no voice in anything except the shops. Many of the workers are children. They certainly have no interest and no voice in the franchise. They are employed in the shops, and of course my idea is that children who work should have a voice in the way they work -- in the hours they work, in the wages that they should receive -- that is, under the present conditions children should have that voice, children who labor. The same is true of women. The political state, the Government, says that women are not entitled to vote -- that is, except in the 10 free States of the West; but they are industrial units; they are productive units; from millions of women. My idea is that they should have a voice in the control or disposition of their labor powers, and the only place where they can express themselves is in their labor union halls, and there they express themselves to the fullest as citizens of industry, if you will, as to the purposes of their work and the conditions under which they will labor. Now, you recognize that in conjunction with women and children.
> The black men of the South are on the same footing. They are all citizens of this country, but they have no voice in its government. Millions of black men are disfranchised, who if organized would have a voice in saying how they should work and how the conditions of labor should be regulated. But unorganized they are as helpless and in the same condition of slavery as they were before the war. This is not only true of women and children and black men, but it extends to the foreigner who comes to this country and is certainly a useful member of society. Most of them at once go into industries, but for five years they are not citizens. They plod along at their work and have no voice in the control or the use of their labor power. And as you

have learned through this commission there are corporations who direct the manner in which those foreigners shall vote. Certainly you have heard something of that in connection with the Rockefeller interests in the southern part of Colorado. You know that the elections there were never carried on straight, and these foreigners were directed as to how their ballot should be placed.

They are not the only ones who are disfranchised, but there is also the workingman who is born in this country, who is shifted about from place to place by industrial depressions: their homes are broken up and they are compelled to go from one city to another, and each State requires a certain period of residence before a man has the right to vote. Some States say he must be a resident 1 year, others say 2 years; he must live for a certain length of time in the country; he must live for 30 days or such a matter in the precinct before he has any voice in the conduct of government. Now, if a man was not a subject of a State or Nation, but a citizen of industry, moving from place to place, belonging to his union, wherever he went he would step in the union hall, show his card, register, and he at once has a voice in the conduct of the affairs pertaining to his welfare. That is the form of society I want to see, where the men who do the work, and who are the only people who are worth while -- understand me, Mr. Weinstock, I think that the workingman, even doing the meanest kind of work, the workingman is a more important member of society than any judge on the Supreme Bench; than any other of the useless members of society. I am speaking for the working class, and I am a partisan to the workers.[40]

For a time, the IWW provided a sense of community, hope, and a shared vision.[41] The Wobblies' crude ideology ("infantile leftism," in Lenin's phrase) expressed in camp speech hitherto inarticulate revolt, and inspired solidarity and determination. Many participated in IWW free-speech fights and strikes more for the brotherhood to be found in IWW halls than for the syndicalist idea of One Big Union. For a time, the red card controlled travel on the boxcar circuit and hampered petty thieves, grafting carmen, and abusive railroad detectives. "You don't remember the Wobblies," Jack Malloy remarked in James Jones' novel,

From Here To Eternity.

> You were too young. Or else not even born yet. There
> has never been anything like them, before or since.
> They called themselves materialist-economists, but what
> they really were was a religion. They were workstiffs
> and bindlebums like you and me, but they were welded
> together by a vision we don't possess. It was their
> vision that made them great. And it was their belief
> in it that made them powerful. And sing! You never
> heard anybody sing the way those guys sang! Nobody
> sings like they did unless it's for a religion."[42]

Song gave voice and spirit to the IWW cause; Wobblies

on the Verona could be heard across the water at Everett

singing "Hold the fort for we are coming/Union men be

strong"; strikers at Lawrence sang "The Internationale";

free-speech prisoners at Spokane or San Diego sang "Solida-

rity Forever!" or "Hallelujah, I'm A Bum" or Joe Hill's

famous refrain,

> You will eat, bye and bye,
> In that glorious land above the sky;
> Work and pray, live on hay,
> You'll get pie in the sky when you die.

These songs sung by American workmen and workwomen were

much different than those Walt Whitman had heard America

singing fifty years earlier: now, "the party of young fel-

lows, robust, friendly,/Singing with open mouths their

strong melodious songs," sang from the Little Red Songbook

of the IWW, whose subtitle was "Songs of the Workers, On the

Road, In the Jungles, and In the Shops -- Songs to Fan the

Flames of Discontent."

190

CHAPTER 8

CONCLUSION:
CORPORATE INDUSTRIALISM, IDENTITY,
AND THE IRONY OF SHARED VALUES

> On looking back fifty years later, at his own
> figure in 1854, and pondering on the needs of the
> twentieth century, he wondered whether, on the
> whole, the boy of 1854 stood nearer to the
> thought of 1904, or to that of the year 1.
>
>   -- Henry Adams, The Education
>   of Henry Adams, 1907

Onward, Christian soldiers! Duty's way is plain;
Slay your Christian neighbors, or by them be slain.
Pulpiteers are spouting effervescent swill,
God above is calling you to rob and rape and kill,
    All your acts are sanctified by the Lamb on high;
    If you love the Holy Ghost, go murder, pray and die.

This anti-war parody was one of the songs the IWW hoped

would "fan the flames of discontent." But some Americans

took it not as satire but as the program of the IWW. When

America entered the war in 1917, such indignation helped to

seal the Wobblies' fate. Holding up the Little Red Song-

book, attorneys read these lyrics to juries as proof that

Wobblies advocated violence, murder and arson.[1] This song

helped ensure the passage of state criminal syndicalism

bills: in Montana, a Helena newspaper published the words

191

while the legislature was in session, and copies were supplied to every member of the 1917 Idaho Senate. In Washington State, the song was read to both houses of the legislature and, "according to one observer, 'appears to have
thrown them into a frenzy.' One legislator who tried to
explain that the song was a satire on militarism and not an
advocacy of violence was hooted down."[2]

This hysteria encouraged the federal government to act
against the Wobblies. But long before this, antipathy to
the Wobblies had been building. It rested upon a contradic-
tion between a cultural outlook and an economic fact, that
is, a clash between an internalized pattern of behavior, the
work ethic, and the reality of an unskilled worker's life.
Wobblies found the bromides about self-help and diligent
industry laughable when they saw themselves cheated out of
their inadequate wages, or blacklisted when they objected to
degrading working conditions, or clubbed and run out of town
when they protested.

By their defiance, the IWW challenged beliefs that had
contributed to the sense of identity of the great majority
of Americans, a challenge so intolerable that only violent
repression of the IWW appeared sufficient to meet it. The
beliefs under attack were crucial to the formation of individual and collective identity in a capitalist society, in
that they filled a primary need for ideas that could help
order the world.[3]

The modern middle class rose to power, as the aristocracy had before it, by asserting a right to property. Liberal-democratic theory, beginning with the natural law philosophers, justified property rights as the natural order, and enshrined sanctity of contract. This theory also held that labor was an alienable property of humans, and thus established market relations based on labor power, in turn creating the possibility of exploiting labor. In short, this set of beliefs held that power in the society could be achieved through acquisition of property; property could be acquired by accumulation of capital; and accumulation could only be ensured by diligent effort, prudent use of resources, thrift, and delayed gratification. This activity required rationalized conduct characterized by regularity of habit, continuous exertion, and emotional withdrawal to maintain control. These personality characteristics were long regarded as masculine, or at least required of all who wished to succeed under a male-dominated society, reflecting the fact that competition for power was long restricted to men of property.

The social system under capitalism depended on the cultivation of the work ethic, and the work ethic in turn acted as a means of social control. Adherence to the work ethic was expected behavior for acceptance into political parties, trade associations, chambers of commerce and the like. The work ethic underlay the roles that men took up in face-to-face relationships with one another, and the loyalty that these associational ties generated reinforced the com-

mitment to the work ethic. Thus the work ethic was a cultu-
rally approved mode of behavior and a fundamental element in
the formation of an identity appropriate for success in a
capitalist culture.[4]

When the Wobblies and others ridiculed this code of
conduct, they threatened the identity of those who had
internalized it. Since the constraints of the work ethic
were imposed in order to acquire property as a means to
power and freedom, the IWW's attack on property -- their
intention, as proclaimed in the IWW Preamble, to "take
possession of the earth and the machinery of production" --
could not have struck a more sensitive nerve. Their threat
to identity and to property was intolerable, a double thrust
whose threat to internal and external reality was total. In
the light of this, it is unsurprising that the Wobblies were
perceived as "alien invaders" and "vicious vagrants."

This intense verbal abuse was a ritual use of language
that turned Wobblies into dehumanized targets for violence;
verbal assault was the psychologically necessary prelude to
violent repression. Tramps and foreigners were thought
inferior by nature, and it was but a short step to see
Wobblies as subhuman.

> These people do not belong to any country, no flag, no
> laws, no Supreme Being. I do not know what to do. I
> cannot punish them. Listen to them singing. They are
> singing all the time, and yelling and hollering, and
> telling the jailors to quit work and join the union.
> They are worse than animals.[5]

This complaint by San Diego's police chief pictures the

194

Wobblies as deviates lacking moral sensibilities, not entitled to the protection of the law.

Because vigilante activity is extra-legal and secre-
tive, it requires community approval and seeks to bind
participants by sharing the work. Thus in many American
towns beset by the IWW, leading citizens encouraged each
other to violence. During the troubles in Minot, N.D., for
example, a contractor who objected to the IWW organizing his
construction crews declared, "I know that by law we can't do
anything to them. But we'll put the God damn sons of bitch-
es out of Minot, if we have to ride them out on a rail."
The cashier of the Second National Bank complained that,
"there ain't no use in treating those fellows with kindness.
The only thing to do is to club them down. Beat them up.
Drive them out of the city." These sentiments were reinforced by Judge Davis, a respected city magistrate of Minot,
who, when asked if something couldn't be done to prevent the
beatings, replied, "Prevent Hell, We'll drive the G-- D--
Sons of B-----s into the river and drown them. We'll starve
them. We'll kill every damned man of them or drive them
together with the Socialists from the city."[6]

In order to act against the IWW, it was necessary to
involve as many people in a town as possible, and in town
after town the opposition was often like that described by
Harris Weinstock in his investigation of the 1912 San Diego
free-speech fight. There, Weinstock found, the Merchants'
Association, city officials and daily newspapers all suppor-

ted the actions of the police and vigilantes. Weinstock,
who compared the city fathers to "despotic and tyrannic
Russian authorities," was shocked to find that those who had

> much of the intelligence, the wealth, the conservatism,
> the enterprise, and presumably also the good citizen-
> ship of the community, felt impelled to play the part,
> as they believed, of patriotic heroes and, in the name
> of law and order, ended in committing the very crimes
> against law and order with which the alleged invading
> offenders were charged.[8]

The press was the agency most responsible for provoking
the public attitude toward Wobblies. Often owned or controlled by the business elements of a community, the local
newspaper reflected their class attitudes. Catering to a
public appetite for sensational news stories, papers all
over the country portrayed the IWW as crazed saboteurs from
the dregs of society. Newspapers' persistent damnation of
the IWW for over a decade provided the public with a focus
for tensions generated by a changing political and social
context. Arizona in 1916, for instance, following the mass
deportations of Wobblies and others into the desert, was
thrown into a panic. A reporter for the New York _Post_,
Robert Bruere, found that the press of Arizona had desig-
nated all laboring men and their organizations as Wobbly.
"This fantastic enlargement of the meaning of WOBBLY we
found to be universal," commented Bruere. His contemporary
description suggests the havoc a hate-filled press can
wreak:

> Very few people had any accurate knowledge of the
> tenets or tactics of the I.W.W. The three letters had
> come to stand in the popular mind as a symbol of some-

thing bordering on black magic; they were repeated over
and over again by the press like the surd tappings of
an Oriental drum, and were always accompanied with the
suggestion of impending violence. It was in this way
that it became possible to use them to work ordinarily
rational communities up into a state of unreasoning
frenzy, into hysterical mobs resorting to violence to
dispel the fear of such violence as happened in Bisbee
[Arizona].[8]

The Wobbly's opportunity to defend himself against

press campaigns that discredited and destroyed him was shar-

ply limited. Ralph Chaplin, the IWW's most able publicist,

commented in his autobiography on the ineffectiveness of

counter-propaganda.

It was not easy to acquaint the public with atrocities
committed against labor in those days. Only a few
voices were raised in protest, and for them there was
no radio, no sympathetic columnists, few understanding
preachers or politicians. Every man's hand seemed
raised against us. At the end of every road, like an
insurmountable barrier, was the 'capitalist press,'
with its 'conspiracy of silence.'

For the Wobblies, this frustration deepened their hatred for

the ruling class. "As a result," continued Chaplin, "our

indignation and outraged sense of justice became intolerably

explosive. We wanted to shout labor's sufferings from the

housetops."[9]

But even the organized labor press attacked the IWW

with vehemence, as it sought to avoid being tarred with the

same brush. "The time has come," the Miner's Magazine edi-

torialized in 1912,

when the labor and socialist press of America must hold
up to the arclight these professional degenerates who
create riots, and then, in the name of "free speech,"
solicit revenue to feed the prostituted parasites who
yell "scab" and "fakiration" at every labor body whose
members refuse to gulp down the lunacy of a "bummery"

197

that would disgrace the lower confines of Hades.[10]
The Wobblies were unable to gain a foothold with workers
other than dispossessed marginals. Many skilled workers,
concerned with "getting ahead" and the bread-and-butter
unionism of the AF of L, saw the IWW as a threat. The IWW's
flamboyant style and socialist rhetoric made many trade
unionists unhappy.

With America's entry into the war, the animus against
the IWW reached white heat. In 1917, the Federal government
decided to move against the IWW, and states began to enact
criminal syndicalism legislation. The press across America,
in addition to representing the IWW as industrial terrorists, now portrayed them as agents of the Kaiser who burned
wheat fields with the aid of German gold. In the wake of
the Russian Revolution, they were depicted as Bolshevists
seeking to Sovietize every American hamlet. The stridency
of the press attack increased as a nation-wide campaign of
repression got under way. Eldridge Foster Dowell, in his
review of criminal syndicalism legislation, remarked on this
increase:

> Throughout the whole period from 1917 through 1919, we
> find the press the great motivating power which created
> through its news and editorial columns a distorted and
> vicious picture of the I.W.W. This stereotype provided
> the psychological stimulus necessary for the acts of
> violence against the I.W.W., their legal persecution
> and prosecution by the Federal Government, and the
> enactment of the State Criminal Syndicalism laws
> against them.[11]

Dowell's statement is based on a canvass of the newspapers of each state that passed a criminal syndicalism law.

198

The headlines and editorial comment he cites in newspaper
after newspaper reflect an irrational press, hysterically
advocating beatings, deportations, hangings, firing squads
at dawn. The Muskogee, Oklahoma, Daily Phoenix declared,
"back to its father Belial with bolshevism and all Bolsheviki in the United States. Everyone of the wild-eyed ought
to be either hung forthwith, or deported right back to
Russia." The Sioux City Journal, in an editorial, "The
I.W.W. As Outlaws," praised the Iowa legislature for enac-
ting a criminal syndicalism law which "did not trifle with
the foolish prattle of reforming the debased criminals."
"Men of the stripe they [the legislators] meant to suppress," said the Journal, "men who take human life regardless of innocence or guilt and who advocate the nationaliza-
tion of women for the beastly purposes of the lousy gang of
loafers -- do not want to be reformed." The Tucson, Arizona, Citizen put it plainly: "Boiled down in a nutshell, it
is about time for the respectable, patriotic, God-fearing
citizens of this country to arise in their might and stamp
out this curse, and if we are to win the war the sooner
drastic legislation is passed to curb this band of social
pirates the better." The Los Angeles Times claimed that
"the Kaiser credits Hearst, La Follette, and the I.W.W.'s as
the most representative Germans in America." According to
the Butte, Montana, Anaconda Standard, "the mere fact that a
man is a member of an I.W.W. organization convicts him of
being an enemy of the United States." The Tulsa, Oklahoma,

<u>Daily World</u> argued that free speech must be suppressed if it was to be preserved:

> If we as a free people are to retain unhampered our prized privilege of free speech we must heartily encourage every reasonable effort to close the mouths of those who habitually abuse the privilege. There have been a number of people in our midst whose rantings have about convinced the people that free speech is a dangerous liberty. If the privilege is to be saved from destruction we must see to it that its sanctity is preserved.[12]

But by the time the <u>Daily World</u>'s editorial appeared in 1919, more than a decade and a half of bitter animosity had stilled the voice of reason where the Wobblies were concerned. The leadership, imprisoned in Leavenworth and other Federal prisons, was reduced to arguing whether accepting pardon would be a betrayal of the working class; the membership was threatened with prosecution or deportation; the various communist parties were claiming the revolutionary limelight; and the Red Scare was beginning. The Great War had aroused a militant xenophobia that signaled the end for the IWW.[13]

In the fifteen years since the IWW first gathered in Chicago, the nation had undergone change. The war had shown what a highly industrialized, bureaucratically organized society could do. Progressivism had shown the benefits of rationalizing social and industrial life: prospective new consumer markets required a prosperous and healthy citizenry, continuous production, and industrial peace. The new corporate order that was emerging had created new possibilities for social mobility, and was moving toward resolving the conflict between capital and labor. But this new order also eliminated or reduced political or economic access for those who, like the floating worker or the small town employer, were being squeezed by changes in the industrial structure.

The technology, transportation, and finance of the late 19th century had evolved a national market structure and new forms of industrial organization. To lower costs and meet competition, many corporations, especially in oil, mining, lumber and other extractive industries, established their own nationwide buying and marketing organizations. They also secured control of their own industries through vertical integration, securing raw materials and buying up various processing companies. Trusts and mergers were a further attempt to rationalize chaotic conditions by setting prices and eliminating competition.

This corporate growth put pressure on businessmen, farmers, and workers. In particular, the shift in power bypassed merchants and small manufacturers not part of the corporate structure, leaving them vulnerable to economic fluctuations whose sources they could neither discern nor control. Strikes and labor agitation by unions were seen as further curtailing employers' ability to compete. They responded by joining forces in local and regional trade associations, which after 1903 concentrated their energies in open-shop drives to crush unionism. These employers were being squeezed in the struggle between labor and the corpo-

rations. To meet competition from cost-cutting corporations, they believed they had no choice but to exploit their
workers. And since unionism already offended their belief
that they alone should control the businesses they owned,
unions easily became a focus for frustrations created by
large-scale corporate development.

As large corporations made decisions affecting distant
communities, the locus of political authority also shifted
away from local control. Many businessmen felt they were at
the mercy of absentee decision-making, cynical manipulation
of markets for their products, discriminatory freight rates,
price fixing, and corrupt political representatives. All of
this was exacerbated by scandalous revelations of manipulation by the "money trust" on a staggering scale involving
oil, railroads, banking and other industries. This gave
rise to a universal feeling that the great corporations were
trying to force out the small business man.

The erosion of local authority was most apparent when
communities faced problems of industrial unemployment and
labor unrest. Providing food and shelter for thousands of
unemployed men during the winters had become an impossible
task for cities to face every year. Harvesting in the grain
belt and the Pacific Coast states had become a nightmare of
corrupt employment agents utilizing uncoordinated and dangerous railroad transport to send hundreds of thousands of
impoverished migrant workers helter-skelter into communities
that had no facilities to house them, had a deep suspicion

of them as foreigners or radicals, and had only a few weeks'
work for them. In communities with year-round industry,
local authority was increasingly bypassed as corporations
relied on state or private police forces, detective agencies, and labor spies to control their industrial workers.[14] Local employers, who resented interference in
their labor disputes by "outside agitators," were willing to
import strikebreakers, and routinely appealed for state
militia or federal troops to control the violence that often
ensued.[15]

The expanding industrial development of the early twentieth century held great promise for the merchants, farmers,
and others who were tied to the community life of city or
town. But the middle class was also worried about the
economy, the labor question, and big business ethics. Muck-
rakers and trust-busters had exposed the predatory side of
corporations, and social reformers kindled fears of social
disintegration and class war. The serenity of life was
increasingly disturbed, and although Progressive reforms
attempted to curb disorder, many citizens were apprehensive.

Their apprehension was a consequence of a shift in the
distribution of authority. With investment capital increasingly controlled by New York banks and insurance companies;
with huge corporations at a competitive advantage; with
packing house combines, milling cartels, and railroad trusts
manipulating the grain and beef markets, the average employer was aware of his diminished influence. When such busi-

nessmen were growing up, firms tended to be small and regional, essentially processing agricultural products. By 1909,
of the 50 largest industrial concerns, over half were in
extractive industries and three-fourths were manufacturing
producers' goods, clear evidence that the business economy
had become industrialized.[16] As early as 1904, almost all
producers' goods carried the trademark of one or another
great corporation; by then, some 5300 separate businesses
had been consolidated into 318 industrial trusts, most of
them formed since 1898.[17] And at the turn of the century,
administrative employees outnumbered those directly engaged
in production,[18] which meant that an increasing proportion
of the nation's industry was dependent upon a bureaucratic
structure to carry on its business and make its decisions.

   As another measure of the shift in authority, the 1914
Census of Manufacturers showed that 1/8 of all businesses
employed more than 3/4 of all workers and produced more than
4/5 of all goods.[19] These giant concerns were most often
owned and operated by distant banks and shareholders, and
their occasional irresponsibility gave further cause for
concern to independent businessmen. Overspeculation and
unscrupulous disregard for the public had resulted in the
severe Panics of 1903 and 1907, underlining the need for
control and reform of trusts and the banking system.

   Thus it is not surprising to find that the businessmen
who formed vigilante committees to deal with the IWW by and
large also supported Progressive reforms and Progressive

politicians. These activities were not incompatible; each was a response to rapid social and economic change. At root, the values of the business class were under attack both from an underclass represented by the IWW, and from the impersonal appetites of big corporations. Because opportunities for the individual entrepreneur to become a self-made man were diminishing, the old-fashioned self-reliant individualism that had formed the self-conceptions of several generations no longer seemed a secure anchor.

Ironically, the Wobblies were also acting out of a perception of their own marginality. Since they represented workers who were the least powerful among an already fragmented and poorly organized labor force, and since they had rejected political action, they were basically outsiders, excluded from the emerging forums that began to regulate labor conflict as the century moved towards the New Deal years. The reform spirit of the Progressive era had yielded a recognition that industrial strife must be better managed. With the passage of child labor laws, state workmen's compensation laws, the Seaman's Bill, the Clayton Act, and other measures that legitimated organized labor, the outlines of conflict regulation took shape, although it would be several decades before collective bargaining was given legal standing in the Wagner Act. But the Wobblies, animated by desperation and buoyed by high fellowship, scorned organized labor, and were without political allies anywhere.

Their impact was dramatic but, in the end, transitory. Their need to believe in the imminent collapse of capitalism and wage slavery was so great, and the misery they opposed so pressing, that they could not stomach any more gradualism. They rejected the accomodating approach of business unionism, which ultimately established a counterbureaucracy to implement workers' needs. Like their predecessors, the Knights of Labor, the IWW had a streak of millenialism and an aversion to compromise. Much of the IWW's drawing power lay in its call for solidarity and brotherhood, and in its creation of a quasi-community wherever it went, in boxcars, jails, jungles or bunkhouse, where otherwise hopeless men could find sympathy and a sense of purpose. Poet and songwriter Ralph Chaplin, one of the Wobblies sentenced to Leavenworth in 1918, recalled this spirit:

> Those of us who gave the best years of our lives in the service of the singing, fighting IWW were enriched in the giving. At all times -- on the soapbox, on the picket-line, and even in prison -- we were aware of being part of something more important than our own unimportant selves, a Cause worth living for and, if needs be, dying for. We didn't enjoy ourselves: we enjoyed one another. We didn't envy the high and mighty of our generation; we pitied them, as the early Christians must have pitied the pagans. At heart we were probably the world's worst snobs, so sure were we that nothing on earth could be deader than a dead tycoon, and that nothing could be more deathless than a

Cause beyond the reach of death.[20]

It is perhaps idle to speculate on whether the IWW
would have succeeded in creating a viable industrial unionism had not the World War and the federal government inter-
vened to wreck their hopes and plans. But Chaplin's reflec-
tion suggests what may well have been a fundamental strate-
gic misapprehension by the Wobblies. They shared with earlier generations of craft workers a sense of impotence at
the imposition of machines and factory methods which alien-
ated them from their jobs by destroying the integrity of
work. And, implicitly acknowledging industrialism as the
modus vivendi of the future, they proposed a large-scale,
vertically integrated enterprise paralleling the nationaliz-
ing business economy. But much of their thought and action
rested on a mistaken belief that a large organization could
be motivated by the emotions of solidarity available only to
a small closely-knit cadre united in outrage over injustices
they had personally suffered.

Their aim was to give workers control. Few of them saw
what would happen if the larger society recognized the
justice of their claims and began to ameliorate conditions
through reform and co-option. They did not see their form
of organization as a competitor of corporate bureaucracy,
capable of balancing competing interests rather than replacing the capitalist structure entirely; nor did they appreciate the yearning for job security and a middleclass standard of living of the average American worker.

Although they envisioned a better world, they were not particularly ideologues; at heart they were sectarians whose hatred for what capitalism had done to them was so strong that it bound them together, and the fellowship thus created was their source of hope. A hatred for a world that had made them underdogs stung the Wobblies to defiance. It occurred to few of them that they could not fuel a mass movement for long on the politics of hatred. Nor did they really see themselves as the revolutionary vanguard of the proletariat with a duty to take power in the name of the workers -- they were rather martyrs for the Industrial Democracy. "We are all leaders!" -- the cry shouted back at the deputies on the Everett dock -- could well have been the IWW's motto.

Thus, the IWW's defiance was at once its strength and its weakness. Wobbly editor Ben Williams called attention to this in a 1913 issue of Solidarity (pointedly reprinted by the open-shop The Square Deal).

> If the Industrial Workers of the World is going to organize the working class then we will have to make a great change in our attitude towards the labor movement and in the methods that we are now using. At present we are to the labor movement what the high diver is to the circus. A sensation, marvelous and nerve thrilling. We attract the crowds. We give them thrills, we do hair-raising stunts and send the crowd home to wait impatiently for the next sensationalist to come along. As far as making Industrial Unionism fit the every-day life of the workers we have failed miserably. . . .
> Had we kept as many organizers in Lawrence after the strike as we had during the strike, we would have an organization that could carry on the next battle without the aid of press agents or sensationalists. In Akron it was the same story; the members cried for sensations; Haywood was sent for. He filled the bill,

> but after the strike was over every organizer was
> called to other points to supply the thrills called for
> by the rank and file. Not one was left to build up an
> organization in Akron.[21]

This theatricalism raised a spirit of sacrifice and camaraderie and put great energies on display. But in addition to misdirecting energies, the roles the Wobblies elected to play proved very hazardous. By choosing to trade on the public's fearful portrayal of them as foot-loose saboteurs, they were aiding the process by which threatened townsmen worked themselves up to violence. Reducing an enemy to a manageable stereotype is a prerequisite to aggression, and the flamboyant rhetoric and stylized performance of the Wobblies in free speech fights depersonalized them in the eyes of the middle class, who saw only a group of singing, yelling, frowsy tramps.

The Wobblies saw themselves as rebels, not as seditionists. The irony of their self-conception is that, without fully realizing it, they shared many of the American values of their opponents in the middle class. Their Marxism was largely confined to a radical vocabulary and a belief in the necessity of class struggle.[22] But fundamentally their cry was for justice, not revolution. They wanted to get the bosses off their backs, but they wanted to do it by bringing the political conception of American democracy into the field and factory. They insisted that the guarantees of the Bill of Rights applied to them, and many a Wobbly was jailed for reading the Declaration of Independence from a soapbox.

Ralph Chaplin, who had been an IWW prisoner in Leavenworth,
could ask in afteryears:

> We of the IWW made mistakes and paid for them dearly,
> but were we so wrong, after all, in contending with
> Thomas Jefferson that "the government that governs best
> is the government that governs least"? Or with Patrick
> Henry, who, spurning the principle of involuntary ser-
> vitude, shouted out to a similarly divided world: "Give
> me liberty or give me death"?[23]

In the Western states where the Wobblies had their
strongest following, an independent frontier tradition still
animated self-conceptions of both the IWW and their opponents. But these states, for all their wild beauty, had
long since come under the industrial plow. Machine technology and distant corporation control had created working
conditions as harsh and exploitative as any Eastern mine or
mill: such conditions had led a number of fed-up radicals
from the Western Federation of Miners to become founders of
the IWW.[24] The development of mining, milling, timber and
agriculture in the western U.S. is better seen as an instance of emergent industrialism in Western culture, with
its attendant occupational and social displacement and interest-group conflict, than as some kind of unique American
response to geography.[25] But the Wobblies, who recognized
that they were outcasts, characteristically rejoiced in that
fact in terms that often celebrated an American romanticism
and a frontier individualism. One writer for Solidarity
ennobled Wobbly vagabondage by casting the bindlestiff as an
industrial frontiersman, as rugged an individualist as any
two-fisted tycoon:

The nomadic worker of the West embodies the very spirit
of the I.W.W. His cheerful cynicism, his frank and
outspoken contempt for most of the conventions of bour-
geois society, including the more stringent conventions
which masquerade under the name of morality, make him
an admirable exemplar of the iconoclastic doctrine of
revolutionary unionism. His anomalous position, half
industrial slave, half vagabond adventurer, leaves him
infinitely less servile than his fellow worker in the
East. Unlike the factory slave of the Atlantic sea-
board and the Central States he is most emphatically
not "afraid of his job." His mobility is amazing.
Buoyantly confident of his ability to "get by" somehow,
he promptly shakes the dust of a locality from his feet
whenever the board is bad, or the boss too exacting, or
the work unduly tiresome, departing for the next job,
even if it be 500 miles away. Cost of transportation
does not daunt him. "Freight trains run every day" and
his ingenuity is a match for the vigilance of trainmen
and special police. No wife or family cumber him. The
workman of the East, oppressed by the fear of want for
wife and babies, dare not venture much. He has per-
force the tameness of the domesticated animals. But
the tang of the wild taints the free and foot-loose
western nomad to the bone. Nowhere else can a section
of the working class be found so admirably fitted to
serve as the scouts and advance guards of the labor
army. Rather they may become the guerrillas of the
revolution -- the francs-tireurs of the class struggle.[26]

How ironic is the celebration of just those circum-

stances of rootlessness, indigence, and alienation that kept

the IWW from becoming a strong competitive interest-group.

Feared and despised for its estrangement from society, and

without access to the self-help of political action, the IWW

felt cheated of an American heritage of opportunity. Like

many other Americans of this day, the Wobbly lamented the

passing of the frontier and the blessings it had bestowed

upon earlier Americans. Wobbly poet Ralph Chaplin summed up

such a sense of loss in an elegy entitled "The West Is

Dead."

What path is left for you to tread
When hunger-wolves are slinking near -
Do you not know the West is dead?

The "blanket-stiff" now packs his bed
Along the trails of yesteryear -
What path is left for you to tread?

Your fathers, golden sunsets led
To virgin prairies wide and clear -
Do you not know the West is dead?

Now dismal cities rise instead
And freedom is not there nor here -
What path is left for you to tread?

Your fathers' world for which they bled,
Is fenced and settled far and near -
Do you not know the West is dead!

Your fathers gained a crust of bread
Their bones bleach on the lost frontier
What path is left for you to tread -
Do you not know the West is dead?[27]

Wobblies and self-made businessmen alike could elegize the passing agrarian glory that seemed in nostalgic retrospect to have been a time of wide-open spaces and ample opportunity for all. While smoke yet curled from the hearths of peaceful home towns that still dotted the landscape at the turn of the century, factory smoke was clouding the vision of the future. American society, under the pressures of industrialization and urbanization, was undergoing profound changes. The common belief in individualism, in self-reliance, in rewards for virtue and hard work, in the salutary effects of property ownership, in the natural and beneficient workings of competitive market relations, had been fatally challenged by managerial forms of corporate capitalism and oligarchical trusts, and by unstable economic conditions with their resultant periodic depressions and high unemployment. The sweet illusion of rural peace had been dashed by unprecedented immigration and the attendant squalor of "dismal cities," and by the hobo legions that floated from town to town.

The Wobblies in disillusion and despair became the most radical and colorful union in American history, who via their crude Marxism asked for decency and fair play. The middle class, determined to defend individualism and the work ethic, sought reform of economic conditions in Progressivism, and tried to control worker unrest via an anti-union campaign and a resurgence of nativism and anti-radicalism. Against the jingoist background of the recent war with Spain, it was unsurprising that men and women of the middle class should bolster their faith in progress by exhibiting their Americanism. Taking umbrage at slurs by radicals and socialists upon American institutions of business, government, and religion, they yielded to a defensive nationalism which called for conformity and loyalty. To them, the Wobblies appeared as malign invaders and visible rebukes to the belief in work and ownership. The more menaced they felt by economic instability, urban growth and immigrant populations, the easier it became to hate the Wobblies, who were perceived as foreigners, tramps, and anarchists.

Wartime hysteria, traded on by a government anxious to mobilize the country for the war effort, ensured the des-

truction of the IWW. Although many Americans rejoiced to
see the Wobblies behind bars, there was little glory in this
intolerant repression of workers; such repression has been a
familiar aspect of the struggle for justice and tolerance
into the twentieth century. With courage and intelligence,
the IWW brought home the truth that there was a great number
of low-waged, ill-treated and disenfranchised workmen and
workwomen who wanted their share of the American dream.
During its brief existence, the Industrial Workers of the
World fought for basic human rights and decent working
conditions, challenging the authority of employers and
others in the middle class. It was in many ways a heroic
movement, and it should be remembered by all Americans, as
should the reasons for the violence of its opponents.

NOTES TO
CHAPTERS
1 - 8

[1]See, e.g., Joseph J. Mereto, The Red Conspiracy (New York, 1920), p. 105, and passim.

[2]Paul F. Brissenden, The I.W.W.: A Study of American Syndicalism (New York, 1919), p. xv.

[3]Quoted in Phillip S. Foner, A History of the Labor Movement in the United States: Vol. IV: The I.W.W., 1905-1917 (New York, 1965), p. 186.

[4]Quoted in Foner, p. 200; and Melvin Dubofsky, We Shall Be All: A History of the Industrial Workers of the World (Chicago, 1969), p. 192.

[5]Harris Weinstock, Report to the Governor of California on the Disturbances in the City of San Diego (Sacramento, 1912), pp. 16-17.

[6]Foner, p. 114; reprinted in The Industrial Worker, June 26, 1912.

[7]Cong. Rec., 21 March 1918, p. 3821.

[8]For an account of a town that decided to negotiate an end to a relatively peaceful IWW free speech fight, see Charles Pierce LeWarne, "The Aberdeen, Washington, Free Speech Fight of 1911-1912," Pacific Northwest Quart., 66. no. 1 (January 1975), 1-12. Also see Norman Clark's Mill Town: A Social History of Everett, Washington (Seattle, 1970), which details the social context of the Everett Massacre of 1916; Donald B. Cole, Immigrant City: Lawrence, Massachusetts, 1845-1921 (North Carolina, 1963); Paul H. Landis, Three Iron Mining Towns: A Study in Cultural Change (Ann Arbor, 1938); John H. Lindquist and James Fraser, "A Sociological Interpretation of the Bisbee Deportation," Pacific Hist. Rev., 38 (1968), 401-422.

[9]Besides the standard histories (Brissenden, Dubofsky, Foner, et al), see William Preston, Jr., Aliens and Dissenters: Federal Suppression of Radicals, 1903-1933 (New York, 1963); Marc Karson, American Labor Unions and Politics, 1900-1918 (Boston, 1958), pp. 176-211; Fred Thompson, The IWW - Its First Fifty Years (Chicago, 1955); John S. Gambs, The Decline of the IWW (New York, 1932). Also see John Higham, Strangers In The Land: Patterns of American

Nativism, 1860-1925 (New York, 1966), pp. 194-263; Paul L. Murphy, _The Meaning of Free Speech: First Amendment Freedoms From Wilson to FDR_ (Westport, Conn., 1972), esp. pp. 38-100; Murphy, _World War I and the Origin of Civil Liberties in the United States_ (New York, 1979), pp. 157, 170-173; Aileen S. Kraditor, _The Radical Persuasion, 1890-1917: Aspects of the Intellectual History and the Historiography of Three American Radical Organizations_ (Baton Rouge, 1981);Michael R. Johnson, "The I.W.W. and Wilsonian Democracy," _Science and Society_, 28. no. 3 (Summer 1964), 257-274; Eldridge Foster Dowell, "A History of Criminal Syndical Legislation in the United States," _Johns Hopkins University Studies in Historical and Political Science_, 57 (1939), _passim_. For a review of IWW historiography, see the Introduction to Joseph R. Conlin, ed. _At the Point of Production: The Local History of the IWW_ (Westport, Conn., 1981).

10These ideas, which inform portions of the present work, draw upon Ralf Dahrendorf's _Classes and Class Conflict in Industrial Society_, rev. ed. (Stanford, 1959); Fred Weinstein and Gerald M. Platt, _The Wish To Be Free: Society, Psyche, and Value Change_, (Berkeley, 1969), and _Psychoanalytic Sociology_, (Baltimore, 1973); Peter L. Berger and Thomas Luckman, _The Social Construction of Reality: A Treatise in the Sociology of Knowledge_ (Garden City, New York, 1966); C.B. MacPherson, _The Political Theory of Possessive Individualism: Hobbes to Locke_ (London, 1962); Erik H. Erikson, "Identity and the Life Cycle," _Psychological Issues_, 1, no. 1 (1959); and various works of Freud.

11This paragraph draws upon David Apter, _Choice and the Politics of Allocation_ (New Haven, 1971); Maurice Stein, _Eclipse of Community: An Interpretation of American Studies_, (New York, 1960); Ted Robert Gurr, _Why Men Rebel_ (Princeton, N.J., 1970); Robert W. Merton, _Social Theory and Social Structure_, rev. ed. (Glencoe, Ill., 1957);

12Readers familiar with the controversy regarding the over-application of the status-anxiety theory to problems in American history will recognize this argument. The emphasis here, and elsewhere in the present work, is on anxiety generated in the context of role-playing and reference group behavior, as proposed by Robert W. Doherty, in "Status Anxiety and American Reform: Some Alternatives," _American Quarterly_, 19 (Summer 1967), supplement, 329-337. For a broad discussion of alienation, social structure, and separation anxiety, see Gerald M. Platt and Fred Weinstein, "Alienation and the Problem of Social Action," in _The Phenomenon of Sociolgy: A Reader in the Sociology of Sociology_, ed., Edward A. Tiryakian (New York, 1971), pp. 284-310. Cf.

Robert F. Berkhofer. Jr., A Behavioral Approach To Historical Analysis (New York, 1969), p. 66: "It matters little
whether the status. . . diminished in reality from the
observer's construction of the situation, and it matters
just as little whether social and political organization of
the situation really changed as a result of industrialism.
What does matter in this argument is whether the actors saw
their situation in that context."

[13]Alfred D. Chandler, "The Beginnings of 'Big Business' in
American Industry," Business Hist. Rev., 33, no. 1 (Spring
1959), 4.

[14]This and the following summary paragraphs are drawn from
Ralph Andreano, ed., New Views On American Economic Develop-
ment (Cambridge, Mass., 1965); Joe S. Bain, "Industrial
Concentration and Anti-Trust Policy," in The Growth of the
American Economy, ed. Harold Williamson (Englewood Cliffs,
1951); Phillip Cagan, "The First Fifty Years of the Banking
System - An Historical Appraisal," in Banking And Monetary
Studies, ed. Deane Carson (Homewood, Ill., 1963); Alfred
Chandler, "The Beginnings of 'Big Business' in American
Industry," Business Hist. Rev., 33, no. 1 (Spring 1959), 1-
31; Thomas Cochran and William Miller, The Age of Enter-
prise: A Social History of Industrial America (New York,
1942), esp. ch. 9; Lance E. Davis, "Capital Immobilities And
Finance Capitalism; A Study of Economic Evolution In The
United States, 1820-1920," Explorations In Entrepreneurial
History, 1 (1963), 88-105; Milton Friedman and Anna
Schwartz, A Monetary History of the United States, 1867-1960
(Princeton, N.J., 1963), esp. pp. 156-173, 189-196; N.S.B.
Gras and Henrietta M. Larson, "Financial Capitalism," in
Casebook in American Business History (New York, 1939), pp.
10-12; Gabriel Kolko, The Triumph of Conservatism: A Rein-
terpretation of American History (New York, 1963); William
Letwin, Law And Economic Policy in America: The Evolution
of the Sherman Anti-Trust Act (New York, 1965); Ralph
Nelson, Merger Movements In American Industry, 1895-1956
(Princeton, N.J., 1959); Doulas North, Growth and Welfare
In The American Past: A New Economic History (Englewood
Cliffs, N.J., 1966), esp. Ch. 12; Glenn Porter, The Rise of
Big Business, 1860-1910 (New York, 1973); Herbert Prochnow,
The Federal Reserve System (New York, 1960); Henry Parker
Willis, "Banking and Monetary Reform," in American Economic
Development Since 1860, ed. William Greenleaf (Columbia,
S.C., 1968).

[15]Chandler, 6.

[16]Bain. pp. 617-621.

[17]Nelson, pp. 6-7, 89-100; Andreano, p. 18.

[18]Cochran and Miller, pp. 189-195.

[19]Quoted in Porter, pp. 89-90.

[20]Davis, 88-89.

[21]Rhodri Jeffreys-Jones, Violence and Reform in American History (New York, 1978), p. 26: "Progressive excitement about violence was unjustified. In the first place, there can be no doubt that it was insignificant compared with other forms of crime. Often-cited Chicago-Tribune figures estimated the total number of murders and homicides between 1894 and 1900 as 62,812. Of these, only 365 were even alleged to have arisen as a result of strikes. In mortal terms, the race problem, though in one of its quieter phases following the demise of Radical Reconstruction, was more serious than the "class" problem. More than a hundred blacks were lynched in each of the years 1891, 1892, 1894, 1895, 1897, 1898, 1900 and 1901. Industrial violence received disproportionate attention (just as racial violence did later) because it was regarded as an important social indicator. As such, it was further twisted and abused by the polemicists of the Progressive period." Also compare H.M. Gitelman, "Perspectives on American Industrial Violence," Bus. Hist. Rev., 47, no. 1 (Spring 1973), 1-23.

[22]Dahrendorf, pp. 68, 245, 268 and passim.

[23]David Montgomery, "The 'New Unionism' and the Transformation of Workers' Consciousness in America, 1909-22," Journ. of Soc. Hist., 7, no. 4 (Summer 1974), 509.

[24]This is the first sentence of the Preamble to the Constitution of the Industrial Workers of the World. See Joyce Kornbluh, ed., Rebel Voices: An I.W.W. Anthology (Ann Arbor, 1964), pp. 12-13.

[25]Jeffreys-Jones, pp. 155-176; Don S. Kirschner, "The Ambiguous Legacy: Social Justice and Social Control in the Progressive Era," Historical Reflections, 2 (Summer 1975), 73ff.

[26]"After the Battle," Survey, April 6, 1912, 1-2.

[1]The most comprehensive account of the San Diego free speech fight is Theodore Schroeder's, "The History of the San Diego Free Speech Fight," in Free Speech for Radicals (New York, 1969), pp. 116-190. (Reprinted from the 1916 edition, itself a compilation of articles appearing in the New York Call Sunday issues, beginning March 15, 1914.) Also see Harris Weinstock, Report to the Governor of California on the Disturbances in the City and County of San Diego (Sacramento, 1912); San Francisco Labor Council Special Investigating Committee, San Diego Free Speech Controversy (San Francisco, April 25, 1912); Ernest Jerome Hopkins, "The San Diego Fight," The Coming Nation, May 4, 1912, 8-9. Also compare Grace L. Miller, "The I.W.W. Free Speech Fight: San Diego, 1912," So. Cal. Q., 54 (Fall 1972), 211-238; Rosalie Shanks, "The I.W.W. Free Speech Movement: San Diego, 1912," San Diego Hist. Q., 19 (Winter 1973), 25-35; Charlotte Benz Villalobos, "Civil Liberties in San Diego: The Free Speech Fight of 1912," M.A. Thesis, San Diego State College, 1966. See Mother Earth, June 1912 (7, no. 4) for firsthand accounts of the treatment accorded Ben Reitman and Emma Goldman; Philip S. Foner, ed., Fellow Workers and Friends: I.W.W. Free-Speech Fights as Told by Participants (Westport, Conn., 1981); also see Melvin Dubofsky's resumé of the Justice Department files relating to the trouble in San Diego (attitudes of Taft, Wickersham, et al) in We Shall Be All (Chicago, 1969), pp. 193-195.

[2]San Diego Evening Tribune, April 2, 1912, p. 3; Mary Anderson Hill, "The Free-Speech Fight at San Diego," Survey, 28 (May 4, 1912), 194; Hopkins, "The San Diego Fight," 8; San Francisco Labor Council, San Diego Free Speech Controversy, p. 10; James Weinstein, The Corporate Ideal in the Liberal State: 1900-1918 (Boston, 1968), p. 179. See Shanks (28) for a suggestion that the San Diego authorities were prompted to suppress the IWW because of apprehension over reports that an IWW contingent was fighting in the Mexican Revolution, and that nearby Tiajuana had been destroyed.

[3]Weinstein, p. 178.

[4]Schroeder, p. 116.

[5]The following list, compiled from various sources, is not intended to be exhaustive, but to illustrate the geographical distribution of confrontations with the IWW, which on

this basis is 9 Western cities, 17 Western towns, 8 Midwestern cities, 8 Midwestern towns, 1 Eastern city, and 7
Eastern towns.

IWW FREE SPEECH FIGHTS OR STRIKES, 1906-1916

Year	Location	Year	Location
1906	San Francicso	1913	Denver
1907	Seattle		Grand Junction, Colo.
1908	Los Angeles		Minot
1909	Missoula		Seattle
	Spokane		Kansas Citv. Mo.
	New Castle, Pa.		Cleveland
	McKees Rocks, Pa.		Detroit
1910	Wenatchee, Wash.		Peoria
	Walla Walla		Philadelphia
	Fresno		Hilo
1911	Duluth		Juneau
	Victoria, B.C.		Omaha
	Denver		Wheatland, Cal.
	Superior, Wisc.		Akron
	Kansas City. Mo.		Paterson, N.J.
	Aberdeen, Wash.		Coos Bay, Ore.
1912	San Diego	1914	Aberdeen, So. Dak.
	Aberdeen, So. Dak.		Kansas City, Mo.
	Vancouver, B.C.		Des Moines
	San Francisco		Victoria, B.C.
	Oakland, Cal.		Butte
	New Bedford, Mass.	1915	Paterson, N.J.
	Minneapolis	1916	Old Forge, Pa.
	Lawrence, Mass.		Everett, Wash.
	Hoquiam, Wash.		Mesabi Range

[6]In addition to the illustration in Appendix II, also see
U.S. Senate, Industrial Relations: Final Report and Testimony Submitted to Congress by the Commission on Industrial
Relations Created by the Act of August 23, 1912, 5:4868-
4871, 4876-4886, 4892-4895; 6:5848-5853. (Hereafter cited
as CIR Final Report.)

[7]William Eugene Hollon, Frontier Violence: Another Look (New
York, 1974), passim. E.g., p. 95, "The murder of Orientals
became such a commonplace occurrence throughout the second
half of the nineteenth century that newspapers seldom
printed the story."

[8]Schroeder, pp. 117-118; Weinstock, p. 10.

[9]San Diego _Union_, Feb. 10, 1912, p. 5. It is likely that
Braly had in mind the upcoming 1915 San Diego Exposition.

[10]To a certain extent, angry editorials and letters to the
editor are hyperbolized releases for aggression and do not
reflect the complexity of human emotions. Thus a citizen
who could both vent his wrath and be forgiving is in a state
of mind that newspapers rarely illustrate. Cf. Freud,
"Mental life is the arena and battleground for mutually
opposing purposes. . . it consists of contradictions and
pairs of contraries. Proof of the existence of a particular
purpose is no argument against the existence of an opposite
one: there is room for both." Quoted in Paul Roazen,
Freud: Political and Social Thought (New York, 1968), p. 64.
However, the printed word also serves the unconscious
purpose of locating the individual in a context of reality,
giving meaning and a sense of order to the world by
rendering dissolving thought into the motionless permanence
of black type on a white page. In this way, sustained
repetition of anti-labor, anti-socialist, anti-Wobbly bias
helped make class prejudice a reality and violence a
probability.

[11]Schroeder. p. 121.

[12]Schroeder, p. 123.

[13]Schroeder, pp. 122-123.

[14]E.W. Scripps owned the _Sun_, and the sugar baron John D.
Spreckels owned the rival _Union_ and _Evening Tribune_; what
one paper was for, the other was usually against. The _Sun_
initially protested police action, but then did little more
than urge moderation: "It was all right to test that law
[the street-speaking ordinance] but most San Diegans want no
violence in connection with any such tests, and are heartily
tired of the disturbances which have resulted. The _Sun_ is
still of the opinion that the ordinance was at least
unnecessary, but that is not the point of this. What the
people want now is a peaceable solution of the question, not
more law violation. That peaceable solution may be had at
the ballot box in a good American way" (March 8, 1912, p.
4). George F. Mott, Jr., _San Diego -- Politically Speaking_
(San Diego, 1932), pp. 18, 72-75; _Dict. Amer. Biog._, VIII,
518; IX, 479.

[15]San Diego _Sun_, April 10, 1912, p. 9. A number of similar
resolutions were passed. For example, the International
Brotherhood of Woodsmen and Sawmill Workers, Local 35,
emulated the Carpenters and the Musicians in condemning

"free speech, so-called; also any other organization who will uphold the I.W.W. in their disturbance," and for good measure, "also other union men whom we have heard making slanderous remarks about our churches." (San Diego Sun, Feb. 28, 1912, p. 9.) The San Diego Typographical Union complained that the IWW was fueling open-shop sentiment, and continued, "Whereas, we do not believe that the right of free speech is being denied lawful citizens of the United States, but that the complaint is being used merely as an excuse for defying the laws of our city and country, and the heaping of abuse upon our regularly elected officials, and openly denying our right to have an established form of government; and Whereas our flag is daily being dishonored and trampled upon and the red flag raised above it, causing the blood of every true American to boil within him. . . ." etc. (San Diego Sun, May 6, 1912, p. 16.) Members of the San Diego Realty Board passed a resolution endorsing the stand taken by the City Council and the Police Department (San Diego Union, April 5, 1912, p. 12; San Diego Sun, April 3, 1912, p. 9); as did the San Diego Ad Club which praised the local police for "ridding the city of the lawless bands of I.W.W.'s and pledging fealty to the Stars and Stripes." (San Diego Sun, May 21, 1912, p. 1).

[16]Cf. Paul Goodman's Speaking and Language: A Defense of Poetry (New York, 1971), pp. 25-26 and passim. "God created the world from nothing with words. A prophet's lips touched with a coal of fire created new ethics. If an ordained priest says 'Hoc est corpus,' the wheaten bread is transfigured. A man can win salvation by repeating the one right syllable, or even spinning it on a wheel." Or Edward Sapir: "The fact of the matter is that the 'real world' is to a large extent unconsciously built up on the language habits of the group. . . . We see and hear and otherwise experience very largely as we do because the language habits of our community predispose certain choices of interpretation." Quoted in Language, Thought, and Reality: Selected Writings of Benjamin Lee Whorf, ed. John B. Carroll (Cambridge, Mass., 1956), p. 134. And Whorf: "Language patterns [and] cultural norms. . . have grown up together, constantly influencing each other. But in this partnership the nature of language is the factor that limits free plasticity and rigidifies channels of development in the more autocratic way." (Ibid, p. 156).

[17]Cf. Sigmund Freud, Totem and Taboo, tr. and ed. James Strachey (New York, 1950), p. 81. The revolutionary's mania for obliterating the past by renaming illustrates the power in names. See Crane Brinton, The Anatomy of Revolution (New York, 1965), pp. 179-180.

[18]Fred Weinstein and Gerald M. Platt, The Wish To Be Free: Society, Psyche, and Value Change (Berkeley and Los Angeles, 1969), pp. 168-196; cf. John R. Seeley, R. Alexander Sim, Elizabeth W. Loosely, Crestwood Heights, A Study of the Culture of Suburban Life (New York, 1956), pp. 382-393; Maurice R. Stein, Eclipse of Community: An Interpretation of American Studies (New York, 1960), pp. 173-174.

[19]The Free-Speech League had a number of women in its ranks. Some, like Laura Payne Emerson, Estelle Kirk, and Rev. Lulu Wightman, were part of San Diego's public life and spoke out on the issue; others attended street-meetings. But few women were arrested and none were harassed, except Emma Goldman. On the other side, although women undoubtedly supported the vigilante activity, they apparently did not participate in it. An exception is the story of Mrs. Earl P. Schnack, as related in a report about Wobblies forced to run the gauntlet. "The determination of San Diego county citizens to run their own government is shown in the daring displayed by Mrs. Earl P. Schnack of Escondido. Mrs. Schnack, known as the 'Barney Oldfield' [a veteran race driver] of that county, is the wife of the proprieter of the Escondido garage. When the party at Escondido was organized for duty at San Onofre, Mrs. Schnack, an expert automobile driver, volunteered to drive a car, her husband being absent in San Diego. She piloted a machine from Escondido to San Onofre in record tine and when she arrived took as much interest in the proceedings as did the men. She was dressed in a natty motoring costume, corduroy skirt, laced shoes, and flannel shirt. And in Mrs. Schnack's shirt are pockets. In one was an automatic revolver. She remained at San Onofre all of Wednesday night and assisted in guarding the prisoners." The story is accompanied by a picture of "Mrs. Earl P. Schnack Who Drove Car For Deputies." (San Diego Union, April 5, 1912, pp. 7, 10.)

[20]Roles are thus like masks. Under stress, roles are more consciously adopted. In this sense, were it not for the unhappy endings to these conflicts, the drama featuring vigilantes and Wobblies might be perceived as low comedy, with each posturing in roles created to intimidate the other. Indeed, there was much theater in the flamboyant career of the IWW. In speeches, songs, newsletters, cartoons, and stickers, the IWW projected an image of the Industrial Worker as strong, determined, brave, defiant, and loyal to the death. Designed to frighten its enemies and encourage its friends, this persona was compensation for the weak position of the unskilled workers for whom the Wobblies spoke. Given the limited fora available to them, the Wobblies exploited their opportunities dramatically: nearly

all the IWW organizers were colorful speakers, and IWW street meetings were always entertaining. The free speech fights were highly theatrical, and laughter often accompanied the roles of soapbox speaker and jailbird. Wobbly theatrics peaked in 1913 with the staging of the Paterson Pageant in New York's Madison Square Garden, where hundreds of silk strikers recreated the events of the strike in an effort to raise funds and sympathy for the strikers. For a related commentary on IWW poetry and the image of the Wobbly as Apocalyptic Rebel, see Donald E. Winters, "The Soul of Solidarity: The Relationship between the I.W.W. and American Religion in the Progressive Era," Diss. Univ. of Minn., Ch. 6.

[21]Cf. Harry Stack Sullivan, The Interpersonal Theory of Psychiatry (New York, 1953), pp. 367-384. "The quicker one comes to a low opinion of another, other things being equal, the poorer one's secret view of one's own worth in the field of the disparagement." (380); Sullivan, "Psychiatry: Introduction to the Study of Interpersonal Relations," in A Study of Interpersonal Relations, ed. Patrick Mullahy (New York, 1949) p. 98-121; Stein. p. 262; John Dollard, Caste and Class in a Southern Town (New York, 1957), p. 367. For a theoretical exposition of roles as social performances requiring mutual cooperation from the members of group, profession, class, etc., see Erving Goffman's The Presentation of the Self in Everyday Life (Garden City, N.Y., 1959). Also Robert W. Doherty, "Status Anxiety and American Reform," Am. Q., 19 (1967), Supp. 329-337; and Peter L. Berger and Thomas Luckman, The Social Construction of Reality: A Treatise in the Sociology of Knowledge (New York, 1966), pp. 72-78. For a comment on workers and roles, see Aileen S. Kraditor, The Radical Persuasion, 1890-1917: Aspects of the Intellectual History and the Historiography of Three American Radical Organizations (Baton Rouge, 1981), pp. 73-74.

[22]See, e.g., Totem and Taboo, p. 64 and passim. Projected hostility and creation of a scapegoat are principal features of a variety of social beliefs, ideologies, and social movements -- millenarianism, nativism, fascism, McCarthyism, red-baiting, paranoid style, conspiracy theory of history, status anxiety, cultural despair, and so on -- that exhibit a fear of internal subversion. One of the few contemporaries who recognized the role assigned to the Wobblies was Max Eastman, "The Great American Scapegoat," New Review [New York], 2 (Aug. 1914), 465-470.

[23]Compare Richard Hofstadter's composite of the ideal-type enemy: "He is a perfect model of malice, a kind of amoral

superman: sinister, ubiquitous, powerful, cruel, sensual, luxury-loving. Unlike the rest of us, the enemy is not caught in the toils of the vast mechanism of history, him-self a victim of his past, his desires, his limitations. He is a free, active, demonic agent. He wills, indeed he manufactures, the mechanism of history himself, or deflects the normal course of history in an evil way. He makes crises, starts runs on banks, causes depressions, manufac-tures disasters, and then enjoys and profits from the misery he has produced." Richard Hofstadter, The Paranoid Style of American Politics (New York, 1965), pp. 31-32. Also see David Brion Davis, "Some Themes of Countersubversion: An Analysis of Anti-Masonic, Anti-Catholic, and Anti-Mormon Literature," MVHR, 97, no. 2 (Sept. 1960), 205-224; Edward Shils, "Ideology and Civility: On the Politics of the Intel-lectual," in Ideology, Politics and Political Theory, ed. Richard H. Cox (Belmont, Cal., 1969) p. 227, for a further description of "the ideological outlook"; John Fraser, Violence and the Arts (Bristol, Engl., 1974), p. 59; Freud, Group Psychology and the Analysis of the Ego, p. 30; Fred Weinstein and Gerald M. Platt, Psychoanalytic Sociology (Baltimore, 1973), p. 95; David Brion Davis, The Slave Power Conspiracy and the Paranoid Style (Baton Rouge, 1969), pp. 24-31.

[24]San Diego Sun, Feb. 13, 1912. p. 1; Schroeder, p. 121.

[25]San Diego Sun, April 4, 1912, p. 1; San Diego Union, April 20, 1912, pp. 4, 9.

[26]Cf. Ruth Miller Elson, Guardians of Tradition: American Schoolbooks of the Nineteenth Century (Lincoln, Neb., 1964); Richard D. Mosier, Making the American Mind: Social and Moral Ideas in the McGuffey Readers (New York, 1947).

[27]Hofstadter, p. 34: "The sexual freedom often attributed to him [the enemy], his lack of moral inhibition, his possession of especially effective techniques for fulfilling his desires, give exponents of the paranoid style an opportunity to project and freely express unacceptable aspects of their own minds."

[28]E.g., Freud comments on the contagious character of taboo: "If one person succeeds in gratifying the repressed desire, the same desire is bound to be kindled in all other members of the community. In order to keep the temptation down, the envied transgressor must be deprived of the fruit of his enterprise; and the punishment will not infrequently give those who carry it out the opportunity of committing the

same outrage under colour of an act of expiation. This is
indeed one of the foundations of the human penal system and
it is based, no doubt correctly, on the assumption that the
prohibited impulses are present alike in the criminal and in
the avenging community. In this, psycho-analysis is no more
than confirming the habitual pronouncement of the pious: we
are all miserable sinners." Freud, _Totem and Taboo_, p. 72.

[29]This psychoanalytical speculation can account for the
vilificaton of Emma Goldman, Elizabeth Gurley Flynn and
other women with radical politics and an unconventional love
life who demanded independence and self-determination. Men
who voiced such demands were understood to be expressing a
kind of natural aggression, and had only to be forced to
curtail it. But women who rejected traditional submissive
roles attacked the core of social control. Rejecting their
status as property, they threatened to expose repressed
sexual impulses regulated through marriage. For many
centuries, rape and adultery have been not only affronts to
"honor" but devaluations of property as well. Women were
expected to be chaste and without carnal passion. Women who
rejected this satellite status were censured on all sides.
(Cf. Weinstein and Platt, _The Wish To Be Free_, pp. 284-285,
n. 21.)

[30]Weinstein and Platt, _The Wish To Be Free_, pp. 202-203.
The Wobblies attacked the hypocrisy of conventional
attitudes. A writer in _The Industrial Worker_ offered these
views on prostitution, marriage, and the property status of
women: "Permit one to enter a respectful protest against the
general attitude. . . toward the 'social evil.' Why 'evil'?
Why not call it the 'social good'? Unmarried women denounce
it because they think it diminishes their chances of getting
married, which is the one aim of nine hundred and ninety-
nine out of a thousand — justly so, because with all its
drawbacks, it is, after all, the most profitable job they
can get. Married women denounce it chiefly from _esprit de
corps_ — that of the Married Women's Union, the most
powerful of all trade unions. To them the woman on the
street is simply a scab who cuts wages. The union price is
life support and no union woman can have a good word for one
who takes less. . . . The whole tendency of the day is to
regard all sex relations as quite devoid of intrinsic moral
significance. As a matter of contract [in marriage] they
may acquire a certain moral significance — that is, breach
of chastity, when chastity is a part of the contract, may be
like any other breach of contract; but the superstitious
attitude toward sex relations in themselves — the attitude
that led the fathers of the church to speak of them, even in
wedlock, as '_stuprum connubiale_' [sic] — is fast fading.

And why should the old prejudice not fade? It was primarily directed against derelictions on the part of woman for the very good reason that, on the part of woman, such derelictions are usually followed by very substantial and very burdensome consequences. There was nothing for it in those days but to scare them out of it with threats of hell. But, nowadays, with prophylactic and remedy both at hand to the intelligent woman, why should she not adopt the man's standard? Why should we not approve her, rather than condemn, when she adopts it?" Quoted in Edmund Weston, "Some Principles of the I.W.W.," The American Employer (July 1913), 714-715; attributed to James F. Clark.

[31]San Diego Union, Feb. 19, 1912, p. 12.

[32]San Diego Union, Feb. 25, 1912, p. 13.

[33]New York Tribune, April 12, 1914, Part V, p. 1. Half of this is reprinted without attribution from a 1912 New York Times article.

[34]Elson, pp. 215-217, 253. Elson (p. 280) quotes Noah Webster from 1835: "The poor have no right to complain, if they do not succeed in business. They all enjoy the same rights; and if they continue in poverty, it is usually for want of industry, or judgment in management of their affairs, or for want of prudence and economy in preserving what they earn. They have no more right to invade the property of the rich, than the rich have to invade the rights of the poor." (From Instructive and Entertaining Lessons for Youth).

[35]Russell H. Conwell, Acres of Diamonds (New York, 1915). "James Roscoe Day," DAB; George P. Bent, "Cooperation and 'Invisible Government,'" American Industry, 14, no. 10 (August, 1913), 18. Andrew Carnegie's ex post apologia for his riches (Triumphant Democracy, 1886; The Empire of Business, 1902; Autobiography, 1920), calls attention to hard struggle and frugality: "Abolish luxury, if you please, but leave on the soil, upon which alone the virtues and all that is precious in human character grow: poverty — honest poverty." The Empire of Business (New York, 1902), p. 129.

[36]Bent, loc. cit.

[37]Sigmund Freud, Civilization and Its Discontents, tr. and ed. by James Strachey (New York, 1961), p. 27, n. 1.

[38]C.B. MacPherson, The Political Theory of Possessive Individualism: Hobbes to Locke (London, 1962), pp. 221-227.

[39]Weinstein and Platt, The Wish To Be Free, pp. 200-206 and passim; MacPherson, pp. 38-61; also see Reinhard Bendix, Work and Authority in Industry (New York, 1963), pp. 99-116, on entrepreneurial ideology. The rationalization of work and the emergence of a complementary economic and social system predate Protestantism and stem from more general assaults on traditional authority, of which Protestantism was but one. The extensive rebuttal to Max Weber's yoking of protestantism and capitalism, in The Protestant Ethic And The Spirit of Capitalism, tr. Talcott Parsons (New York, 1958), includes Ephraim Fischoff, "The Protestant Ethic and the Spirit of Capitalism -- The History of A Controversy," Soc. Research, 2 (1944), 53-77; Robert K. Merton, "Puritanism, Pietism and Science," in Social Theory and Social Structure (Glencoe, Ill, 1957), pp. 574-606; Kurt Samuelsson, Religion And Economic Action: A Critique of Max Weber, tr. E. Geoffrey French (New York, 1961); Robert E. Kennedy, Jr., "The Protestant Ethic and the Parsis," Am. Jour. Soc., 68, no. 1 (July 1962), 11-20; Gabriel Kolko, "Max Weber on America: Theory and Evidence," in Studies in the Philosophy of History, ed. George H. Nadel (New York, 1965). For a summary review, see Irving M. Zeitlin, Ideology and the Development of Sociological Theory (Englewood Cliffs, N.J., 1968), pp. 122-138. Samuelsson's critique is the most telling; e.g., in regards to certain features of the work ethic and Protestantism: "The doctrine of diligence and thrift that was preached to mankind for three centuries -- roughly the 16th, 17th and 18th -- was not unique to Protestantism, Calvinism and the free religious sects. It constituted a most important feature of the moral outlook of mercantilism, which everywhere reigned supreme. It was preached in Catholic France with the same zeal as in Switzerland and the Netherlands" (p. 81). Weber revised his ideas on the origins of occidental rational capitalism in his later writings on world religions and economic history: see his General Economic History, tr. Frank H. Knight (New York, 1961) pp. 233-270; and the Introduction to The Protestant Ethic And The Spirit of Capitalism, written just before his death. Exhortations to diligence and thrift can be found in other cultures, viz., early 17th century Japan: "When a man has capital, small though it may be, he must allow himself no relaxation in his attention to household problems or the running of his business, and must continue to make the earning of his living his principal concern. This is his lifelong duty. If, when one has capital, one begins to relax, to buy things one longs for, to behave in a wilful manner, to live in style, and to do all the things which one wishes to do, the money is soon spent. . . . One must set to work from the moment one has capital." (Samuelsson, p. vii, from the Introduction by D. C. Coleman.)

[40]Weinstein and Platt, The Wish To Be Free, p. 202; Weber, The Protestant Ethic, pp. 47 ff.

[41]Kolko, pp. 192-193.

[42]Samuelsson refutes Weber's correlation of diligence, thrift, economic progress, and Protestant doctrine: "Practical reality was as far removed from the frugality enjoined by Calvinism and Puritanism as it was possible to be. The palatial old residences of businessmen in one mercantile city after another -- Berne, Geneva, Zurich, Amsterdam, Antwerp, London, Lubeck, Danzig, Stockholm -- are testimony enough. Summer residences, country estates, and pleasure yachts, records of servants, vehicles, clothes, funerals, weddings and other festivals complete the picture. A way of life verging on the lavish was far more typical than the pathological niggardliness that Calvin, Colbert and the Free church fathers all exalted as the ideal. Rockefeller and Carnegie are often instanced as examples of an almost morbid thriftiness. Yet the effective role of this trait -- when it existed at all -- was surely negligible. The great palaces, the princely courts with which such seigneurs surrounded themselves must not be obscured by the vision of the frugal meals or turned suits they may have affected. . . . The possession of great wealth and the command of really important capital assets -- and this is what we must consider, not the painfully hoarded coppers of small traders and craftsmen -- can scarcely have derived, even exceptionally, from 'saving up' in the connotation usually implied by this expression, a connotation which Weber must also have intended if his argument is to make any sense at all. Although hard work has certainly and often made its contribution, great fortunes are, and for the most part always have been, the product of 'fortunate speculations,' of vast profits from vast risks and vast luck -- in short, of speculation and capital gains usually in association with extensive structural changes and innovations in economic life. . . . The determining factors were the volume and fortune of business, enormous capital gains on unexploited, or previously ill-exploited, natural assets, and the monopolization of markets or credit. With few exceptions, all great fortunes, far-flung economic empires and individual concentrations of economic power have been built up at tremendous speed, in the course of a single generation, not of two or three (although time may have increased wealth still further) in a single decade or even a single year" (Samuelsson, pp. 83-85).

[43]Weinstein and Platt, The Wish To Be Free, pp. 200-202.

[44]Weinstein and Platt, The Wish To Be Free, p. 203.

[45]Editorial, "Why San Diego Has Taken Some of the Law Into Its Own Hand," San Diego Evening Tribune, May 10, 1912, p. 4.

NOTES TO CHAPTER 3

[1]Theodore Schroeder, "The History of the San Diego Free Speech Fight," in Free Speech For Radicals (New York, 1969), pp. 125-150.

[2]San Diego Sun, April 12, 1912, p. 3.

[3]Schroeder, pp. 149-150.

[4]Schroeder, pp. 156-162; San Diego Union, May 15, 1912, p. 8; Ben L. Reitman, M.D., "The Respectable Mob," Mother Earth, 12, no. 4 (June 1912), 109-114.

[5]Schroeder, pp. 163 165, 167-168.

[6]Hyman Weintraub, "The I.W.W. in California, 1905-1931," M.A. Thesis, Univ. of Cal., Los Angeles, 1947, p. 38; Miller, 223; Schroeder, p. 152.

[7]San Diego Sun, February 17, 1912, p. 1; April 5, 1912, p. 2; San Diego Union, April 6, 1912, p. 9; Miller, 217-218.

[8]Transposition of suspicion and repression inwards upon the conspirators is a function of guilt over excursions outside

the law, and has been oft-remarked by Freud and others.
Compare, e.g., Weinstein and Platt's description of Robes-
pierre and the Reign of Terror (The Wish To Be Free, pp.
108-136); or Crane Brinton's discussion of the Thermidorean
reaction, Stalin's purges, and the like (The Anatomy of Revolution, pp. 176-236); or Franz Fanon's analysis of
violence as initiation and bonding in revolutionary groups
in "The Wretched of the Earth," in Reader in Political
Sociology, ed. Frank Lindenfeld (New York, 1968), pp 486-
505.   There is also a first-hand account from San Diego.
The Reverend Willard B. Thorp, of San Diego's First Congre-
gational Church, described the effects of vigilantism in the
wake of his shock over the Reitman-Goldman affair: "It has
been necessary to resort to extraordinary measures to protect our community against those who were coming here for
the express purpose of breaking down our laws. It was under
this plea that volunteer vigilance committees came forward.
That good men were on these committees and were actuated by
conscientious motives, cannot be questioned. But this is a
method which is exceedingly dangerous. Human nature cannot
be trusted to act in matters like this without the res-
traints of law and responsible direction. When soldiers are
called out, we know who is commanding them and we know the
soldiers themselves by their uniforms and they are held
strictly accountable for what they do. But when self-
constituted vigilance committees undertake the work, we know
not who they are, and a feeling of distrust and intimidation
runs through the community. We have been playing with fire.
We hoped we would not be burned. But alas, we have been
disappointed. Human nature among us has turned out to be no
better than elsewhere." (San Diego Union, May 20, 1912, p.
7).

[9]San Diego Sun, May 2, 1912, p. 16; May 24, 1912, p. 1; San
Diego Union, May 21, 1912, p. 13; May 15, 1912, p. 8. The
San Diego Evening Tribune carried this item: "Mother With
Socialist Views Is Not Considered Fit to Raise Children.
Los Angeles, June 12. -- Karl Marx Walker and Moyer Hayward
[sic] Pettibone Walker, the children of Mrs. Eunice Walker,
who said she was a Socialist writer, were removed from the
custody of their mother, when she testified that she had
taken them from the home of a Christian family, because she
did not want them 'reared with false religious views.' Mrs.
Walker made the statement in the juvenile court yesterday.
The court promptly ordered the children placed in an institution. Mrs. Walker said she named her children after the
men tried in Idaho on a charge of having conspired to slay
Governor Steunenberg" (June 12, 1912, p. 1).

[10]San Diego Union, May 8, 1912, p. 7. There seems little

reason to doubt that the Union's reporter, Francis Bierman, was an active vigilante, as he was so identified in numerous accounts and sworn affidavits. E.g.: "The Cossack Regime in San Diego," 108; Reitman, "The Respectable Mob," 113; Emma Goldman, "The Outrage of San Diego," Mother Earth, 7, no. 4 (June, 1912), 117; Schroeder, pp. 130, 132 (affidavits); Hopkins, "The San Diego Fight," 9.

11"The Cossack Regime in San Diego," 108; Miller, Mott, Shanks, Schroeder, Weinstein, et al, passim; San Diego Sun, Union, Evening Tribune, passim.

12"The Cossack Regime in San Diego," 108; Shanks, 33, n. 16. Abram Sauer, the kidnapped editor of the San Diego Herald, reported that "the personnel of the vigilantes represents not only the bankers and merchants but has as its workers leading church members and bartenders. The Chamber of Commerce and the Real Estate Board are well represented. The press and the public utility corporations, as well as members of the Grand Jury are known to belong." Philip S. Foner, A History of the Labor Movement in the United States, Vol. IV: The I.W.W., 1905-1917 (New York, 1965), p. 198.

13Schroeder, p. 129.

14Bruce C. Johnson, "Taking Care of Labor: The Police in American Politics," Theory and Society, 3, no. 1 (Spring 1976), 98. Cf. Melvin Dubofsky, We Shall Be All, p. 37, concerning labor conflict in Western mining regions, 1894-1904: "[I]n most mining communities local farmers, businessmen, and professionals allied with labor unionists; and public officials, including judges, elected by union votes, often supported labor's goals. Instead of class being pitted against class, local communities united in coalitions cutting across class lines to combat 'foreign' capitalists."

15George F. Mott, Jr., San Diego -- Politically Speaking (San Diego, 1932), pp. 72-75.

16Samuel Walker, A Critical History of Police Reform (Lexington, Mass., 1977), p. 11.

17Walker, p. 8.

18Walker, pp. xv, 3.

19American Civil Liberties Union, The Police and the Radicals: What 88 Police Chiefs Think and Do About Radical Meetings (New York, March, 1921), pp. 3, 6-7. The IWW and the Salvation Army both directed their appeal to the same audi-

ence. The IWW often heckled the "Starvation Army," adopted
street-preaching techniques, and wrote parodic or inspiring
lyrics to familiar hymns. That the Salvation Army was
rarely included in street-speaking bans was a propaganda
point for the IWW.

[20]A.C.L.U., p. 3. That police attitudes reflected views of
the business community can be seen in a colloquy between the
Industrial Relations Commission's Counsel and James W.
Cooke, treasurer of a Paterson, N.J. construction firm.
During the 1913 IWW-led silk strike, local authorities had
shut down the meeting halls. Mr. Cooke was asked his view
of that action:
     MR. COOKE: I viewed that as justifiable action under
the circumstances.
     MR. THOMPSON: Did you view it, however, as a legal or
illegal action?
     MR. COOKE: Why, strictly speaking, it would be consi-
dered a denial of liberty.
     MR. THOMPSON: And of the right of free speech?
     MR. COOKE: Yes, sir.
     MR. THOMPSON: And you thought that it was justifiable
to close the halls, nevertheless?
     MR. COOKE: I did; yes, sir.
     MR. THOMPSON: From your point of view, what was the
justice, or the cause, which made it seem justifiable?
     MR. COOKE: Why, I think the good that was to be gained
to the community by stopping this disorder and instigation
to trouble and stoppage of work and all the mills which
followed it justified the restriction at that time.
     MR. THOMPSON: Then looking at it from the ends that
should be attained, social peace and quiet, you felt that
this slight infraction of free speech and liberty was justifie
     MR. COOKE: Yes, sir.
     MR. THOMPSON: I don't wish to characterize that action,
but just to show the comparison between what has been said
here by yourself and others, that it would be a sort of mild
political sabotage justified by the ends to be attained?
     MR. COOKE: I think there is all the difference in the
distinction as to whether it is for a beneficent end or an
evil end. (CIR Final Report, 3:2610)

[21]Editorial, "These People Must Not Disturb Our Peace," San
Diego Evening Tribune, May 17, 1912, p. 4. This argument
becomes irrational, claiming that peace was insured by vio-
lently preventing violence that had not yet occurred from
occurring: "There is no lawlessness in San Diego that is not
provoked by lawlessness, and whatever violence has been
necessary to preserve the general peace of the city is mild
in comparison with what would have ensued if the law brea-

kers now clamoring for 'justice' had been permitted to go
the lengths they intended, even within the law and what they
are pleased to call their 'constitutional rights,' although
in all their wild oratory and their every act these same
appellants from _lex talionis_ of natural justice have insisted that the constitution is a mockery and the statutes
shackles on the limbs of a people that are and of right
ought to be free to do as they see fit irrespective of the
rights of others. . . ."

[22]Cf. Paul L. Murphy, _The Meaning of Freedom of Speech:
First Amendment Freedoms from Wilson to FDR_ (Westport,
Conn., 1972), pp. 11-22.

[23]A.C.L.U., p. 8. Murray Levin, in _Political Hysteria in
America_ (New York, 1971), an account of the psychology
behind the Red Scare of 1919-1920, comments on the equation
of _verbum_ and _factum_: "Radical literature became the equivalent of radical action. As millions of revolutionary words
were produced, circulated, captured, and reprinted, an aura
of credibility began to emerge that the word -- particularly
the written word -- was not only father to the deed, but an
action in itself. . . . The discovery of a statement of
revolutionary aims in a radical pamphlet was perceived as if
it were _prima facie_ proof of the actual existence of a
revolutionary conspiracy. . . . Words were captured by the
Justice Department in raids and then exhibited, just as an
enemy might be captured and exhibited" (p. 101).

[24]A.C.L.U., pp. 10-11. A number of replies did show a
different understanding of the role of police vis-à-vis free
discussion. The Charleston, S.C., Police Chief said, "We
always adhere strictly to the policy in this community of
not interfering with the constitutional rights of any individual of free speech, etc. The department thinks it far
better, although we may disagree with their propaganda, to
give them the right of public expression. For if what they
advocate be good, it will be commended by the public.
Otherwise they will condemn themselves by their own expressions" (p. 11). And in Haverhill, Mass., the police commissioner replied, "We regard the duties of the police as the
preservation of law and order, not the suppression of ideas"
(p. 11).

[25]San Diego _Evening Tribune_, May 15, 1912, p. 4.

[26]San Diego _Sun_, April 29, 1912, p. 6.

[27]San Diego _Union_, May 6, 1912, p. 5. Reverend Thorp
typified the confusion of the middle class of San Diego. He

deplored violence, but also destested the IWW. His involvement in this affair climaxed with a retraction of his criticism of the vigilante treatment of Ben Reitman: "To the
public: In my address last Sunday evening, I spoke of Dr.
Reitman as having been taken out of the city and subjected
to abuses and indignities of the most insulting character.
I was not then aware of the assertions Reitman has been
making that acts of personal torture and unprintable inde-
cency were perpetrated upon him. Inasmuch as my words might
be construed as covering accusations of this character, I
feel it my duty to state that I am convinced that nothing of
this kind occured. With two other gentlemen, I have had an
extended interview with one of the men who took Reitman out.
He related to us in detail everything that was done, offered
to supply his statements with an affidavit, and to take us
to the scene and corro?orate his story by such evidence
could be obtained. This we did not feel was necessary, for
we were entirely satisfied of the truthfulness of his narra-
tive. A coat of tar, even if applied cold, as it was in
this case, is a bad enough indignity to deserve the words I
used. But for the credit of our city, let it be known that
it was not accompanied with branding or anything to cause
physical pain or bodily injury, except that once the end of
a lighted cigar was touched to his flesh. WILLARD R.
THORP." (San Diego Sun, May 22, 1912, p. 1.)

[28]San Diego Union, April 7, 1912, p. 15.

[29]The emergence and definition of civil liberties in public
policy is the subject of Paul Murphy's World War I and the
Origin of Civil Liberties in the United States (New York,
1979). Cf. pp. 30-31. A San Diego editorial urged state
legislators to frame a sedition law, arguing states' rights
to curtail civil liberties. "The Fathers of the Republic
were wiser in their generation than some of us are in ours.
They provided in their constitution that Congress shall not
abridge the right of free speech or popular assembly. This
provision therefore applies strictly and exclusively to the
powers of the federal body, leaving the several states free
to frame such statutes as they may deem suitable to any
circumstance in which they may find themselves. It is,
therefore, the constitutional right of the states to abridge
the right of free speech and to prohibit or regulate the
privilege of popular assembly." (San Diego Evening Tribune,
June 6, 1912, p. 4). This argument was accepted by the
judiciary until 1925, when Gitlow v. New York protected
First Amendment freedoms from impairment by the states.

[30]Cf. Murphy, World War I and the Origin of Civil Liberties
in the United States, p. 40. "The attitude of a majority of

public and private leaders of the late nineteenth and early twentieth centuries towards civil liberties, as well as the attitude of great numbers of rank-and-file Americans who supported those leaders, held that such liberties were only to be protected for those citizens who had demonstrated, both by their attitudes and their behavior, that they were prepared to utilize those freedoms in positive and constructive ways. The decision as to whether a citizen deserved to have his civil liberties formally protected was to be made by those responsible elements within the society that were knowledgeable in the proper use of personal freedom. Liberty, in short, was a condition conferred by the community at its discretion, usually only to 'good people' who had earned their prerogatives." Also see Weinstein and Platt, The Wish To Be Free, p. 203; MacPherson, The Political Theory of Possessive Individualism, pp. 221-227.

[31]San Diego Sun, February 23, 1912, p. 2. Superior Court Judge W.A. Sloan, presiding over the various vagrancy and conspiracy trials of the IWW, revealed bias in a statement directed to the defense attorney: "I might as well tell all the people here that I am in sympathy with the police department in enforcing the laws of the city. The situation we all know has arisen through you people stepping outside the law. Not satisfied with stepping outside the law yourself, you have also endeavored to induce others to step outside. I refer to violation of the street speaking ordinance." (San Diego Evening Tribune, April 10, 1912, p. 1). Jury-packing was not uncommon in labor trials. Cf. CIR Final Report, 3:2536- 2537: Robert Hunter, Violence and the Labor Movement (New York, 1922), p. 289.

[32]Schroeder, p. 190.

[1] The Socialist: The Workingman's Paper, (Seattle) Jan. 22, 1910, p. 4.

[2] Richard Brazier, "Looking Backward to the Spokane Free Speech Fight," typescript, p. 1, in the Archives of Labor History and Urban Affairs, University Archives, Wayne State University, The Industrial Workers of the World Collection, box 46, folder 13. (Hereafter cited as Wayne State, I.W.W. Collection.)

[3] Letter to the editor, Spokane Spokesman-Review, Dec. 4, 1909, p. 4.

[4] Brazier (p. 11) claims 500 were arrested the first month, and slightly fewer in subsequent months; an Industrial Relations Commission investigator puts the figure at 320. Daniel O'Regan, "Free Speech Fights of the I.W.W.," HF 1424, 06, "The Free Speech Fight in Spokane," p. 1. U.S. Dept. of Labor, General Records, "Report of the United States Commission on Industrial Relations, 1912-1915," National Archives Record Group 174, Microfilm publication T4. (Hereafter cited as CIR, Unpub. Rpts.) The Spokesman-Review for Jan. 3, 1910 reported: "The sick report of I.W.W. prisoners who were held in the city jail and attended by Emergency Physician John H. O'Shea has been completed and shows that there were 334 men on the hospital list and that Dr. O'Shea gave 1,600 treatments. None died."

[5] From a letter published in the Spokane Daily Chronicle, Jan. 10, 1910, p. 6. A classic form of sinister foreign conspiracy was displayed in a letter received by the Police Chief: "All over Europe, especially the southern part, they [the IWW] have scouts who induce members to come, cultivate the anarchist spirit, and when highly developed, if necessary pay their fare into this country with money levied as dues or a special assessment. In the large seaports of the Atlantic and Gulf states they have offices which see to nothing else but the welfare of members arriving here. At least 70 percent of the steerage passengers coming into the southern and Gulf seaports are members of some society affiliated with the main body. I give you this information as a patriotic American citizen, but, knowing the fatal results to me, I beg you to withhold my name." (Spokesman-Review, Nov. 16, 1909, p. 7).

[6]Spokesman-Review, Nov. 24, 1909, p. 7.

[7]Spokesman-Review, Dec. 10, 1909, p. 7.

[8]The Socialist: The Workingman's Paper (Seattle), March 19, 1910, p. 4. Other Anglo-Americans in the city's administration, besides Judge Mann, included Mayor Pratt, City Comptroller Fairley, Prosecuting Attorney Pugh, Police Chief Sullivan, Detectives Burns, McDonald, Shannon. Wobblies, too, needed scapegoats. Elizabeth Gurley Flynn characterized Officer Shannon as "with face and form like an African gorilla, showing no sign of either human compassion or intelligence." Flynn, "The Shame of Spokane," International Socialist Review, 10, no. 7 (January 1910), 612. Juries that convicted Flynn and other Wobblies in Spokane were of the business class and had Anglo-Saxon names: Flynn was found guilty of conspiracy by "George T. Crane, businessman; W.J. Nichols, mining man; A.R. Babb, retired farmer; J.M. Comstock, president Spokane Dry Goods Company; James B. Gray, real estate; J.H. Abrahams, retired farmer." (Spokesman- Review, Dec. 10, 1909, p. 1). Another jury, out for five minutes before it found a verdict of guilty, included "W.H. Kipp, of the Palm Confectionery Store; J.F. Hoyt, Clerk of the Woodmen; T.M. Reid, a North Monroe grocer; L.H. Wolfe, of the German Bakery; R.B. Paterson, of the Spokane Dry Goods Company; and A.W. Edington, a retired businessman." (Spokane Daily Chronicle, Jan. 18, 1910. p. 7.)

[9]Fred W. Heslewood, "Barbarous Spokane," International Socialist Review, 10, no. 8 (Feb. 1910), 711. Heslewood was one of those "unkempt Ciceros" (Spokesman-Review, Nov. 3, 1909) jailed for street-speaking; he noted that President William Howard Taft was permitted to speak on the street for two hours, although the ordinance was in effect at the time (710).

[10]There are numerous accounts of the Everett Massacre. Among the most reliable are David C. Botting, Jr., "Bloody Sunday," Pacific Northwest Quarterly, 49 (1958), 162-172; Norman H. Clark, "Everett, 1916, And After," Pacific Northwest Quarterly, 57 (1966), 57-64; Clark, Mill Town (Seattle, 1970); Harvey O'Connor, Revolution In Seattle: A Memoir (New York, 1964); Walker C. Smith, The Everett Massacre: A History of the Class Struggle in the Lumber Industry (Chicago, I.W.W. Publishing Bureau [1917]); Robert L. Tyler, Rebels of the Woods: The IWW in the Pacific Northwest (Eugene Ore., 1967). For first-hand accounts, see Philip S. Foner, Fellow Workers and Friends: I.W.W. Free-Speech Fights as Told by Participants (Westport, Conn., 1981).

[11]Smith, p. 91.

[12]Clark, "Everett, 1916, And After," 60.

[13]Clark, "Everett, 1916, And After," 61.

[14]O'Connor, p. 37.

[15]Everett Daily Herald, Sept. 29, 1916, p. 3.

[16]Everett Daily Herald, Oct. 10, 1916, p. 3.

[17]Everett Daily Herald, Oct. 7, 1916, p. 4.

[18]O'Connor, p. 47.

[19]Clark, Mill Town, pp. 154, 192; "Everett, 1916, And After," 62.

[20]Smith, p. 166.

[21]Clark, Mill Town, pp. 192-193.

[22]Cf. Melvyn Dubofsky, "The Origins of Western Working Class Radicalism, 1890-1905," Labor History, 7, no. 2 (Spring 1966), 138.

[23]Clark, Mill Town, pp. 41-42, 235-236.

[24]Clark, Mill Town, p. 195.

[25]Smith, p. 286.

[26]Smith, p. 278.

[27]Smith, p. 143.

[28]Smith, p. 278.

[29]See Irvin G. Wyllie, The Self-Made Man in America: The Myth of Rags to Riches (New Brunswick, N.J., 1954); and John G. Cawelti, Apostles of the Self-Made Man (Chicago, 1965).

[30]Cawelti, p. 189.

[31]Russell H. Conwell, Acres of Diamonds (New York, 1915), p. 18. Conwell was an influential Protestant cleric. Born in Massachusetts, the son of a middle-class merchant, he was of the same generation as Henry Adams. Conwell served in the Civil War, met Lincoln, and rose to prominence as presi-

dent of Temple University. He was on the same lecture circuit as Ralph Waldo Emerson, and delivered "Acres of Diamonds" over 5,000 times in 50 years. His championing of the pursuit of wealth as a "Christian and godly duty" was tempered by the respectable ends that he believed riches should be used for: "A man is not really a true man until he owns his own home, and they that own their homes are made more honorable and honest and pure, and true and economical and careful, by owning the home" (pp. 19-20).

[32]Wyllie, pp. 56-57. The homogeneity of business groups is underscored by the lack of Catholic participation. Wyllie points out that "since there were relatively few Catholics in the American business elite, probably never more than 7 percent prior to 1900, the Church had no special interest in glorifying this group" (p. 57).

[33]O.H.L. Wernicke, "Sorry For The Boy," _American Industries_, 12 (Oct. 1911), 10.

[34]Wernike, 10.

[35]Wernike, 10.

[36]Ruth Miller Elson, _Guardians of Tradition: American Schoolbooks in the 19th Century_ (Lincoln, Neb., 1964), p. 279.

[37]Conwell, p. 21.

[38]Conwell, p. 19.

[39]Conwell, pp. 21-22.

[40]Clarence E. Bonnett, _Employers' Associations in the United States: A Study of Typical Associations_ (New York, 1922), p. 84.

[41]Testimony of William S. Wollner, in U.S. Senate, _Industrial Relations: Final Report and Testimony. . . ._, 6:5101, 5106. (See bibliography for complete citation. Hereafter referred to as CIR _Final Report._)

[42]Elbert Hubbard, _A Message to Garcia_ (East Aurora, N.Y., 1899), pp. 6-7.

[43]Wyllie, pp. 86-87; Cawelti, pp. 172-174. Also cf. Richard Hofstadter, _Social Darwinism in American Thought_ (Boston, 1955), pp. 143-169.

[44]Hubbard, pp. 7-8.

[45]U.S. House, Hearings on the Lawrence Strike, Document 671, 62nd Cong., 2nd Sess., 138:6320, (GPO, 1912), 262-263.

[46]Hearings on the Lawrence Strike, 263.

[47]Donald B. Cole, Immigrant City: Lawrence, Massachusetts, 1845-1921 (Chapel Hill, 1963), p. 178.

[48]Cole, p. 203.

[49]Melvyn Dubofsky, Industrialism and the American Worker, 1865-1920 (Arlington Heights, Ill., 1975), pp. 10, 18.

[50]Hearings on the Lawrence Strike, 416.

[51]Hearings on the Lawrence Strike, 417.

[52]Hearings on the Lawrence Strike, 416.

[53]Hearings on the Lawrence Strike, 417.

[54]"Socialism in the Colleges," American Industries, 13 (July 1913), 11. Reprinted from The Century Magazine (July 1913).

[55]National Tribune, Aug. 2, 1888. Quoted in Wallace Evan Davies, Patriots on Parade: The Story of Veteran's and Hereditary Organizations in America, 1783-1900 (Cambridge, Mass., 1955), p. 294.

[56]Davies, p. 49.

[57]Davies, p. 294.

[58]Hezekiah N. Duff, "The I.W.W.'s; What They Are and What They Are Trying to Do," The Square Deal, 10 (May 1912), 304. Duff's ideas were echoed by eminent citizens. Cf. President Woodrow Wilson's 3rd annual message to Congress (Dec. 7, 1915): "The gravest threats against our national peace and safety have been uttered within our own borders. There are citizens of the United States, I blush to admit, born under other flags but welcomed by our generous naturalization laws to the full freedom and opportunity of America, who have poured the poison of disloyalty into the very arteries of our national life." Quoted in Michael R. Johnson, "The IWW and Wilsonian Democracy," Science and Society, 28 (Summer 1964), 266. Two months later, in a confidential memo to Wilson, Attorney General Gregory reported on a probe of the

IWW: "The investigation has shown that the membership of the Industrial Workers of the World is made up for the greater part of agitators, men without homes, mostly foreigners, the discontented and unemployed who are not anxious to work, and men of a very low order of intelligence and morals." Attorney General Gregory to President Wilson: Feb. 17, 1916 (Personal and Confidential), "Investigation into the I.W.W. on the request of the governors of California, Washington, Oregon, and Utah," U.S. Dept. of Justice, General Records, National Archives Record Group 60, File no. 150139.

[59]Duff, 305.

[60]Selig Perlman, "Preliminary report of an investigation of the relations between labor and capital in the textile industry of New England," in U.S. Dept of Labor, General Records, "Report of the United States Commission on Industrial Relations, 1912-1915," National Archives Record Group 174, Microfilm publication T4, HF1423, P4, p. 4. (Hereafter cited as CIR Unpub. Rpts.).

[61]Perlman, p. 6 [6'].

[62]Cole, p. 184.

[63]Perlman, pp. 5, 6 [6'].

[64]Cole, pp. 196-197.

[65]Lawrence Evening Tribune, March 11, 1912, p. 4.

[66]Paul F. Brissenden, The I.W.W.: A Study of American Syndicalism (New York, 1919), pp. 294-295. The IWW banner was a mistake that cost the support of strikers who feared to be thought unpatriotic and atheist. "NO GOD! NO MASTER!" was quoted in countless articles on the menace of the IWW. (The banner also read: "XX Century civilization. For the progress of the human race we have jails, gallows, guillotines . . . and electric chairs for the people who pay to keep the 'soldiers' to kill them when they revolt against Wood and other czars of Capitalism.").

[1]Ruth Miller Elson, Guardians of Tradition: American Schoolbooks in the 19th Century (Lincoln, Neb., 1964), p. 248

[2]Elson, pp. 248-249.

[3]Elson, p. 301.

[4]Elson, p. 251.

[5]Carleton Parker, "The IWW," Atlantic Monthly, 120 (1917), 657.

[6]John A. Fitch, The Causes of Industrial Unrest (New York, 1924), pp. 121-122.

[7]Leo Wolman, Growth of American Trade Unions, 1880-1923 (New York, 1924), p. 33.

[8]David Montgomery, "The 'New Unionism' and the Transformation of Workers' Consciousness in America, 1909-1922," Journ. of Soc. Hist., 7. no. 4 (Summer 1974), 509.

[9]Clarence E. Bonnett, Employers' Associations in the United States: A Study of Typical Associations (New York, 1922), p. 24.

[10]Quoted in Marguerite Green, The National Civic Federation and the American Labor Movement, 1900-1925 (Washington, D.C., 1956), p. 101 (n. 40).

[11]George G. Suggs, Jr., Colorado's War on Militant Unionism: James H. Peabody and the Western Federation of Miners (Detroit, 1972), pp. 66-67.

[12]Green, p. 105.

[13]Green, pp. 95, 124 (n. 99).

[14]Quoted in Graham Adams, Jr., Age of Industrial Violence, 1910-1915: The Activities and Findings of the United States Commission on Industrial Relations (New York, 1966), p. 36. Also compare any of Kirby's many pronouncements in American Industries, the NAM's principal publication; e.g., his attack on the National Civic Federation, "A Disloyal and Unpatriotic Organization," Am. Ind., 12 (Aug. 1911), 10.

Kirby wound up an embittered and bankrupt conservative associated with Gerald L.K. Smith, Eugene Talmadge, and the American Liberty League during the Roosevelt years. See George Wolfskill, Revolt of the Conservatives: A History of the American Liberty League, 1934-1940 (Boston, 1962), pp. 240-242.

[15]George Pope, "A Message From Colonel Pope," Am. Ind. 13, no. 11 (June 1913), 7.

[16]James Weinstein, The Corporate Ideal in the Liberal State: 1900-1918 (Boston, 1968), pp. 18-20.

[17]Weinstein, p. 16. The NAM preferred to accentuate the positive: "The National Association [of Manufacturers] is for the most part composed of average manufacturers. Though many of the great combinations are represented here, they are rather as survivors of memberships taken by their constituent concerns in the past. The great combinations have taken no very active part and no very deep interest in our Association. The life of it, the vitality of it, depends on the average man." (Quoted in Bonnett, p. 291.).

[18]Kirby, "A Disloyal and Unpatriotic Organization," 10.

[19]Adams, p. 2; Bonnett, p. 291.

[20]Robert F. Hoxie, Trade Unionism in the United States (New York, 1931 [1919]), pp.

[21]Quoted in National Civil Liberties Bureau, The Truth About the I.W.W. (New York, April, 1918), pp. 24- 25. This publication is included in the State Historical Society of Wisconsin Collection of Materials on and about the Industrial Workers of the World Microfilm P34898, IV, no. 18. (Hereafter cited as SHSW Collection.) This interview is from a series of articles Bruere did for the New York Evening Post entitled "Following the I.W.W. Trail" in the Post's Sunday Supplements from Nov. 1917 until March 1918. They also appear in SHSW Collection, Misc. pub. end of reel.

[22]The Truth About the I.W.W., 24-25.

[23]M. O'Sullivan, "Is There Opposition on the Part of Large Industrial Corporations to Labor Unions? If So, What Are the Reasons Therefor?" (Submitted Dec. 12, 1914), CIR Unpub. Rpts., HF1458 08, pp. 11-13.

[24]"Socialism in the Colleges," 11. Anti-socialist bias was inculcated by 19th century education. Elson (p. 287) points

out that among schoolbooks of the 1880's, "socialism or communism is mentioned only once by name, in a paragraph headed 'Communism' in which the railroad strikes of the 1870's are blamed on the 'Communists.' Socialism, like labor organization, is identified only with unscrupulous agitation and violence. After the Haymarket affair in 1886, anarchism, still undefined, is sensationally portrayed in action. Even practice sentences in the Spellers introduce the child to the violence of anarchism: 'Some bombs and other missiles were found by the police in the anarchists' magazines.' The Haymarket affair itself is described as 'an awful scene of murder' in which foreign agitators created tragedy and senseless destruction. The child could have no idea from his schoolbooks of nonviolent forms of socialism and anarchism. The Populist party is mentioned rarely, and only in a few books written by professional American historians. Such political doctrines are without question alien to political concepts approved in schoolbooks."

[25]A. Parker Nevin, "Some Problems of American Industry," American Industries, 14 (March, 1914), 13.

[26]The history of the Commission is the subject of Graham Adams' Age of Industrial Violence (see n. 14). For an additional analysis of the political significance of the Commission's work, see James Weinstein's The Corporate Ideal in the Liberal State, pp. 172-213.

[27]CIR Final Report, 1:19-20. Hearings were held in Washington, New York, Paterson, Philadelphia, Boston, Chicago, Lead (S. Dak.), Butte, Seattle, Portland, San Francisco, Los Angeles, Denver, and Dallas.

[28]CIR Final Report, 5:4643-4647.

[29]Banfield's contempt for the Commission's efforts was typical; when the Commission issued its report in 1915, many newspapers around the country ridiculed it. The Rutland [Vt.] Herald asked, "Was there ever a clearer case of wasting time and money on worthless investigation of subjects of which men like Walsh and his associates know nothing, or being informed, are deliberately partisan? The Walsh report transcends the wildest dreams of the socialists, anti-militarists, single-taxers and direct-action anarchists who call themselves labor unionists. Waste basket fillers!" The Wheeling [W.Va.] Intelligencer, under a headline of "Demagogy Run Riot," concluded "Neither Walsh nor his Commission recommendations can be taken seriously by Congress, or by the patriotic, order loving, law abiding American citizenship." Other headlines bespoke similar sentiments: "The

Board of Industrial Anarchy" (Boston Transcript); "When Rhetoric Blinds Reason" (New York World); "The Industrial Commission Fiasco" (Chicago Daily News); "Mr. Walsh Investigates His Own Mind" (Brooklyn Standard-Union); "Failure of a Fool Commission" (Oakland [Cal.] Tribune). These extracts were reprinted in "Industrial Relations Commission Reports," American Industries, 16 (Sept. 1915), 12.

[30]Walker C. Smith, The Everett Massacre, A History of the Class Struggle in the Lumber Industry (Chicago, I.W.W. Publishing Bureau, [1917]), p. 102.

[31]Robert W. Bruere, "Following the I.W.W. Trail," New York Evening Post, February 23, 1918, p. 4. (Also in SHSW Collection, see n. 21).

[32]Bruere, February 16, 1918, p. 16; Philip S. Foner, History of the Labor Movement in the United States, (New York, 1965), IV, 192.

[33]Bruere, February 16, 1918, p. 16.

[1]Lines 101-102, Preface 1855 to the first edition of
Leaves of Grass.

[2]Walt Whitman, "I Hear America Singing," Leaves of Grass
(New York, 1914), p. 17.

[3]Walt Whitman, "The Tramp and Strike Questions," in
Complete Prose Works (Boston, 1907), p. 325.

[4]Robert A. Hunter, Poverty (New York, 1917 [1904]), p. 60;
Harold U. Faulkner, The Quest for Social Justice, 1898-1914
(New York, 1931), pp. 21-26. Cf. Jacob A. Riis, A Ten
Year's War (Boston, 1900); The Battle with the Slums (New
York, 1902); How the Other Half Lives (New York, 1957
[1890]).

[5]Leslie H. Marcy, "800 Per Cent and the Akron Strike,"
The International Socialist Review, 13, no. 10 (April 1913),
717-718.

[6]In 1900, farmworkers totaled 11,050,000; non-farm workers
15,906,000. By 1916, while the number of farm workers
remained stable at 10,802,000, non-farm employees numbered
27,212,000. U.S. Bureau of the Census, Historical Statistics of the United States, Colonial Times to 1970, Bicentennial Edition, Part 1 (Washington, D.C., 1975), Series D:
1-10, p. 126.

[7]This figure is for manufacturing industries, 1890-1914,
and is an average derived from Albert Rees, Real Wages in
Manufacturing, 1890-1914 (Princeton, 1961), Table 10,
Column 3, "Average Days in Operation per Year [1890-1914],"
p. 33. Since 312 days were apparently regarded as a full-
time work year during this period (365 days less 52 Sundays
and one holiday), 288 days is the equivalent of eleven 26-
day months (ibid., p. 34).

[8]John A. Fitch, The Causes of Industrial Unrest (New York,
1924), pp. 54-55.

[9]Hist. Stat., Series G 554-563, pp. 309, 321.

[10]U.S. Senate, Industrial Relations: Final Report and
Testimony. . . ., 1:22-23. (See Bibliography for complete
citation. Hereafter referred to as CIR Final Report.)

[11]Fitch, pp. 41-42.

[12]Hunter, pp. 54-55.

[13]Fitch, p. 43.

[14]Carleton H. Parker, "The I.W.W.," Atlantic Monthly, 120 (Nov. 1917), 660.

[15]Frank Hatch Streightoff, The Standard of Living Among the Industrial People of America (Boston, 1911), p. 67; Scott Nearing, Income (New York, 1915), p. 106.

[16]Hist. Stat., pp. 148-149.

[17]Hist. Stat., p. 148.

[18]Lebergott, Table A-5.

[19]Hist. Stat., p. 151; Rees, p. 31; Lebergott, p. 484, n. 2.

[20]Fitch, p. 44.

[21]CIR Final Report, 1:23; Parker, 660.

[22]W.F. Ogburn, quoted in Fitch, p. 59.

[23]4,478,000 manual laborers; 1,851,000 service and domestic workers; 5,370,000 farm laborers; and about 1,000,000 miners. Hist. Stat., Ser. D 182-232.

[24]Carleton H. Parker, "The Economic Basis of the I.W.W.," in Wisconsin State Historical Society, Collection of Materials on and about the Industrial Workers of the World, Microfilm P 34898, sec. 1, no. 34 ("More Truth About the I.W.W."), p. 10.

[25]Paul Brissenden, "Underemployment," Business Cycles and Unemployment (New York, 1923), p. 68. For employees on non-agricultural payrolls, see Hist. Stat., Ser. D 127-141.

[26]W.M. Leiserson, "The Labor Market and Unemployment," CIR Unpub. Rpts., HF 1452 L5, p. 6.

[27]Leiserson, p. 12.

[28]Cloice R. Howd, "Industrial Relations in the West Coast Lumber Industry," Bulletin of the U.S. Dept. of Labor Statistics No. 349, Misc. Series (Wash., D.C., 1923), p. 47.

[29]Howd, pp. 48-49.

[30]Howd, pp. 51-53.

[31]Howd, p. 50.

[32]Howd, p. 53.

[33]Howd, p. 53.

[34]Daniel O'Regan, "Free Speech Fights of the I.W.W.'s," CIR Unpub. Rpts., HF 1424, 06, p. 2.

[35]O'Regan, p. 6.

[36]O'Regan, p. 16.

[37]O'Regan, pp. 16-17. O'Regan relates an incident in the Fresno affair that illustrates the exasperation of the authorities, the determination of the Wobblies, and the heavy-handed humor that occasionally made its appearance. "There were as many as two hundred in jail at one time and these two hundred made it as unpleasant for the jailors as possible. One fellow, named Lefferts, had a pair of heavy boots and he'd spend the whole night pounding on the bars with these boots, making it impossible for any one in the vicinity of the jail to sleep. He was put in a cell by himself (the others were confined in a long detention room, called the bull-pen) but he kept up the racket. Ed. Jones, the jailor, warned him to be quiet or some extreme measures would have to be taken with him. Lefferts told him to go ahead, so Jones tied him hand and foot, then took off one of Leffert's socks and put it in his mouth as a gag. The severity of this punishment can be understood by one who is familiar with the rank and file of I.W.W.'s and knows how rarely they bathe. In a short time the gag was removed and Lefferts [was] asked if he'd behave. He said he would and gave no trouble afterwards." (pp. 15-16)

[38]CIR Final Report, 5:4324.

[39]CIR Final Report, 5:4254.

[40]John R. Commons, et al, History of Labour in the United States (New York, 1926), I, 4. Cf. Frederick Jackson Turner: "The most important effect of the frontier has been in the promotion of democracy here and in Europe. . . . The frontier is productive of individualism. . . [and] frontier individualism has from the beginning promoted democracy." The Frontier In American History, (New York, 1920), p. 30.

[41]CIR _Final Report_, 5:4121.

[42]Ole Hanson, _Americanism Versus Bolshevism_ (New York, 1920), pp. 247, 253.

[43]Hanson, p. 253.

[44]Cf. C.B. MacPherson, _The Political Theory of Possessive Individualism: Hobbes to Locke_ (London, 1962), pp. 222-223: "[John] Locke's proposals for the treatment of the able-bodied unemployed are fairly well-known, although when they are mentioned by modern writers it is usually to deprecate their severity and excuse it by reference to the standards of the time. What is more to the point is the view they afford of Locke's assumptions. Masters of workhouses ('houses of correction') were to be encouraged to make them into sweated-labour manufacturing establishments, justices of the peace were to be encouraged to make them into forced-labour establishments. The children of the unemployed 'above the age of three' were unnecessarily a burden on the nation; they should be set to work, and could be made to earn more than their keep. All this was justified on the explicit ground that unemployment was due not to economic causes but to moral depravity. The multiplying of the unemployed, Locke wrote in 1697 in his capacity as a member of the Commission on Trade, was caused by 'nothing else but the relaxation of discipline and corruption of manners.' There was no question in Locke's mind of treating the unemployed as full or free members of the political community; there was equally no doubt that they were fully subject to the state. And the state was entitled to deal with them in this way because they would not live up to the moral standard required of rational men."

[45]See Lynn H. Lees, "The Study of Cities and the Study of Social Processes: Two Directions in Recent Urban History," _Journal of Social History_, 7, no. 3 (Spring 1974), 334. Lees concludes that the casual laborers of London were "given pariah status by the middle class, which saw them not as badly-housed, badly-paid human beings but as demoralized semi-criminals. In continued analyses of the poorest of the poor, moral condemnations of their life style or a Social Darwinist explanation of their unfitness was substituted for attention to the economic circumstances that produced the problem. Although the palliatives offered changed from slum clearance and "remoralization" of the shiftless to more slum clearance and detention colonies for those whose weaknesses menaced national efficiency, the casual poor continued to be excluded from the body politic. They were to be eliminated by non-economic means without substantial alteration of the

labor market that produced them." Also see Gareth Stedman Jones, <u>Outcast London: A Study in the Relationship Between Classes in Victorian Society</u> (Oxford, 1971).

[46]E.g., "In the heady days of the New Imperialism [1898+], lawmakers were increasingly in favor of an American Devil's Island for such undesirables. Senator Hoar of Massachusetts proposed to his colleagues that they send all the anarchists to an 'island Paradise.' Senator Vest of Missouri offered a resolution to the Judiciary Committee asking it to determine the expediency and necessity of amending the Constitution in order to establish a penal colony for anarchists 'on some suitable island.'" Richard Drinnon, <u>Rebel in Paradise: A Biography of Emma Goldman</u> (Chicago, 1961), p. 90.

[47]CIR <u>Final Report</u>, 1:368-369.

[48]CIR Unpub. Rpts., HF 1452.

[49]Peter A. Speek, "Psychological Aspects of the Problem of Floating Laborers (An Analysis of Life Stories), June 25, 1915," CIR Unpub. Rpts., HF 145, S7, p. 14.

[50]Speek, "Report on Conditions in Labor Camps, June 4, 1915," CIR Unpub. Rpts., HF 145, S7, p. 4.

[51]"Salvaging the Unemployable," <u>The New Republic</u>, 4 (Oct. 2, 1915), 221.

[52]"Salvaging the Unemployable," 221.

[53]"Salvaging the Unemployable," 221-222.

[54]"Salvaging the Unemployable," 222. To be sure, some in the IWW were also concerned that the IWW attracted too many down-and-out types: "It is up to every local union of the Industrial Workers of the World to see that the real 'slum' element, the degenerates, the drunks, and those men who are so far gone that they have lost all manhood, are kept away from the halls and meeting places of the I.W.W. The element which makes up the drunks, and those who are too lazy to keep clean are simply a drawback to the human race and a detriment to any union or association." "The Unemployed and the IWW," <u>Industrial Worker</u>, June 24, 1909. Quoted in Aileen S. Kraditor, <u>The Radical Persuasion, 1890-1917: Aspects of the Intellectual History and the Historiography of Three American Radical Organizations</u> (Baton Rouge, 1981), pp. 118-119.

[55]"Salvaging the Unemployable," 222.

[56]Quoted in Daniel Bell, The End of Ideology (New York, 1965), pp. 232-233.

[57]Cf. CIR Final Report, 1:127 ff. This critique of scientific management was based on Robert F. Hoxie's research; see his Trade Unionism in the United States (New York, 1931 [1919]), pp. 298 ff. For a comprehensive view, see Samuel Haber, Efficiency And Uplift: Scientific Management in the Progressive Era, 1890-1920 (Chicago, 1964), passim. Ironically, the IWW, cautiously looking for ways to survive in its last days following the debacle of the 1918-19 persecutions, dabbled in scientific management, establishing a Bureau of Industrial Research to conduct industrial surveys, studying production and management techniques, and briefly featuring the Technocratic ideas of Howard Scott. (Haber, pp. 154-155.)

[58]Cf. Fitch, pp. 140-156.

NOTES TO CHAPTER 7

[1]Peter A. Speek, "Psychological Aspects of the Problem of Floating Laborers (An Analysis of Life Stories), June 25, 1915," CIR Unpub. Rpts., HF 145, S7, p. 6.

[2]Speek, "Psychological Aspects . . .," p. 38.

[3]Speek, "Psychological Aspects . . .," pp. 5-6.

[4]CIR Final Report, 5:4933. A larger study of 222 typical migratory workers yielded similar results. See Carleton H. Parker, The California Casual (New York, 1920), pp. 69-74.

[5]CIR Final Report, 5:4763.

[6]CIR Final Report, 5:4251.

[7]Speek, op. cit., pp. 89-90. The State employment service, part of the "Wisconsin Plan," was a fledgling attempt to correct abuses of private employment agents.

[8]James Foy, "A Migratory Workers Diary," Industrial Pioneer (Feb. 1924), 29. From Wayne State University Archives of Labor History and Urban Affairs, The Industrial Workers of the World Collection, Box 148, folder 8. (The Industrial Pioneer was a late IWW paper, formerly the One Big Union Monthly.)

[9]Parker, The Casual Laborer, p. 121. Parker commented on the migratories in California: "As to the numbers on the road constantly throughout the State, or the numbers who resort to this migratory life between periods of work, it is impossible to reach an approximation. Only can it be said that there is a great shifting army of them, tramping, riding, back and forth, every train bears them. I have counted from forty to sixty on single freights. Every railroad town has its 'jungles,' frequented by an ever-flowing stream of itinerants." Carleton Parker, "Preliminary Report on tentative findings and conclusions on the investigations of seasonal, migratory, and unskilled labor in California, 1914," CIR Unpub. Rpts., HF 145, P2, p. 20.

[10]Peter A. Speek, "Report on Transportation of Laborers, July 15, 1915," CIR Unpub. Rpts., HF 145, S7, p. 21. An additional question in this survey soliciting suggestions from the railroads brought the response that no problem existed: "The prevailing opinions in the answers were that the annual migration of floating labor is not necessary and the method of travel is not necessary. Those who travel are usually tramps and will not work if offered the opportunity. . . . The opinion is that the hoboes could be eliminated; that, if they were arrested whenever possible and put to work they would soon disappear; that if they had to work they would better do it of their own volition" (p. 35).

[11]Parker, The Casual Laborer, p. 121,

[12]Speek, "Report on Transportation. . . ." pp. 5-6.

[13]Parker, "The I.W.W.," 661. The "jungle" accomodations were preferable to most of the poor housing available in the cities. "In one San Francisco lodging-house, out of two hundred and fifty beds, there were eight with outside ventilation. A New York study disclosed that the lodging-house inmates were eleven times more tubercular than the average population. The beds seldom have linen, and the covers are usually dirty quilts which have to be repeatedly fumigated

during the winter on account of vermin" (661). See also Peter A. Speek, "Report on cheap lodging houses in the cities," July 25, 1915, CIR Unpub. Rpts., HF 145 S7.

[14]Wm. M. Duffue, "Labor Market Conditions in the Harvest Fields of the Middle West," Dec. 1, 1914, CIR Unpub. Rpts., HF 145 D9, p. 7. At their worst, these conditions in the harvest fields were frightful, as evidenced by the Wheatland Hop Riot of August, 1913. The farmer had lured some 2800 people, men, women, and children, with promises of good wages and pleasant vacation surroundings. In reality conditions were unbearable: unspeakably bad and completely inadequate toilets, no water in 122° California heat, low wages held back on a phony bonus system. An arrogant rejection of the workers' grievances and the hotheadedness of a motley collection of armed "deputies" led to a spontaneous eruption that left several dead, and put two innocent Wobblies in prison. At root, this tragedy rested on the contemptuous attitude of the community towards migratory workers -- "these damn hoboes." Considerable literature exists on the Wheatland affair: cf. Woodrow C. Whitten, "The Wheatland Episode," Pacific Hist. Rev., 17 (Feb. 1948), 37-42; Carleton Parker, The Casual Laborer, contains his official Report on the incident, pp. 171-199; for a dramatic account, see James P. Thompson's testimony in the 1918 I.W.W. trial, WSU IWW Collection, Box 109, folder 2, pp. 5069-5084.

[15]Duffue, pp. 39-43.

[16]CIR Final Report, 2:1359.

[17]CIR Final Report, 5:4378.

[18]CIR Final Report, 2:1361.

[19]CIR Final Report, 3:2586.

[20]WSU I.W.W. Collection, Box 111, folder 6, pp. 6907-6908.

[21]CIR Final Report, 6:5123.

[22]CIR Final Report, 5:4219.

[23]CIR Final Report, 1:110.

[24]Wm. M. Leiserson, "The Labor Market and Unemployment," CIR Unpub. Rpts., HF 1452 L5, pp. 38-40. Also see CIR Final Report, 1:110-111.

[25]Report of the President's Mediation Commission to the

President of the United States (Washington, D.C., 1918), pp. 13-14. (The "womanless, voteless, jobless" quote is from Carleton Parker).

[26]Robert W. Bruere, "Notes on the I.W.W. in Arizona and the Northwest," Journ. of the Nat. Institute of Social Sciences, 4 (April 1918), 100.

[27]Mediation Commission, Report, p. 14.

[28]CIR Final Report, 5:4385.

[29]CIR Final Report, 5:4385.

[30]CIR Final Report, 5:4386.

[31]CIR Final Report, 5:4253, 4383.

[32]CIR Final Report, 5:4383.

[33]CIR Final Report, 5:4553.

[34]CIR Final Report, 5:4324.

[35]CIR Final Report, 5:4325

[36]CIR Final Report, 5:4389-4390.

[37]CIR Final Report, 5:4382.

[38]Edward Townsend Booth, "The Wild West," Atlantic Monthly, 126 (Dec. 1920), 786.

[39]Proceedings, 1st Convention of the Industrial Workers of the World (Chicago, 1905), p. 1.

[40]CIR Final Report, 11:10588-10589.

[41]For the flavor of life with the Wobblies, see the collection of materials in Joyce Kornbluh, Rebel Voices: An I.W.W. Anthology (Ann Arbor, 1964), pp. 65-93 and passim.

[42]James Jones, From Here to Eternity (New York, 1952), p. 640.

[1]Donald M. Barnes, "The Ideology of the I.W.W.: 1905-1921," Diss., Univ. of Washington 1962, p. 168.

[2]Eldridge Foster Dowell, "A History of Criminal Syndicalism Legislation in the United States," Johns Hopkins University Studies in Historical and Political Science, 57 (1939), 76-77.

[3]The term "ideology" has not been used because the beliefs under discussion were not held as part of a consciously developed intellectual system of concepts. As Samuel Barnes points out, "most people acquire the belief systems of those around them," which, while they often have ideological content, are of a more instrumental nature. See Samuel Barnes, "Political Ideology and Political Behavior," in Ideology, Politics, and Political Theory, ed., Richard H. Cox (Belmont, Cal., 1969), pp. 350-361. Erik Erikson has expressed the connection of ideology with personality formation in a way that avoids these difficulties. He defines ideology as "an unconscious tendency underlying religious and scientific as well as political thought: the tendency at a given time to make facts amenable to ideas, and ideas to facts, in order to create a world image convincing enough to support the collective and the individual sense of identity." Erik H. Erikson, Young Man Luther: A Study in Psychoanalysis and History (New York, 1958), p. 22. Freud reasoned that "it is not to be supposed that men were inspired to create their first system of the universe by pure speculative curiosity. The practical need for controlling the world around them must have played its part." Freud, Totem and Taboo, tr. and ed. James Strachey (New York, 1950), p. 78.

[4]This mode of organizing personality was not unique to capitalist culture. Compare the Bolsheviks under Lenin, who took a businesslike attitude toward achieving their aim. See Fred Weinstein and Gerald M. Platt, The Wish To Be Free: Society, Psyche, and Value Change (Berkeley, 1969), p. 206ff.

[5]San Francisco Labor Council, San Diego Free Speech Controversy (San Francisco, April 25, 1912), p. 8.

[6]Arthur LeSueur, "Riot in Minot, North Dakota, July, 1913," CIR Unpub. Rpts., HF 1424, S6, p. 1. Philip S. Foner, History of the Labor Movement in the United States (New York,

1965), Vol. 4, p. 212. Also see Appendix II of the present work.

[7]Harris Weinstock, <u>Report to the Governor of California on the Disturbances in the City and County of San Diego</u> (Sacramento, 1912), pp. 17-19.

[8]<u>New York Evening Post</u>, November 17, 1917, p. 4.

[9]Ralph Chaplin, <u>Wobbly! The Rough-and-Tumble Story of an American Radical</u> (Chicago, 1948), pp. 156-157. The opposition the IWW encountered was formidable and sometimes cynical. Robert Bruere, in his series for the New York <u>Post</u>, reported that: "At the conference between the Western lumber men and the President's Mediation Commission in Seattle, it was the practically unanimous opinion of experienced men that the I.W.W. had forced upon the serious attention of the lumber-industry evils which had long needed correction. The operators frankly admitted that their opposition to the I.W.W. was simply an expression of their general opposition to all attempts of organized labor to interfere with their exclusive management of their business, and that the peculiar reputation for violence and lawlessness which had been fixed upon the I.W.W. was largely the work of their own ingenious publicity agents. Their most effective publicity man told me that they had been able to find no evidence of destructive sabotage -- of driving spikes into the logs to damage the saws, or of putting emery into the machines. Such examples as they have discovered they attribute to the malice of disgruntled individuals rather than to the organized propaganda of the I.W.W." Robert W. Bruere, "Following the I.W.W. Trail," <u>New York Evening Post</u>, Saturday, February 16, 1918, p. 1.

[10]Quoted in Paul F. Brissenden, <u>The I.W.W.: A Study of American Syndicalism</u> (New York, 1957), p. 324. Compare "Why the I.W.W. Is Dangerous," San Francisco <u>Labor Clarion</u>, April 5, 1912, p. 8; "Menace of the I.W.W.," <u>Houston Labor Journal</u>, Nov. 2, 1912, p. 1; Samuel Gompers, "Destruction The Avowed Purpose of the I.W.W.," <u>Amer. Federationist</u>, 20, no. 7 (July 1913), 533-537; Samuel P. Orth, <u>A Chronicle of the Organized Wage-Earners</u> (New Haven, 1919), pp. 212-219.

[11]Dowell, 37.

[12]Dowell, 41-42, 75-76.

[13]In the Pacific Northwest, Wobblies who escaped prosecution during the war could join a government-organized labor union in the timber industry. Ironically, this union, the

"Loyal Legion of Loggers and Lumbermen," legislated over-
night all the reforms the IWW had long agitated for --
including an eight-hour day. See Robert L. Tyler, "Four
L's," MVHR, 47 (1960), 434-451; Harold M. Hyman, Soldiers
And Spruce (Los Angeles, 1963).

[14]Cf. Samuel Walker, A Critical History of Police Reform
(Lexington Mass., 1977), p. 29; Bruce C. Johnson, "Taking
Care of Labor: The Police in American Politics," Theory and
Society, 3, no. 1 (Spring 1976), 98. For contemporary views
on industrial espionage, see Sidney Howard's The Labor Spy
(New York, 1924); Edwin E. Witte, The Government In Labor
Disputes (New York, 1932), pp. 183-190; Robert Hunter, Vio-
lence and the Labor Movement (New York, 1922 [1914]), pp.
283-291; John A. Fitch, The Causes of Industrial Unrest (New
York, 1924), pp. 171-185.

[15]The paranoia over labor violence and unionism was exploited by detective agencies during this period and on into
the New Deal years. Such agencies provided spies who would
often act as agents provocateurs, and then provide strikebreakers and armed guards, thus practically guaranteeing
violence. Advertisements like the following were placed in
newspapers and trade papers around the country and illustrate the open expression of bias against unions common to
these years. "!!ATTENTION!! Gentlemen: We wish to call your
attention to the present labor situation in the coal mining
industry. Should a strike take place we are in a position
to furnish you with guards, or special policemen for the
preservation of life and property. We can further furnish
all classes of non-union help to take the places of men on
strike. Should you wish to be relieved of the responsibility we can take entire charge of the situation, establish a
regular military system, and feed and lodge all help. We
wish to call your attention to the fact that we are posi-
tively the LARGEST STRIKE-BREAKING BUREAU IN THE WORLD.
Among the hundreds of strikes we have successfully broken we
might mention the following: Pressed Steel Car strike at
McKees Rocks, Pittsburgh; Philadelphia trolley strikes;
Lehigh Valley RR. Co.; Delaware and Hudson Co.; Central RR
of New Jersey; New York, Ontario & Western; Vermont Central
RR; Baltimore and Ohio RR; Baldwin Locomotive Works, and the
Erie RR. Our offices can be reached night and day by telephone and should you desire any further information we would
be glad to send a representative. BERGHOFF BROS. STRIKE
SERVICE AND LABOR ADJUSTERS 140 LIBERTY ST NEW YORK." This
ad was placed in the San Diego Sun during the height of the
I.W.W. disturbances there (April 8, 1912). For a thorough
treatment of this subject, see Rhodri Jeffreys-Jones, Violence and Reform in American History (New York, 1978), Chs.

1 and 2. For a historical overview of strikebreaking and violence, see H.M. Gitelman, "Perspectives on American Industrial Violence," Bus. Hist. Rev., 47, no. 1 (Spring 1973), 1-23.

[16]Alfred D. Chandler, Jr., "The Beginnings of 'Big Business' in American Industry," Bus. Hist. Rev., 33, no. 1 (Spring 1959), 30.

[17]Harold U. Faulkner, The Quest for Social Justice, 1898-1914 (New York, 1931), pp. 28, 32.

[18]U.S. Bureau of the Census, Historical Statistics of the United States, Colonial Times to 1970, Bicentennial Edition, Part 1 (Washington, D.C., 1975), Series D 127-141.

[19]Faulkner, p. 29.

[20]Ralph Chaplin, "Why I Wrote 'Solidarity Forever,'" American West, 5, no. 1, (Jan. 1968), 27.

[21]Solidarity, Aug. 23, 1913, p. 2; "The Industrial Workers of the World Make Confession," The Square Deal, 13 (Oct. 1913), 236-237. Cf. Melvyn Dubofsky, We Shall Be All (Chicago, 1969), p. 288. For a contemporary view of the Wobblies as sensationalists, see "Organization or Anarchy," The New Republic, 11 (July 21, 1917), 320-322.

[22]Barnes, "The Ideology of the I.W.W.," p. 5. On shared values, see Robert L. Tyler, Rebels of the Woods: the I.W.W. in the Pacific Northwest (Eugene, Ore., 1967), p.3, passim; Joseph R. Conlin, "The Case of the Very American Militants," American West, 7, no. 2 (March 1970), 4-10, 62-63.

[23]Chaplin, "Why I Wrote 'Solidarity Forever,'" 27.

[24]Cf. Vernon H. Jenson, Heritage of Conflict (Ithaca, N.Y., 1950); Rodman W. Paul, Mining Frontiers of the Far West, 1848-1880 (New York, 1963).

[25]Melvyn Dubofsky has suggested that the industrial incursion into the West, largely completed by 1893, had a greater impact because it occurred so rapidly. But he points out that the disturbance in social and authority relations in the West had also occurred in the East and in the earlier industrialization of England. The historical ties which the Western worker had had with the middle class -- "local merchants, professionals, farmers, and party politicans" -- were being sapped by corporations. Melvyn Dubofsky, "The Origins of Western Working Class Radicalism, 1890-1905,"

<u>Labor History</u>, 7, no. 2 (Spring 1966), 139, 154. An instructive comparison can be drawn between the United States and Germany, the two most dynamic pre-war industrial societies: cf. George L. Mosse, <u>The Crisis of German Ideology: Intellectual Origins of the Third Reich</u> (New York, 1964).

[26]<u>Solidarity</u>, Nov. 21, 1914, p. 3; attributed to F.S. Hamilton.

[27]Chaplin, <u>Wobbly</u>, p. 91. Chaplin wrote years later, "Even at this late hour I am more grimly convinced than ever that neither the song ['Solidarity Forever'] itself nor the organization that sparked it could have emerged from any environment other than the Pacific Northwest in the afterglow of the rugged period of American pioneering." Chaplin, "Why I Wrote 'Solidarity Forever,'" 24, For additional expressions of frontierism, see Dubofsky <u>We Shall Be All</u>, p. 25; Joseph R. Conlin, <u>Bread And Roses Too: Studies of the Wobblies</u> (Westport, Conn., 1969), p. 148.

APPENDIX I

MINUTES OF THE BUTTE COUNCIL OF DEFENSE

"Stenographic Report of Meeting of County Council
of Defense, Labor and Financial Interests," Butte,
Montana, February 13, 1919. Archives of Labor
History and Urban Affairs, Wayne State University,
The Industrial Workers of the World Collection.
Box 99, folder 24.

These are the partial surviving minutes of a meeting of
business, labor, religious, and community leaders with a
U.S. army adviser called to discuss declaring martial law in
the current labor disturbances involving the IWW. Meeting
participants included:

John Berkin, Businessman and Mine Superintendent
F.A. Bigelow, Member of the County Council of Defense;
    Editor of the "Free Lance," a conservative labor
    publication; Organizer for the Montana Federation
    of Labor
Eugene Carroll, Businessman (Water Company)
D.J. Charles, Banker; Ex-county Commissioner
Colonel Donahue, U.S. Army
Judge Dwyer, Judge of the District Court
Mr. Farrell, Secretary of the Teamsters Union
John Gillie, Mine Manager, Anaconda Copper Mining
    Company
Major Halloran, U.S. Army
Charles S. Henderson, President of the Rotary Club
Seph R. Jackson, County Attorney of Silver Bow County
J. Bruce Kremer, Mining Company Attorney
F.L. Melcher, Businessman; Manager of the Western Iron
    Works
Mr. Partelow, Secretary of the Montana Federation of
    Labor
Raymond Rhule, Businessman; Manager of McKee Printing
    Company
Roman Catholic Priest (unnamed)
J.R. Wharton, Manager of the Street Railway Company

Butte, Montana, February 13, 1919

MEETING OF COUNTY COUNCIL OF DEFENSE,
LABOR AND FINANCIAL INTERESTS.

EUGENE CARROLL, nominated and elected Chairman.

BY MR. CARROLL: Mr. Jackson has told you the business of
this meeting. The Major [Halloran, U.S. Army] has just
gotten into town and wants to get a line on the situation
here, as I understand it. In order that there can be no
question as to what you say or as to what takes place at
this meeting, there is a stenographer here who will take
down and transcribe the full proceedings, so that there can
be no question in the future as to what is said or done.

I think that in order to open the proposition I will
call on the oldest man here in time of residence, John
Gillie, Manager of Mines of the Anaconda Copper Mining
Company, the largest producing company in our district. I
will ask Mr. Gillie to give us a general talk on conditions
past and present.

BY MR. GILLIE: Mr. Chairman, Major Halloran and gentlemen:
During the past two years or four years, we will say approx-
imately two years, this district has been called upon to
produce every pound of copper and zinc that it possibly
could for war purposes. This district produces about one-
sixth of the copper of the world and a large proportion of
the zinc and it was very necessary that it make capacity
production in order to meet requirements for war purposes
for ourselves and our allies.

From the time we entered the war up to the time of the
armistice the government, through its different departments,
was very insistent on all copper producers to make maximum
production. Accordingly we were forced to employ practically every man that came into the district with the result --
I would state the district normally employs from eighteen to
twenty thousand men in and about the times [mines?] and
mining is the chief industry here.

On account of employing every one that came in we were
loaded up with an element here that at different times before has made onslaughts on this place and is known as the
"I.W.W.," and in connection with them the pro-German and
revolutionary element. We kept them at work in order to
produce. When the armistice came of course, the necessity
for copper ceased. It left [in] the hands of the producers
a very large stock of copper which was made at a very high
wage cost and a high cost for supplies. The same is true of
zinc.

264

We ran along normally during the month of November and produced our maximum production and in December we curtailed production to about 80%. In January we curtailed further to about 2/3 and ran along, paying the same war-time wages, until the 7th of this month.

The authorities at Washington, realizing the condition of the copper market and zinc as well and the inability of the companies to continue producing copper under these conditions and no sale, there was practically no sale of copper from the first of November up until early in February. There was no hope of receiving orders and it was inevitable that the producing companies must shut down or something down [done?] to relieve the condition of those producing copper, as it was costing them much more than they would ever realize and not able to sell it. No concern on earth can go ahead and produce indefinitely unless it sells its production and gets some money in return to meet costs of wages and supplies. The Labor Department in Washington in the latter part of January had put forth a plan asking the representatives of labor through the Rocky Mountain region, Arizona, Utah, and Montana, heavy copper producers to meet with some of the copper producers in Washington, which they did about ten days ago. The result was it was shown there that there was over one million pounds of copper in stock, exclusive of that held by the government of this country and other countries and in the market. The producers made the statement to the War Labor Board that they would sell copper in the neighborhood of eighteen cents per pound, provided they could make a reduction in wages.

I will say here that the mines here for the past eight or ten years have always worked under contract with its employees on a sliding scale for copper. That the sliding scale provided that when the price of copper was fifteen cents or under the nominal wage was to be $3.50 per day and that the wage advanced 25¢ per day for every advance of 2¢ per pound for copper. At the time that copper was selling at 26¢, wages, instead of being $3.50, the miner and mucker got $5.75. That wage prevailed for two or three years.

In addition to the amount the wage would be with copper at 18¢ the companies (all companies I mean, others as well as the Anaconda Companies) were paying fifty cents bonus, that is, the wage at 18¢ would be nominally $4.25 for the ordinary mucker and miner. That [w]as the minimum wage for the man that worked underground. But they agreed they would pay an additional sum of fifty cents as bonus.

After this meeting or conference was held in Washington and practically agreed to and consented to by the representatives of the laboring people and they had returned to Butte, the company cut the scale last week, on February 7th,

265

reducing the wages to $4.75, which is the minimum wages paid to men in the mine.

All of the companies here made it a point and published at all the Butte mines that the returned soldier would have the preference for employment at the Butte mines and then would come the hands [heads?] of families to the exclusion of the unmarried or those that did not have dependents. This has been carried out during December, January and part of February and was going to be pursued while there was any employment. It seemed to be an opportune moment for this disturbing element to take hold and they immediately got out and called a strike. No demands were made upon the company of any kind, but they struck against any reduction, notwithstanding this reduction was practically agreed upon by representatives -- the real representatives of labor.

The element that has brought about the conditions here now is that same element that started the trouble in 1917. This same element to prevent the production of copper organized a pro-German movement all through this country.

As to the immediate conditions here or what is going on, -- picketing etc., you are all familiar. These men are not permitted to work. No later than yesterday one of our pumpmen was assaulted. This district is peculiarly situated. There are a lot of trails to the mines, embracing about three square miles of territory or rather three miles square. There are a lot of trails running devious ways to those mines. It is almost impossible to go out and protect every one of these trails over which men go to work.

Here is the condition of picketing. It is not alone that they will stop these men and beat them up or something like that, which they do whenever they can. They will go further; if men have got a phone in his house, who is out at work, whether it be a pumpman, engineer or miner, they will call him upon the 'phone and say: "Tom has gone to work to-day." The wife answers "Yes". "Don't look for him back to-night. If he comes back to-night he won't be back to-morrow night. We are going to set that mine on fire."

We have a number of men who have been assaulted. We cannot get the assaulted parties to appear. We would not force them. They say their lives would not be worth anything if they appeared. If they have not got a telephone at their house, these women, these foreign women go out and make it their business to notify these people at their houses that "if your man goes out to work he will not come back," by saying the mine will be set on fire or something like that. The poor wife will say, "Don't go out. We will get along some way." You cannot blame them for staying home and cannot blame them for not appearing against a fellow for

266

assault. Cannot blame them for staying home.

BY CHAIRMAN CARROLL: There have been a great many meetings since Major Jones has been here. We have drawn from every angle the necessity of martial law or that the military take control of the situation and the answer we are met with is: Why don't the state and county authorities handle the situation. I think we hope to show to-day why the state and county authorities cannot and have not taken charge of the situation and why the necessity of the military doing it exists at this time.

What the citizens of Butte want is that we want to see men who desire to work allowed to work. It is not only the mining companies who have had men called off but all companies. The water company, who I represent, have had their machinists called out, which cuts off all repairs to trucks. They have pulled the men out of the ditches and taken the tools away from them and have done other depredations to other concerns which could be shown here.

I am going to call on the professional end of it. J. Bruce Kremer, one of our prominent attorneys here. He is familiar with the situation and has been in legal affairs of the mining companies for several years.

BY MR. KREMER: I think that Mr. Gillie has outlined our present conditions quite fully. However, I do not think it would be amiss to refer to one other feature in connection with this difficulty that has been fomenting here for a good many years. (The speaker refers to the blowing up of the old Miners Union Hall on June 13th, 1914.)

It does not matter whether there is a strike on or not, the fact remains that men are not allowed to work. Industry is paralyzed, business is stagnant and the community faces a crisis that must mean financial ruin. Far greater and beyond that hunger and privation stands knocking at the door of many householders in this community.

I am not here to suggest a panacea for these ills but I do believe that organized co-operation is necessary. I believe it is important that something be done to the end that we seek to establish as nearly normal business and industrial conditions in this community as is possible. If it is apparent to us that the only way it can be established is to have the civil authorities step aside and the military authorities step in, then certainly that is the course that should be pursued. If it should be determined by you, after your investigation, Major Halloran, that such is the condition here, I am satisfied that through the medium of the army officials anything that may confront it with reference to the method will be speedily faced.

267

D.J. CHARLES, BANKER, Ex-County Commissioner: As to the conditions of the mining companies I cannot speak, but from my own personal knowledge I believe that Mr. Gille [sic., Kremer?] and Mr. Gillie have covered the ground thoroughly.

I have been a resident of Butte for practically 37 years and I believe that Butte as an industrial center will have more or less disturbance from time to time.

I believe that since the troubles of 1914 there has come into this community an element that is not in favor of good government. I believe there is an element in Butte to-day that are not taxpayers nor heads of families but who are the disturbing element, who make their wage by keeping up disturbance and who have nothing to lose.

I believe that if the men are going to be beat up and families disturbed and their wives threatened in order to keep men from employment, I think it has come to a point where something radical should be done. If we have to meet fire with fire, possibly this is the time. It was said a few days ago,-- I happened to be at a meeting of a committee that met with Major Jones and that after he had looked over the situation (he had been here about 24 hours, possibly 48 hours), and at that meeting it was said that if the fire department would stay at their stations and pay attention to their duty and that if the police department would keep at their work, he believed he could cope with the situation. I do not know whether it has become worse or not. I have not been around the mines. I did see one man day before yester-day, who said he was employed on the "hill." He showed me his face where he had been beat up. Said he was a mechanic and that someone had stopped him from going to work on the "hill." He said that three men stepped up against him and asked him where he was going. He said he was going to work. "No you're not," and told him that he should not go. He stepped to one side and another fellow came up and struck him in the face and he showed me marks across his nose. He is a man about fifty years of age and an old-timer here.

If these conditions are existing and the sheriff and the city authorities are not able to cope with the situa-tion, perhaps this is the time to start martial law and allow people to be employed that want to work. I believe if these things continue there will be a great deal of suffer-ing here in Butte. I believe there are a great many fami-lies who have lived here a number of years, who own their own homes and whose credit is limited, that if this con-tinues a week or ten days are going to be short of food and their wives and children are going to suffer.

If this is the proper time let's go to it.
CHARLES S. HENDERSON, President of the Rotary Club: There

was a meeting of the Rotary Club to-day, which represents a very large number of men who are members of all the different business organizations of the city. The proposition was put up to them today as to what was best to be done. The statement was made that as far as the Bolshevists and Wobblies were concerned they have practically done their work up to this time, paralyzed industry and stopped work. What more can they do?

It seems to me we are in a position of standing up and saying that all we can do is wait and see. Taking the same position as we would if someone came into our house and run it and we stood by and permitted them to do it. I believe something should be done to relieve the situation. The fact that these people have gained their point, are we going to stand up and see them get away with it? The Rotary Club composed of men of different lines of business went on record today and passed a resolution asking that martial law be started in this community as soon as it can be done.

BY MR. CARROLL: I call on Judge Dwyer, who is judge of the District Court, and who has had charge of the criminal department for the past two or three years.

BY MR. DWYER: My experience with the Criminal Department, of course, would simply be a presentation of the extreme results of the troubles that we have had here.

Muckie McDonald one of the leaders in the 1914 trouble told me personally that they had enough dynamite to wreck Butte and the same rumor is current here now. We got things under way and Muckie McDonald disappeared and was sent to the penitentiary. Going back to the cause of conditions. It is a little bit socialist and the rest radical element. In fact [it] "is a thing that was made in Germany for outside consumption and we are the consumers here." We have five thousand people in Butte at present who have no sense of right or wrong.

They claim that they cannot live on what they make but these men who run the miners off the hill, these Finlanders and others, sleep three shifts in the same bed and live on one dollar a day and save more than ever before heard of. They are not affected so much by the cost of living. 85% of the miners of this community think it costs too much to live. It is not due directly to the merchant here, it is due to conditions throughout the country generally. While I say it is not due directly, they contribute to it. There is no question but what on many things prices are high in this community and many working in the mines cannot live on the wages. These radicals seize on that as one of their causes and get to their support a lot of persons they otherwise would not get. The dangerous element to contend with here

269

is those that know no other restraint than fear of the law. That is the conditions you have to meet with.

I sometimes think it is obvious, so obvious that we run by it looking for something else, the principle of give and take, of live and let live. By the way, that is one side of it. You cannot teach Wobblies that principle. They have to be handled.

MR. PARTELOW, Secretary of the Montana Federation of Labor: We who represent labor at this time are placed in a somewhat peculiar position. We are not directly selected to represent labor at this meeting and as a result we can simply speak from a personal view-point. (Cites an instance of three boys, 17, 18, or 19 years of age, carrying fifty pounds of dynamite on June 13, 1914.)

I have stated my view point as a laboring man without authority to speak for my organization.

F.A. BIGELOW, Member of the County Council of Defense. Editor of the "Free Lance" conservative Labor publication: As Mr. Partelow has just stated, a laboring man speaking at this time is in a peculiar position.

I say that I believe some drastic steps are necessary to rid the atmosphere at this time. If we could get rid of one hundred men in this community it would clear up the atmosphere, so we could get along for possibly five years.

As I said before, if some steps are taken to rid the town of that element I believe organized labor and the business representatives can get along as well as we have in the past. We have never come to blows and have gotten along fairly well and we are willing to take a chance with the business men in this town as far as the A.F. of L. is concerned.

I know the civil authorities in this town can never straighten things up. Sheriff O'Rourke cannot straighten it up. He is helpless. The Mayor with his policemen cannot clear things up. These men have no respect whatever for a deputy sheriff, nor policemen, nor plain-clothes men.

BY MR. CARROLL: Q. What effect did that proclamation have on the men who wanted to go to work?
A. No more effect than this cigarette smoke.
Q. What effect would it have if martial law was declared and the U.S. government would give protection to the men going to work?
A. Lots of men won't want to be placed in the position of being called "Scabs." I believe many miners feel like going to work. I know a number of craftsmen who are

not working and who are afraid to go to work.

Q. Would the government taking charge here remove the fears of these men?

A. It is my opinion it would.

Note: Mr. Bigelow is also organizer for the Montana Federation of Labor.

F.L. MELCHER, Business man and Manager of the Western Iron Works: There is not much to be said. Our men did not show up. The only excuse we had from them was that they were going to play safety first. Friday some of the blacksmiths, machinists, and molders came to work. The molders helpers came to work and came in and made a demand on us that their wages be restored or that the cost of living be reduced 25%. That is the demand they made on us.

The majority of our men are willing to work and will come to work as soon as they can be guaranteed protection. I mean protection that they will not be molested. I think that is the attitude of the machinists and mechanics of this community.

There is one thing that came to my ears today. That officials at Washington had called representatives of Labor there within the last two weeks. Those representatives have come back here. One of them undertook to talk last night to of the unions and he was hissed and called down. They would not listen to him.

If this condition exists in this community it is time something was done. I suggest that we stop these things. Put the military in power and clean this thing up. Find out who the disturbers are and get them out as soon as the law will provide.

J.R. WHARTON, Manager of the Street Railway Company: Last Monday morning our men went to work and had four cars out of the barn. A mob of about four hundred men came down there and lined up in front of the gate. Watchman, who is a nervy fellow said "this is private property. Stop where you are." Immediately called the sheriff's office. The sheriff got there with his force and some soldiers but they pulled our men off the work. The men told me they did not take the cars out and did not believe they could run the cars. I don't believe they could do it today except under your protection.

Our men are placed in a peculiar position. You leave here next week or month and then they would be in a worse position. Unless they can feel that they will be protected, not only now but in the future, they do not dare work. I believe the majority of them would go back to work. I don't know and am not sure.

271

We have had strikes. We met the strikers in our own rooms and came to terms with them. But with the element now in control there is no talking. They are not trying to shut down the street railroad. It means it is no strike, it is revolution. They want a change of government and if they are not stopped they are going to succeed.

MR. FARRELL, Secretary of the Teamsters Union: As said by other members of labor here, we are in a peculiar position. While we cannot say we are representing labor yet whatever we say may be quoted as an expression of opinion by that organization. Any man who is not in accord with the wild ideas or radical ideas of the Wobblies or Bolshevists is immediately abased and ridiculed and humiliated from end to end of the world as being opposed to the interests of the laboring classes and they use their best efforts to discredit those people. I speak simply as an individual. I do not pretend to represent the sentiments of the teamsters union. At the same time most of you know the action of the teamsters union Tuesday evening. I might say for the teamsters union that the sentiment of the teamsters is against a sympathetic strike.

They are in this position. Nobody can deny that it was a hard shock when the miners were cut the one dollar a day. No laboring man may take the position that seems to favor the employer who makes that cut or he is immediately put down as working in the interest of the employer and endeavoring to make all laboring people subservient to the employer. The teamsters union had several members affected by the cut in wages.

I might say that the committee who represented the Soldiers', Sailors & Workmen's Council, stated their case that we strike against a cut in wages. One member reported that the laboring man has to strike and protest against infringement of rights. One of the members, a returned soldier advised the members of the teamsters union that they had better strike, because he said he would advise them things would happen in the morning if they did not strike; that their teams would be taken away from them etc. (Mr. Farrell cites a few instances of increase in cost of gloves, shoes, provisions, etc.). It seems to me that some concerted effort should be made to bring down the cost of living. I would like to hear some explanation of why the prices go up and down with the wages.

SEPH R. JACKSON, County Attorney of Silver Bow County: Mr. Chairman, Major Halloran and gentlemen: For your information Major I might state that I do not represent any mining company. I do not represent any body of laboring men and my sole interest in this meeting is the good and welfare of the entire community, and to point out to you, if I can what I deem to be the clear and incontrovertible truth about the situation as it exists here.

I am one who feels that the citizens of Butte have been following the doctrine of let good enough alone for so long a period that some of us have to almost vomit in disgust. We are following the path of least resistance and have done so all during my nineteen years in this community. Side-stepping a condition when it comes instead of meeting it fair and putting it down if possible. That is what we did in 1914. We did not remove the cancer. We made an opening but left the roots there and a new growth was permitted. Right here today is the same condition or situation. We respect to the men who are out in good faith. They undoubtedly have a just cause for complaint as to the high cost of living and existing conditions.

When I was in Helena recently I was talking to the chairman of the Senate investigation committee and if the facts and figures he showed me are correct, many of your wholesale houses are as big as robbers as Tom Stagg.

I cannot see how the workingmen of the community have existed during the past year. It is not the retailer. The wholesaler, jobber, he is the man. He holds the community by the throat and calls the military to come in and kick the heads off the men that are down.

To my way of thinking, my mind is clear as crystal, we must stand absolutely and squarely on one or the other side of the line.

I want to show you, Major, that this is not an economic strike. It is not a strike against any industry or to better the conditions of the men who are out, but is surely and absolutely one of the levers that is being used by this corrupt pack of theorists who come in here off and on and whose object is the overthrow of the American state of Government.

About picketing. Last night the Wobblies decided there would be no more picketing; rather dangerous to go up on the hill; but the men are going to be notified over the 'phone, through their wives or through their children, that if they insist on going out harm is going to befall them.

Now the king-pin, the hub of the entire difficulty, sits over in the legislature under the name of William Dunn. Dunn blew in here two years ago after having been driven out of Chicago.

He told me, himself, in Helena, not more than two weeks ago, the present order of society is about to crumble. We

273

are living in a capitalistic age and it refuses any more to function. That the Soviet form of government in Russia is the most ideal form of government.

His sole idea is to make this one of the spots where the big Soviet revolution is going to start.

(MR. JACKSON READS A PAPER GIVING THE PRINCIPLES OF THE ORGANIZATION OF THE I.W.W.)

That gives you, without any possible doubt of any kind or character, just the quality of the man and organizations you are up against.

Now the core of the situation is the Finlander and Sinn Feiner.

The only way to get rid of it is to get the Finlanders, get the undesirables to more real opportunity. Take these men as undesirables and deport them. Let's get them out of the community, out of our country. The minute that martial law is declared these men get out, they go out to the wood camps, the country. When things are quiet and order restored they come back again; and in every instance where the Wobblies strike an industrial center there is some little sore spot and they irritate the sore and they are the masters who make their fellows jump.

You talk about civil authorities. I am your prosecuting attorney. You can arrest these men. You get a complaint in my office for a misdemeanor, over which the Justice of the Peace has jurisdiction. You file your complaint and these men are out on bonds, in ten minutes doing exactly the same thing. They get a jury trial and in this town a jury is drawn entirely from our working people.

I can say there is only one thing to be done and that the civil authorities cannot do. The thing to do is to put squarely all the power of the county into the hands of one man who is strong enough to handle the situation. I am in favor of putting them in and bringing them before the representative from the Immigration Department when he arrives here, for examination and see if they can be deported.

I did go into the subject of state martial law with the Governor and as regards the Federal Martial law with Major Loran. I take it that the Federal martial law which would exist here would be somewhat different than when Mr. Donohue was in charge.

When the condition here is of such a character that the Governor of the state will clearly know to be in a state of --

This is not a labor trouble, it is a revolutionary movement, it is treasonable and I for one do not propose to stand for it under any circumstances.

COLONEL DONAHUE: I think I have had a little experience here in Butte. Had control of it for ten weeks in 1914. The element that is behind this strike movement is the same element that was behind the troubles at that time. Joe Shannon, one of the leaders, I had in jail here nearly three months. He was the only one of the bunch that was acquitted. Muckie McDonald served his term in the penitentiary. At that time we had martial law. As Mr. Jackson says, without martial law you are at the mercy of the justice courts.

At the present time the movement is composed of the Wobbly element. This man Dunn is the prime mover and probably has more influence than any other man. I believe Dunn to be a fanatic on the subject. Personally, I believe he is sincere. I believe he is a fanatic along these lines.

This thing has to be properly handled. My personal opinion is that martial law should be put into effect quietly. The great amount of the Wobblies here are Finlanders with a few Sinn Feiners Irish furnishing the brains to lead them. You will find when the wash comes that the Sinn Fein Irish will not be there. Dunn is not a citizen of Butte; Campbell is a citizen of Canada; Joe Shannon is an agitator and Fisher does not belong here. These men flock in here and cause disturbances. At the present time there is no doubt but what we have at least two hundred Wobblies, gunmen waiting to do slugging.

My personal opinion is that the sooner the situation is taken in hand by the military the quicker we are going to have peace in this town.

RAYMOND RHULE, BUSINESS MAN. MANAGER McKEE PRINTING COMPANY: One point comes up in regard to the "Bulletin." The printers, as you all know, are a very radical union. They have plans on foot now to go out tomorrow. They are not going on strike; they are going to go out because to go to and from work on account of no street cars. Then you get the condition that the Miner, Post and other papers are closed down and the Bulletin is the only paper running. That is the condition we are going to have unless we get some action and get it pretty quick.

MR. BIGELOW: I think that can be verified. I have been told the same thing as stated by Mr. Rhule. On Sunday the printers did a very despicable thing. They had $300.00 of Liberty Bonds and at Sunday's meeting they gave these Liberty Bonds to the Bulletin. Some of the printers are pretty sore about it.

Fisher is editor of the Bulletin. Dunn writes very
little of that stuff for the Bulletin.

MR. GILLIE: I would like to call the attention of one point
made by Mr. Jackson. If anything is done under military law
it must be done right off. They will disappear like snow as
as soon as martial law is declared.

JOHN BERKIN, MINE SUPERINTENDENT AND BUSINESS MAN: I would
say that immediate action should be taken if it is done at
all. As the Doctor stated, in 1914 the soldiers came in
here about eight or nine o'clock. The dope was given that
the soldiers were here and the ring-leaders scattered like
cockroaches and we could not find them. The same thing will
occur now. It has started tonight. As soon as martial law
is declared they will get out of this town. Fisher will
leave this town. There is where we want to grab these
fellows. That paper goes to five thousand people twice a
day.

I agree with the man from the teamsters union as to the
cost of living. When that time came and I heard of it, I
wished the cut had not come for sixty days. If we could
have got the committees out and the cost of living down the
miners would not have taken exceptions and would not have
complained as they did. However, it is done.

The average miner, working man, the man who is a citizen of the United States, with a family depending on him,
wants to go to work.

There is another element controlled by five leaders. In
addition to that five there are fifteen or twenty that are
helpers or muckers to the man who works the machine. These
men are the leaders of this entire organization, followed by
2500 people and the majority of those people are aliens.

The county Attorney has covered the ground that I was
going to cover. He said all the trouble is this power of
the man who you have representing you in the legislature.

These five men you must destroy, by what action I am
unable to say. I do believe there is not any other way than
by declaring martial law. For all times take out root and
core of this proposition. I have been here 52 years. We
blazed trails and made it possible for these disreputables
to come here and I will not stand for it. All right if they
get me but I am going to get my part before I go. They got
to walk over my dead body to do it. Get to this Butte Bulletin and destroy it. I have been working for three years
night and day, as different people will bear out. I know
every man at the head of this organization. They are not
going to do anything. If the street cars start tomorrow

they will not molest the street cars, simply because the Major is here.

"Wait until the son of a gun goes out of town then we will blow it up altogether."

ROMAN CATHOLIC PRIEST: I think opinion has come to the point where we can say what is the best thing to do. I am very familiar with the conditions in homes in the city of Butte. I think we should not only protect these people for the future but that we make some guarantee that this protection will be effective. Through my observation during the last week or so I do not think there is an effective way of handling it through our present civil authorities.

Knowing, as I do, the good will of the company here employing labor to try to bring us over the period of difficulty that we are under just after the war, it is a case where people would become impatient. We must not delay to start these people learning whose duty it is to provide necessaries for helpless children. I suggest that we handle this matter under the protection of the United States Government.

COMMUNITY PRESSURE
IN MINOT FREE SPEECH FIGHT

Grant S. Youmans was President and General Manager of the Savings Loan and Trust Co. of Minot, North Dakota. This extract from Youmans' "The Labor Troubles" illustrates pressure exerted by the community during an IWW free speech fight in Minot, North Dakota, July, 1913. His statement describes his experiences with the business element after he had donated $5.00 to the harvest hands' fund and posted a notice in his bank window declaring "We Believe In Free Speech." In "Report of the United States Commission on Industrial Relations, 1912-1915," HF 1424, I5. (See List of Works Consulted for complete citation.)

The consequences of my actions came quickly. About 2:30 the next day while hard at work at the bank three representative business men called upon me. They were J. A. Roell, a hardware merchant; F. W. Youngman, a real estate broker, and F. L. Householder, a dentist. They stated their mission briefly. They had been appointed as a committee, chosen by the Commercial Club Members then in session, to invite me to the meeting as there was something to be brought up in which I would be interested. My suspicions were at once aroused, for I expected the experience would not be pleasant so in a kindly way I declined the invitation. They pressed me to go. So I stated my objection, namely, that I wished to have no words whatever with my former business associates. So earnest were they that they convincingly assured me that there would be nothing unpleasant at all. They stated the Club simply wished to ask my advice regarding the Labor Troubles. That at this moment seventy-five of the members were seeking some means of compromise, through this session and they wanted me to help in securing a settlement of our Labor Troubles. After this explanation, I gladly went with them to the meeting.

As we entered the room, I was surprised to see that the presiding officer was D. G. Greenleaf, a local Attorney, who

a few nights before in a drunken condition, had done all in
his power to interfere with the street meetings. We all
went quickly to some vacant chairs near and when seated,
Greenleaf arose and in his haughtiest manner addressed me,
"Mr. Youmans, we understand you are in favor of Free Speech.
We have invited you up to make a speech." He then sat down;
the room became instantly tense and quiet. I looked care-
lessly around and found the entire body glaring at me with
unfriendly eyes. So this was their game, and broken were
all the promises of the three men who so kindly invited me
to this friendly session. I accepted the challenge.

"I think that request somewhat unfair. I don't fully
understand the purpose of this meeting, and until it is
explained to me I do not see that I have anything in particular to talk about." No answer from the presiding officer.
The silence of the room became oppressive. Finally, J. M.
Devine, former Governor of the state, arose and began to
mumble an explanation. He told them what a good citizen I
had been, what a fine neighbor and understanding me as he
did it seemed incredible to him that I should so far forget
my social standing, my duty towards the business interests,
as to help feed a bunch of bums who had come to the city --
here he was interrupted by angry growls and hisses directed
against me. The uproar became so violent, Mr. Devine could
not be heard. The cry was raised, "Let Youmans speak, Let
Youmans speak, speech, speech," demanded angry voices. "Let
him speak, he believes in free speech," snarled others. I
arose and waited for silence, then addressed them in this
manner:

"Mr. Chairman, Gentlemen. This having to make a speech
without any warning or preparation and especially upon a
subject about which I fear you all have the same opinion, is
anything but pleasant. I will, however, do the best I can.
I understand that you have called this meeting for the
purpose of discussing the unfortunate labor condition in
this city. I feel perfectly safe in saying that all this
trouble could easily have been averted if the men had been
left alone and not treated to showers of rotten eggs and
other insults." (Groans, growls, hisses and jeers.) "Instead of certain business men plotting to prevent, disrupt
and abolish these meetings, they should have displayed the
same energy and interest in showing the workers some little
consideration. These toilers were entitled to fair play,
which they did not get. They were entitled to police protection which was denied them. Had you men been only human
and allowed them to have in Minot that liberty guaranteed
them under the Constitution a labor union might have been
perfected, the leaders have gone quietly to other cities,
and all this unpleasantness and bitterness been avoided. I
have only done what I firmly believe to be right. These men
are mostly harvest hands, who have come for the harvest and

279

threshing. They come here seeking work." (Cries of "No, no, they don't want work, they only want trouble.") "I admit I gave $5.00 one day and later gave larger sums because men were hungry and needed help. I did for them what I have done for almost every man here. Nearly all of you have come to me at some time or other with a subscription paper or request for money; I have always been generous with you. Never have any of you been turned down." (Voices of "That's true, we admit that.") I continued: "If even now a little tact and kindness be used in dealing with this situation, further conflict can be avoided." (Cries of "What would you do?") "Why bless you, that's easy. I'd negotiate with these fellows for a friendly settlement. They are after all very human. I would arrange for a conference between the labor leaders and the -----." I got no further, for I was here silenced by roars of "Never, never, not by a damn sight. Not with those damned bums. We'll hang them first, we'll drive them from the city."

Though still standing waiting to continue, I was deprived of the floor by L. D. McGahan, one of our leading citizens. He is the editor of the weekly Democrat, a politican by nature, former Police Commissioner, who found it very convenient to resign over night. It is said his decision was hurried because of a polite request from the State's Attorney. When he arose he was in a highly excited state. He worked himself into a furious passion, swinging his arms as though guarding off demons. After comparing the present situation to the days of the French Revolution, he made the following threat: "There are just two sides to this question, either a man is on the side of the business man or on the side of the anarchy. Any man who is not on the side of the business man is a TRAITOR to his country, and should be driven out at the head of the vags, bums and scum who call themselves Working Men." (Spirited applause, cries of "That's right. That's the dope. Give 'em hell. Show no quarter.") An uproar was created and when quiet came again, I thanked the committee for their kindness in inviting me there to be insulted. Then I quietly left the room. No good could be accomplished by remaining longer, as anything I could do or say would simply fan their bitter passion or class hatred into hotter flames.

The situation was plain. I stood alone among my former friends. I was with the workers and firmly believed in their right to organize, and fully intended to give my best judgment in bringing about a satisfactory termination of the trouble but not at the sacrifice of principle. Being called a traitor did not exactly apply to my case. During the year 1898, I had resigned my position as clerk in the First National Bank, of Winona, Minnesota, to enlist as a recruit in the Spanish-American War. As a soldier, I served creditably but without distinction. I thought of my sacrifice in

280

army life when McGahan called me a "Traitor." The confidence I formerly held among my business associates and friends can best be established by the letters which follow. They were given only a few weeks before that session at the Commercial Club rooms. I came from that meeting bearing this one impression "That I was a marked man." Later developments justify that impression.

REIGN OF TERROR PROTESTED IN SAN DIEGO

Henry Austin Adams was a well-known California speaker and writer who lived in the vicinity of San Diego. He addressed a letter to Commissioner Harris Weinstock, who had been sent by the Governor of California to investigate the trouble in San Diego. Printed in the San Diego Sun (April 22, 1912, p. 4) in an edited version, the full letter appears in San Francisco Labor Council, Special Investigating Committee, San Diego Free Speech Controversy (San Francisco, April 25, 1912), pp. 5-8; and State Historical Society of Wisconsin, Collection of Materials on or about the Industrial Workers of the World, Microfilm P34898, Addendum of Miscellaneous Publications (end of reel).

"We have always fools and appearances against us."
-- Nietzsche.

H. A. ADAMS, M.A.
Educational Journalist,
La Jolla, California,
April 17th, 1912.

Harris Weinstock, Esq.,
    Special Commission,
        San Diego, California.

Dear Sir:--

In common, I believe, with a considerable portion of the people of San Diego I hail your advent among us as the authorized commissioner sent by His Excellency, the Governor of California, to investigate the "reign of terror" which has disgraced our city for some weeks past. Your presence in this official capacity gives us the hope that now, at last, we who feel as I do may be allowed to enter our protest and voice our sorrow and indignation without running the risk of being subjected to the indignities perpetrated by a brutalized police force and the inhuman and utterly lawless private vengeance of a gang of organized anarchists calling themselves "vigilantes." Absence from the city and serious illness has prevented me from doing what I would

have wished to do had I been at home and able to be about.
I have, however, written an Open Letter, which is now being
printed and will shortly be circulated.

By way of identifying myself I may state that I am not
of the "working class," but an author, lecturer, and scho-
lar. The services of probably no other private citizen have
been more frequently in demand than my own, in the good work
of "boosting" every public cause, by delivering orations,
speaking at banquets, and contributing articles to the public press. As to my personal standing I can refer you to
the Hon. Lyman J. Gage (ex-Secretary of the Treasury), G.
Aubrey Davidson (President of the Southern Trust and Savings
Bank), the officers of the Panama-California Exposition, and
practically every banker and prominent attorney in the city.
Politically, I am (like so many millions of Americans to-
day), a free lance, having belonged to no party for years,
but holding myself ready to support any and all men and
measures that I believe will make for more just and more
democratic conditions. I mention this to show that in this
local issue I represent no faction and have no axe to grind.
By birth and education I belong to the class which has been
perpetrating these humiliating acts of lawlessness here; and
I realize with profound sorrow that in venturing to testify
as I am now doing I shall no doubt risk the loss of very
many of my closest personal friends, who, misled by the
prostituted and mendacious press, seem to me to have been
swept off their feet by this wave of what is known as "the
madness of the herd" or the "psychology of numbers." Nothing in my experience has so filled me with pessimistic
dread of the future as has this simply incredible outbreak
of primeval brute instincts in men commonly ruled by reason
and the sane dictates of civilized society.

The troubles began when our City Council (at the request of a number of merchants, and over the protest of a
much larger number of workingmen) passed an ordinance prohibiting street speaking within a defined area, where meetings
had always been held. Feeling that this was an unlawful
infringement of their rights a number of organizations (including the Socialists, the Single Taxers and the I.W.W.)
decided to test the constitutionality of the ordinance, by
continuing to speak within the prescribed area and thus
subjecting themselves to arrest and trial. This customary
method of testing an obnoxious law was at once shrieked at
as "Anarchy"; women as well as men were clubbed (one man
into insensibility); treated with dignities which would be
disgraceful even if shown to desperate criminals; and (will
you believe it?) the charge against these ladies and orderly
citizens was not the simple one of violating a city ordinance, but of "conspiracy!"

Then came rumors that members of the I.W.W. were coming

to San Diego to swell the number of those willing to be arrested for speaking on the streets -- and hell was let
loose! These unarmed and penniless wanderers (whose only
weapons are their tongues) were proclaimed as a "horde of
dangerous anarchists." The usual yellow journal tactics
were begun. A "plot" to dynamite us all was "discovered" --
in the cerebellum of the police, who of course must find
some excuse for their brutality. An officer of the Exposition was heard to say that if he were the chief of police he
would line all the I.W.W.'s against a wall and shoot them
like the dirty dogs that they are! Merchants and real
estate speculators (fearing that their merry little carnival
of greed and "prosperity" might be hurt by any labor agitation) swapped horrific stories about "those damned anarchists." Over their cocktails at the club, bankers and
"leading citizens" exchanged ominous opinions as to the
"outrage of letting anarchists run at large." And, just
naturally, it required only the half-jesting hint of a
newspaper genius to start the "Vigilante" infamy. In a
moment the basest instincts of the brute within men asserted
themselves and these cowardly ruffians enlisted eagerly in a
"patriotic crusade" in which they could indulge all their
blood-lust and brutish cruelty without the slightest danger
of having their own craven skulls cracked by their defense-
less and unarmed victims. Automobiles were eagerly offered
for the glorious work and dozens of "influential citizens,"
armed to the teeth, tackled the heroic work of trampling all
semblance of law and order out of San Diego -- and all
semblance to humanity out of themselves. The press cheered
them on; the pulpit remained silent or joined in the praise;
and the police and "Vigilantes" had saved us!

In the meantime what were the "anarchists" really
doing? Beyond singing a few songs in a crowded jail and
asking to have the vermin suppressed and the vile food
improved, their conduct was like that of the "drunks" and
criminals with whom they were herded; that is to say, they
made no trouble. Outside the jail NOT A SINGLE ACT OF
VIOLENCE OR EVEN OF WANTONNESS has been committed! Not a
blow has been struck; not a weapon used; not a threat of any
kind made by any I.W.W. or other sympathizer with the Free
Speech movement. Such patience under the most infamous and
galling inhumanity and injustice speaks well for the discipline maintained by the leaders of these men.

Backed by public opinion and confident that any act,
however lawless, or any cruelty, however bestial, would be
not only safe from prosecution but actually heralded by the
"kept" press as heroic and patriotic, the police then ventured even farther. They ceased arresting violators of the
ordinance, contenting themselves with clubbing them or, if
arrests were made, turning them over at dead of night to
"Vigilantes," who then carried them out into the country and

after subjecting them to frightful treatment and diabolical indignities, drove them off with threats of death if they ever dared to exercise their constitutional right to live wherever they choose! Newspapers which (printed in other cities or published by the Labor Unions) presumed to tell the other side of the story were confiscated and their vendors beaten unmercifully by the power-crazed police. A scholarly gentleman, sitting in a neighboring restaurant, witnessed the brutal clubbing and kicking of a poor youth who was selling some of these objectionable newspapers. It was all that my friend could do to restrain himself from going out and felling the blue-coated thug. And this eyewitness is no Socialist or I.W.W. but a highly educated and refined gentleman of leisure who takes no part in either the political or commercial life of the city. The SAN DIEGO UNION printed a large picture of an enormous pile of newspapers, seized (it did not have the honesty to say "confiscated"), and then, in answering the criticism of an eastern paper, this same UNION had the simplicity to state that only "one copy" had been seized as "evidence" against the vendors!

Then came the climax of our local Blood and Thunder regime. The editor of a weekly newspaper, which had ventured to print its own views on the issues in this fight, was attacked when about to enter his house late in the evening, overpowered, thrown into an automobile, carried into the country, strung up by the neck to a tree, and then suffered to save his life by promising to leave his home of twenty years and never return! Some of his captors are known (they are prominent citizens) but it seems that they have terrified Mr. Sauer into doing nothing to send them to San Quentin, where many of our "leading citizens" should be sent and will be sent if the outraged working-class is wise and captures the political machinery which can once more set up the forms of law and justice in San Diego. As things are now, not even the attorney who dares to represent any sympathizer with the working-class is safe from insult and possibly worse at the hands of the officers sworn to carry on the legal and proper processes of the law.

In turning over his prisoners to a wholly unauthorized and illegal gang of conspirators the chief of police was guilty of a serious crime. In lending the apparatus of the fire department for the illegal deportation of prisoners awaiting trial the chief of that department became an accessory. And in conspiring to deprive many men of their liberty without due process of law every "Vigilante" in the whole murderous and cowardly crew has laid himself open to conviction under the Federal statutes, which provide for such a heinous crime a long term of imprisonment. Will they be prosecuted? Certainly not until the working class develops sufficient class consciousness to realize that the "law" is

285

but the expression of those who now rule us and that no
working man need expect anything but the club of the policeman, the kick of the jailer, the contemptuous sneer of the
judge, the lying report of the cub reporter, the curse of
the "leading citizen" -- and the pious silence of the
pulpit.

On Friday, April 12th, the SAN DIEGO UNION printed a
proclamation signed by the "Vigilantes," which warned us
that nobody has a constitutional right even to criticize the
police or any officer of government; and that if anybody
dared to do so they, the "Vigilantes," would capture them,
rub tar into their hair, and drive them out of holy San
Diego. It is incredible that any American could write such
an outrageous piece of dangerous imbecility; but still more
incredible that a reputable paper would print it without
denouncing it. Believe me, sir, these tactics are sowing
the seed of a class war so terrible in its possibilities
that I (a student of economics and sociology for twenty-five
years) solemnly and with a deep sense of responsibility at a
time like this declare to you, and through you to the Governor, that it is my profound belief that if the officers of
the law do not abandon their present practice of treating
the working class like outlaws, why then, sir, nothing but a
bloody revolution can ever put an end to conditions which
have become beyond human endurance. And booming, boosting,
boastful, bourgeoise San Diego has just been doing its
stupid best to precipitate such a social catastrophe.

In closing, let me point out to you, sir, that none of
my statements is "ex-parte," but may be fully corroborated
by the news items printed for several weeks past in the
public (and anti-labor) press of this poor hypnotized and
hysterical community. I have everything to lose (friends,
influence, even money), and nothing to gain by testifying as
I have. The Socialists do not trust me, because I have frequently in speech and print criticized their tactics; the
business element make use of my eloquence and enthusiasm,
but fear me nonetheless because of my known independence and
contempt for their lack of ideals; and the general public
(always scatter-brained) does not know just where to place a
man who keeps informed of world-movements and naturally
shapes his views in the light of a wider outlook than that
of the ward, the parish, and "our city." So you see, sir,
that I shall be able to count upon only myself in thus taking an attitude of scornful and outspoken protest against
what has been going on here in San Diego. But sometimes the
"minute minority of one" (the fortunate outcome of being
singularly free from the influences and immediate interests
which sway other men) sometimes, I say this microscopic
minority has shown in history surprising powers of rapid
growth. You will find, sir, that now that one man (not
directly interested on either side) has told the truth,

286

others will creep out from behind their caution and prudence and begin to say that "really something ought to be done about it!" And if history has not always lied, our recent hysterical debauch will ere long be classed with those innumerable other instances of popular injustice and lawless terror which have been the immediate precursors of the dawn of a larger and deeper life for the unprivileged and despised many.

Very respectfully yours,

HENRY AUSTIN ADAMS

LIFE STORIES OF FLOATING WORKERS

Peter Speek was an investigator for the Commission on Industrial Relations. His reports, based
on interviews of more than one thousand itinerant
workers, formed the basis for many of the Commission's conclusions and recommendations. This
appendix reprints excerpts from his "Report on
the Psychological Aspect of the Problem of Floating Laborers (An Analysis of Life Stories), June
25, 1915," CIR Unpub. Rpts., HF 145 S7, pp. 38-
62, 92-98, 104-113. The first excerpt is Speek's
composite profile of the "life story" of a typical unskilled itinerant; following are his field
notes of the "life stories" of two migratory
workers.

When a country boy under such conditions is grown up,
say 20 years of age, he naturally begins seriously to think
about his future, of establishing himself in life independently. He may be in love with a girl in the neighborhood,
who has grown up in much the same way and whom he dreams of
marrying at the first opportunity, to establish a family,
his own home. But where, how, by what means? He possesses
nothing. To hire out as a farm hand, or, if somebody would
help him, to rent a farm or acquire a piece of new land
(from lumber companies -- cut-over and burnt-over land)
might be a solution. But what is the use of doing this? he
asks. His parents have tried to make good by hiring out as
farm laborers, or by working by themselves on land either
"rented" or "bought." They, together with their children,
have struggled hard all their lifetime and now what or where
are they? Just where they were at the beginning, he acknowledges, hardly more than keeping alive! He even must care
for them in their old age! No, in the country there is no
opportunity open for him. Thus concludes our young fellow-
citizen in his reasoning.

But he has heard from distant relatives, or migratory
harvest hands, lumber jacks, or other boys who know more
than he, or has read in the Sunday newspapers or in maga-

zines, that the best opportunities for a young, strong
beginner are in the city -- the larger the city the more
opportunities are there for not only earning a good living
but making a fortune. Besides, the boy may have visited the
city, or at least his country town, where he saw the attrac-
tions -- theaters, clubs, poolrooms, varied social life.
etc. -- which the country does not provide. These attrac-
tions, however, the so-called "lure" of the city, are only
secondary considerations with him. The main reason of his
deciding to go to the city and to try his fortune there,
consists, as stated, in his desire to establish himself in
some trade or calling, to earn and save money that he may
acquire a home -- is economic need. Indeed, not all country
boys are so moderate in their ambitions. Many of them dream
of building up fortunes, of becoming a Rockefeller, or some
other great power in the future.

Of his resolution to go to the city our boy first tells
his sweetheart. She reluctantly and with some apprehension
agrees to his plan, for his arguments are too strong to
oppose. He has no difficulty in getting the blessing of his
father and mother, for they do not want their boy to repeat
the fruitless life struggle they have endured in the country. A sum of money for railway ticket and for expenses for
a week or so in the city is secured. Either the father has
succeeded in saving so much, or the money is borrowed from
some good neighbor. And our boy arrives, say, from the
State of Kansas or Nebraska, in Chicago -- one of the largest centers of all sorts of supposed opportunities.

Nearing the city, he sees smoking factory chimneys. He
notices their location and plans to be at the offices of
these factories the next day. Early in the morning he is
there -- awkward, shy, and at the same time, with a strong
hope of securing a "good promising" job with fair wages and
rapid advancement. But the employing officials when they
learn from his story that he is just a green country boy,
with no experience in any city trade and knowing nothing
about factory work, refuse him everywhere. The boy, although slightly discouraged by his failures the first day,
continues his search for a likely job by direct application
at factory gates and various work places during a number of
days. The only definite result is that he learns not to
speak the truth about his inexperience, but to lie -- to
state that he has had some experience, for instance, in
carpentry, or mechanical work, whatever may be the nature of
the desired job. By this kind of lie he at last secures a
helper's job, but he is fired after a few hours of work.

Meanwhile his money is rapidly melting away. Alarmed
by this, he appeals either to the owner of the lodging house
where he sleeps, or to some fellows in the same house, telling his trouble and asking advice. His attention is called

to the newspaper "want ads" and employment offices. He
first turns to the "ads", for there is no need of paying
fees. In trying to secure a suitable job through want ads
the following may happen: He may run from office to office
during several days and still fail for a number of reasons.
He may not be qualified for the job advertised; the job may
be taken before he arrives; he may be pushed aside without
ceremony by the physically stronger applicants later joining
the crowd before the office; or there may not be any real
job behind the want ad -- it was only an advertisement of
the concern, for instance, a private employment office. Or
he may easily fall a victim of a swindler who had advertised
for agents to sell, for example, an "article which everybody
needs and buys, and which anybody can sell and earn $100 a
week or more." The only thing the boy has to do is to buy
samples. If he still has left several dollars, he buys and
goes to make his fortune -- to find out that nobody wants
the article, even the concern itself does not want to take
it back, for its business consists solely in selling the
"samples" to naive would-be agents.

Now, our boy is broke, and still without a job. A
postal to his homefolks brings a small sum to him. He turns
for aid to the employment agencies. He pays $2 or $3 for
fees, to find out soon that he does not get a job nor are
his fees refunded. He tries other agencies, being careful
not to pay fees before he is assured of a job. One agency
has to offer jobs in a railway section gang, $1.50 a day.
It is not the work our boy is looking for, still, knowing
that he has only a couple of dollars left, and knowing
already by experience, how hard it is to get a suitable job,
and figuring that he will work on such a low-paid and unpro-
mising job only temporarily, earning a sum of money, after
which he will return to Chicago and continue his efforts to
find a real job with a future for him, he accepts a railway-
track-work job, pays his last dollars for fees, and is
shipped out, say, to North Dakota, to work in a railway
construction camp. What conditions he experiences there are
seen in fh< "Report on Labor Camps," by your investigator.
Only our boy is not accustomed to such conditions. They are
much harder for him to bear than for seasoned laborers.

Take, for instance, the board. He has been accustomed
to eat meals prepared by his mother at home, -- poor it may
be, but clean, wholesome and tasty. The board in the camps
is entirely different. He eats meat and can not tell of
what kind -- from what animal it is. The reddish-gray mass
having no taste but that of salt, is called "canned salmon";
the coffee he drinks is just a warm bitter water, etc.
After several dav< he has stomach trouble -- his first
experience in the so-called "camp disorders." He sleeps in
a wooden bunk, on straw bedding, at the side of another
fellow. If he has not got vermin in the lodging house in

Chicago, he gets it in his bunk now. He has never slept
before in such an overcrowded room as the bunk car, in which
14 men sleep. He notices a "bad taste" in his mouth and a
dizziness in his head every morning. He works 11 hours a
day, 7 days a week -- for the same pay on Sundays. Although
he works hard, the foreman is never satisfied with him,
cursing him and his fellow laborers with a profanity he has
never heard before. Notwithstanding all these hardships he
is cheerful, hopeful, takes things as they are, with a
spirit of humor, comforting himself that this job is only a
temporary one. In the same spirit he sends a few lines to
his sweetheart and homefolks, written either on his bunk or
on his knees, because there is no other place, no table for
reading and writing, provided for laborers in the camp.

So he keeps on working hard and stoically enduring the
conditions. He expects to work several months so as to earn
money enough for returning to Chicago. But after a month he
begins to feel very tired every evening. One morning he
finds that he is not able to get up -- he has a slight fever
and headache. Recovering after a day or two he goes again
to work although he is weak and has lost appetite; he still
lingers on, working a week or two more, finally to discover
that he is entirely exhausted or "all in," as the camp
laborers say. He quits. In getting his wages he may have
some trouble; either the commissary runner has made an over-
charge, or the reduction for the time of bad weather is more
than it should be; or he is given a check to cash which he
must go to a distant town where the main office of his
employer, usually a contractor, is located; or he has to
wait even for a check several days in the camp -- which
often happens in the interest of the boarding company,
especially when it charges a higher price for meals to
laborers who have quit or are discharged and must wait in
the camp for their pay. He feels helpless, intending to go
to the local police or court office, and telling his trouble
to other laborers, who perhaps say: "To the court! Yes, if
you were a millionaire, you possibly would beat the company,
but as a laborer -- no!, we have tried, it was of no use.
Get what you can, and go!"

He accepts the wages, whatever is left after the deductions, just and unjust, and goes. Either he buys a ticket,
or, when one or more fellows who know how to steal a ride
come along with him, he "freights" back to Chicago, tipping
the carmen -- this being his first lesson in the art of
stealing rides on railways.

Arriving in Chicago with from $15 to $20 left, he
cleans himself up and rests a couple of days. He then
begins his hunting for a "real" or "promising" job. A week
passes of hard labor of search, but no such job is to be
found for him. All better paid jobs require experience,

291

and, in many cases, union membership is needed. He feels a
keen desire to learn a trade, but how?

To enter apprenticeship? Either the wages paid are so
small that he can not live on them or there are no wages
paid at all. To enter a trade school? He can not, for it
requires considerable money to do this. He is again dead-
broke. He has already pawned his watch. The only thing
left for him now is to accept again a job in a railway construction camp, which a private employment office offers to
him somewhere in southern Illinois. Wages are $1.75 a day;
shipment is free; fees for the job, $3, may be deducted from
his wages afterwards. He arrives, works three days, and is
fired -- "no more work for him." He complains about his
"hard luck" to another fellow, who, bitterly smiling, tells
him that "it's a fee-splitting business of the foreman, in
collusion with the employment agent. Didn't you see in the
three days how the men were coming and going like an endless
chain? See how much you will get!" And really the boy
gets, instead of the $5.25, his three days' wages, only 11
cents, for the fee of $3, the board bill of $1.94, and 20
cents for the purchase of trifles in the commissary store,
were deducted. He being still broke, "freights" back to
Chicago, and pawns his Sunday suit.

The next day he is at the employment office demanding
that his fees be refunded. This is refused on the ground
that the office provided him with a job and if he has been
fired so soon it is because he is "not much of a laborer" on
the job. He protests. The employment agent points toward
the office door, threatening to "break his neck if he does
not clear out at once." He tries to get a policeman. The
first he meets refuses. The second directs him to a certain
office in the city hall. He is told there that if he sus-
pects splitting of fees he must bring effective evidence and
witnesses, which he can not do. So his three days' earnings
are lost -- he is materially worse than before. He also has
lost his faith in the honesty of private employment agents.

He continues to hunt for a job by direct application at
the work places. This is a difficult task. From early
morning he is rushing from factory to factory, to any place
where he believes a job may be found, where he had seen or
sees want signs in the windows, or where he is directed by
rumors among his fellow-job-hunters. Meanwhile the money
secured for his suit in a loan office is rapidly melting
away. Being almost broke, he decides to accept any job,
even at 50 cents a day. In a restaurant he finds and
accepts a dishwashing job, at $6 for seven days' work. He
also gets three meals a day. The work itself is not hard,
but his workday is 13 hours. There is no time left for him
to look for anything better. On the first pay day he finds
out that he gets, instead of $6, only $5.25, for 75 cents is

charged to him as fines for broken dishes. During the
second week his health begins to suffer from the effects of
the long hours and the heat and smells of cooking in the
kitchen, where the ventilation is very poor. As a result he
is losing appetite and sleep. At the end of the third week
he has to quit his "hell of a job." He has seven dollars
left. Resting a couple of days and thinking over his situation, he is visited for the first time by a doubt of his
own abilities to beat his way through. He almost regrets
that he left the country for the city. To quit his efforts
and return would shame him in the eyes of his homefolks;
they would think him a quitter, a failure, not a real man.
But this is not true -- he comforts and convinces himself;
he has not found any real chance as yet. Everybody comes to
Chicago. Here are too many young men unemployed. Why not
try some other, smaller city, for instance Detroit? He
freights there.

After two days' search he finds a floor-sweeper job in
an automobile factory, at $9 a week for 10 hours work six
days a week. At last he has struck his chance. He will
demonstrate that he is a good laborer. He will little by
little -- by more observing -- learn some simple mechanical
work, get advancement to a better job, then to a still
better job -- up to his goal. Besides, he can save a little
money on this job.

He works cheerfully, writes optimistic letters to his
sweetheart and homefolks, sending them a few dollars as
presents on their birthdays. He also tries to redeem his
watch and suit in Chicago, but he finds that the loan office
charges more than 200 percent interest on loans. The suit
he leaves, but the watch he buys out, as it is connected
with some happy memories of his home.

He works faithfully on this job about a year, during
which he eagerly tries to learn something, but can not do
so; he is always busy with his cleaning and sweeping and by
merely seeing others work one can learn very little. He
tells the foreman of his desire to learn but is told that
there is no such job for him; as for an apprenticeship, he
is rather too old.

He is not going to be a floor sweeper all his life. He
inquires in regard to other factories and opportunities but
without result. As far as his future career is concerned
his present job is worthless. Still, it enables him to save
a little money. His bank account has crossed the hundred
mark, which gives him considerable pride. He keeps on working at the same job just for the sake of saving money a
half-year more. His savings are now very nearly $200. With
this money he could let his sweetheart come to Detroit,
marry her, and establish his family life, but to support a

family upon $9 a week seems impossible to him.

He begins to dream of a profitable investment of his savings, planning to find an opportunity for a small business enterprise. Walking the streets in the evenings and dreaming how he would prosper in his little business, he enters shoe-shining parlors, barber shops, poolrooms, and talks to all sorts of peddlers, inquiring about the conditions of their business. All the information, correct and incorrect, that he is able to gather, shows that a certain amount of experience and much more money than he has are required, and that even then success is doubtful, for he learns from his fellow-laborers that many of them have at one time or another attempted business and failed. Finally he decides to invest his money in learning a trade, either by securing an apprenticeship or by entering some trade school. He quits his job as a steady unskilled laborer, determined to learn a trade and become a skilled workingman.

He again visits the employing offices of factories and work shops, but no opportunity of learning is to be found. Everywhere there are applicants waiting for such jobs. In the union offices he is told that he is old for a formal apprenticeship, and even if he were not so old he would have to secure an apprenticeship job by his own efforts.

He decides to return to Chicago. With money he might succeed there. Searching a day or two as he did in Detroit, and failing, he turns his attention to advertisements of trade and business schools, institutes and academies. He sends postals asking for particulars. Not only does information come, but it is followed by agents. One of these explains his trade school in the most attractive and promising way. The student would first have exercises in reading and writing, arithmetic, and drawing; the school then would put him into a shop to practice in mechanical work. After the course is finished, the school would help him to find a job as a skilled mechanic. All this training would require only three months. The tuition fee, $50, must be paid in advance. He accepts the proposition and begins to attend school. As his previous schooling has been very meager, he has great difficulty in keeping up with other students. He studies hard.

After a week or so a stock-selling agent pays him a visit, telling him that a company has recently been organized for the manufacture of refrigerators, with assured and tremendous success in the near future; the stock will double in value in a few weeks; the governor and other prominent men are among the stockholders; a great bank is backing the enterprise; if he does not believe the words of the agent or the literature of the project and reports of the company, which the agent heaps before him on the table, he may go to this bank and inquire about the wonderful opportunity of investment in the stocks of this company.

Keenly interested in so easy a way of making money he goes to the bank to find out if the agent spoke the truth. In appearance it is a prosperous bank, with marble stairs, several offices, and many important-looking officials. He is directed to one of these, who, with an air of confidence and authority, assures him that investment in the stock of the new company is the opportunity of a lifetime, advising him to invest, to the last dollar he may possess. The investment seems safe and promising. He will ask the school authorities to postpone his course of trade study for a couple of months, and in the meantime he will earn money to finish his course. So he invests all his money except a few dollars.

He is now ready to accept any job, working on which he can save money. An old Irishman who is earning his living by doing odd jobs, and who sleeps in the same lodging-house where he lives and has befriended him before, helps him out. This man teaches him how and where to find odd jobs, floor mopping, window cleaning, furniture moving, canvassing, and what not, and what prices to charge for his labor. At first they go out together and work together, then separately. Some days the younger man earns on these jobs $5 a day; some days he does not earn a cent. He is not able to save much, because the search for that kind of work requires a tremendous waste of time. In one week he may save $5 or even $10, in the next he may eat up all his previous savings. Besides, his old friend drinks and is more often out of money than he is. In such cases he must help his friend, by paying for meals and lodging.

After a month or so of such fruitless struggle, he is informed that the bank which backed the new refrigerator company has failed, and with it the new company itself; his invested money, to the last cent, is lost. This news, coupled with his failure in earning and saving money, makes him desperate. He asks himself: What's the matter with me? Am I a child, not a man, that I don't succeed in anything I undertake? Is it only hard luck or am I a weakling? What rosy dreams I had about this investment! What confident hopes I wrote to my home-folks! What should I write to them now? That I am stupid, good for nothing!

Still, not all hope is lost. He continues on odd jobs. As he feels at evenings lonely and restless, he learns little by little to drink whiskey, sometimes in company with his old friend, sometimes alone. When a little drunk he feels all right. After a time he notices that the drinking is developing into a regular habit with him. A fear of becoming a drunkard and of going down, gets hold of him. He decides to break with his old friend and to leave Chicago altogether.

Through a private employment agency he is shipped out to a lumber camp in Northern Michigan. He is to receive twenty-five dollars a month and board, for an eleven-hour work-day, and no Sunday work; the fee of the employment agent and transportation expenses are to be deducted from his first wages. The life and labor conditions in this camp are a little better than in the railway construction camp in the Dakotas where he worked several years before. On Sundays and when not working because of bad weather, he feels lonely and sad. To get rid of such feelings he drinks whiskey, which is secretly, against the company's rule, brought into the camp. He also plays poker once in a while. At the end of the second month he is exhausted -- "done" or "all in" -- and he quits.

He has forty dollars left. He freights back to Chicago in the hope of continuing his trade learning. But his school had been closed. Desperate, he drinks. After two weeks his money is gone. He is shipped out to an ice camp. The conditions there are still worse than those in the railway camp. After two weeks the work is done and he has only $15 to show for it. From that camp he goes to Milwaukee; buys some clothes and the rest of the money he "blows in." He visits a number of the employment offices. No shipments are being made. He turns to odd-job work. Some days he is quite successful, some days he is starving. On several occasions he has to spend the night in the park. When he succeeds in earning some money he drinks in company with similar casual and odd-job laborers.

When he is sober, he hears within himself a voice saying: You are a failure, a failure, a good-for-nothing! As he was not able to send any money as a present for his mother's last birthday, he was ashamed even to write a letter, and since then he has not written to his home. Occasionally he sends a letter to his sweetheart, informing her as to where he is and what he is doing. He is sorry for her.

When he is drunk his saloon friends invite him to see "the girls" sometimes; the day following such a visit, when he is sober, he suffers keenly for what he has done. And to get rid of this suffering he drinks again.

Disgusted with such a "dog's life," he tries to get a job in the country as a farm hand, which he finds through the local public employment office. The farm is in the vicinity of the city. The wages are $20 a month, with board and washing. He enjoys the farm work so familiar to him. He is a good laborer; the farmer is well pleased with him.

After a time he discovers, to his horror, that he is affected by a secret disease. He is so frightened by this discovery that he almost breaks down or becomes insane. Convinced that he is no longer fit to marry his sweetheart or any other woman, he sends a last letter to the girl, telling her that she must look for another, that he is done for as regards family life, and that she must forget him forever.

This is the most pathetic moment in his life. A temptation to commit suicide visits him for the first time. Only fear of death-pain -- "cowardice," as he puts it, telling his story to your investigator afterwards -- prevents his ending his "miserable life."

In regard to his health there is yet a little hope left. He remembers advertisements in the saloon toilet rooms in the city that such and such Dr. Applebaum or Niffelfield cures all secret diseases in a very short time. Although, taught by bitter experience, he is skeptical in regard to any advertisement, still who knows? There may be some truth in it; why not try? A drowning man grasps at a straw -- so does he. Given a day's leave of absence and a small sum of money by his employer, he goes to the city. He tells his trouble to his former saloon friends. Some of these laugh at him. Telling him that it is not worth bothering with at all; it is just like a cold -- no danger whatever. Some say that, danger or no danger, it is incurable, "there ain't any physician in the world who can fix it -- we have tried; no use in filling the pockets of doctors, better drink!"

He, being too much disturbed by his misfortune, does not drink at this time; he takes the address of the advertised doctor, and goes to him. The doctor assures him that his disease, though dangerous, is entirely curable, but that the entire healing will take some time. The patient is given medicine and invited to come again -- regularly every week. The compensation is fixed by the doctor as high as the patient's wages will permit. So he continues regularly to visit this physician, every Saturday. All his wages go to the curing of his disease, which sometimes disappears, only to return again.

At length the farming season, which lasts five months, is over. He is laid off. He has only a couple of dollars left. Losing hope of curing his disease, and seeing that it really does not bother him very much -- at least as far as his ability to work is concerned -- he ceases to care for it. He desires to be shipped out of Milwaukee. The next day he is sent to a lumber camp in northern Wisconsin. There he works the season through, though in different camps and for several concerns. When he is "all in" he goes to nearby towns to "rest," which practically means to remain in a drunken condition, sometimes in prostitution, or, as he says, "blowing in his money." He can not rest soberly, for he is, when not working, too lonely and sad.

After the lumber season he works in the ice camps; then in the spring on farms, plowing and seeding the fields. In early summer he freights to the wheat belt to do the harvesting work, beginning in the southerly States and finishing in the Dakotas in the fall. Then again the lumber camps, the ice camps -- and so goes his circle, year in and year out.

He is now a seasonal laborer. All ties between him and his home are broken; his family has moved meanwhile to another state, but he could hardly find where, even if he should care to do so. As far as his own personality and his ability for aggressiveness are concerned, his ambition is gone. If he has any criticism to make for his failures, he criticizes himself alone. He is now a self-confessed failure.

Only one faint hope is left him -- a strange expectation that he may strike in some way, somewhere, a tremendously promising opportunity. This is something like the alluring dream of a rich gold strike to a prospector. If this hoped-for opportunity were such that its realization might reasonably be expected, it would recreate in him a strong enthusiasm and confidence, as a result of which he would cease drinking, and would work and battle till he won out and became a victor in life, instead of a beaten man. But if one asks him of what nature is the opportunity he expects to find, he hardly has any definite object in his mind. He answers that it may happen that he will by chance become a prospector and strike a rich gold mine; or he may become a fisherman, at first for wages, afterwards independently; or he may find a very good job, working on which he will save lots of money; or he may specialize in some line of highly paid work; or he may by chance secure a homestead; or -- or -- and so on.

Led by such faint hope -- very faint, almost nothing in his mind, but strong enough in his sentiment -- he begins restlessly to roam over all the country, from north to south, from coast to coast, back and forth, working on this and that, moving from place to place by freighting or walking, seldom paying his way. Whatever money he succeeds in earning he "blows in" in short order.

He is now a migratory casual laborer. Migration -- constantly being on the move -- has become his habit. No matter how good the wages and other labor conditions on a certain job, he can not stay there longer than required to make a "stake" -- to earn a certain sum of money, specified in his own mind at the acceptance of the job. This stake is destined to help him to prosecute his immediate plans, to buy clothes and shoes, to have a "good time," to buy meals on his travels, or what not. But the main thing is, he must move; he must change his environment so as to see something new, interesting. To this end he has always a plan in his mind where to go and how to go.

When, years before, he had real ambition and real hope for his future, he enjoyed life, everything was bright and he was happy, joyous. But on meeting failure after failure his real ambition and hope broke down; life became dark and gloomy for him -- no natural enjoyment whatever was left. Labor is not always an enjoyment to him. It has only this advantage -- that he has no time to think very much about his situation, therefore he may feel indifferent to his lot. But when not working -- in the time of rest, travel, or unemployment -- how may he escape, then, his gloomy thoughts and sad feelings? By drinking? This artificial substitute for natural enjoyment lasts only short periods of time. A man can not always be drunk even if he has the money to buy drinks. What to do then, when not working and not drunk? The wonderful human nature invents other, one might say in common parlance "artificial," substitutes for "natural" enjoyment, and these are: The dream of a wonderful chance and the craving for environment, the new, the interesting. This partly explains why he can not stay long in the same place, but must keep moving.

Up to this time in his life he has never begged, never applied for charity, and never stolen anything except rides on railways, which is not considered at all immoral by laborers. His strong self-respect will not allow him to resort to illegitimate means of securing a livelihood. To these he prefers starving and he approaches starvation many times. He has asked for meals or lodging at doors -- yes, but always in exchange for his labor.

Now, he is getting older; he feels more tired; and meets more troubles with his health, than ever before. In addition to this an industrial depression sets in, creating serious unemployment. He happens to be in Philadelphia, at the time, still keeping up by doing odd jobs. As the number of the unemployed is rapidly increasing, the competition for jobs, especially for odd jobs, becomes keener and keener. He fails to find work and is starving. As a result he finds himself begging in the streets -- for the first time in his life. This humiliates him greatly in his own eyes, but he must choose between starving to death or asking alms. He chooses the latter, intending to beg only once and hoping to find some sort of work the following day. However, the next day he has to beg again; the repetition is a little easier

-- the rubicon of self-respect was crossed yesterday. And so it goes.

In the next city or during the next winter, when he again fails to find work and is hard pressed by want, he begs. He also has learned to apply for charity. Once or twice he steals small sums of money from his drunken saloon friends, not to speak of stealing meals which he successfully attempts a number of times. So he falls lower and lower, in his self-respect.

Still he is a laborer -- a hobo, one should say. He prefers to earn his livelihood by labor whenever he has a chance to do so, and really most of his living is so earned -- by work in railway construction camps, harvesting fields, on odd jobs, and so forth. Only his periods of remaining on a job are rapidly shortening. He no longer works for a large stake; he desires to earn "just a few dollars" on one job and then quit. Time goes on. The less he works the more he roams and begs -- until he quits work altogether.

Now he is a tramp -- a down-and-out of the common type. Physically he is still able to work, but psychically he is not. He has come to hate labor. If one asks why he does not want to labor he will answer: To labor? Why should I labor? I have labored, worked hard -- years, tens of years, but the labor did not help me; it let me fall down where I am as you see me!

An almost similar answer he would give to the question as to why he has lost religion: I believed in God, I was a regular church-goer, and prayed fervently up to 25 years of age. I prayed, sometimes with tears, that God would help me; but no help was forthcoming. I perceived that either there is no God or if there is a God He does not care for me -- why, then, should I believe in Him?

The same negative philosophy he expresses toward the labor movement: Labor unions, labor parties and organizations! What good are they doing? Years ago, on several occasions, I wanted to join a labor union. The first thing was, they demanded from me a trade training, money for dues, and, if I had both, I still must find a union job by myself. Unions may be good for their own members, not for outsiders, for common laborers!

He does not believe in Government laws and institutions; he has a very low opinion of courts and the police. He is a wild individualist with the philosophy of "every man for himself and the devil take the hindmost."

In his movements as a tramp he has some sort of regularity according to climatic conditions. In the summer time

300

he frequents the cities and country towns around the Great Lakes in the North. In the fall he migrates toward the South, spending the winter in the cities and country towns around the Gulf. He is there called the "snow bird."

He still carries with him his old child-like dream of a wonderful chance waiting for him somewhere, although he does not consider it so seriously as before. Soberly talking, he admits that there is no hope whatever left in him, and that he is just "human wreckage," nothing else. He would have done away with himself altogether, long ago, if it had not been for his cowardice before the death-pain.

After a number of years he ends his days in a poor-house, a correction farm, a jail, or an asylum, or he lies in a city morgue, unidentified, among others similar to himself.

TWO EXAMPLES OF THE "LIFE STORIES"
OF MIGRATORY WORKERS,
FROM THE FIELD NOTES OF PETER A. SPEEK

November 20, 1913. Milwaukee

Number 1. Age 33 years. Strong and healthy in appearance.

Says that he is not a tramp, nor even a hobo; just a
"rounder" or casual laborer; English-Scotch; steamship fireman; has lived in the United States several times, three
years altogether; this time, since May of this year.

Parents live in Liverpool, England; he does not corres-
pond with them; he used to send them money, but not any
more. He has no home in America, no relatives, no friends
except other "rounders" like himself. He quit his foreman
work on the steamships because of the dirt, heat, darkness
and small pay -- in general, the "dog's life." He wanted to
earn more money by working "on land." But he very soon
discovered that he can't keep jobs, no matter how good they
are. Although he likes work, he can't stand its monotony;
he wants constant change, has a wandering feeling; besides,
the "whiskey fever" gets hold of him sometimes. He can not
work on a "steady" job longer than two weeks; if the job is
very good he can work one month -- this is the limit for
him. When he works he does not drink, does not even think
of whiskey; but when he quits a job, and gets paid, his old
enemy the whiskey fever comes "darn quickly" upon him, and
in a few days all his money is gone. He does not drink
alone, but in company with other "rounders." His company
hangs around saloons and red-light districts, but he never
had any sexual disease.

Last fall he was a fireman on a steamship in Argentine
waters. After six weeks he deserted the ship in Bratford
City, because he was locked up for having got a "little
drop." He and two other deserted sailors lived in a railway
shack; some days they were starving, other days they would
go "around the market" and had plenty to eat -- "mighty good
people are down in Argentina." But most of their living was
earned by making copper rings from two-cent coins and selling them to the natives, getting from one peso to three
pesos (about $1 to $3) for each ring. This kind of life he
continued three months; he then became disgusted with it,
especially when one of the trio was arrested for fighting on
the street.

He then went to Buenos Ayres and through the Sailors'
Home got a fireman's job on a ship; conditions of work and
wages were the same. The ship sailed to Hull, England.

From there he went to Cardiff. There he got another job but
missed the ship because he was drunk. For this a mark was
made in his book which meant that he could not get a job on
any ship in Cardiff. He lived six weeks in Cardiff, during
which time he was supported partly by his friends and partly
by a sailors' organization. He walked 160 miles to South-
ampton; on the road he slept in haystacks and barns; worked
on odd jobs for his meals -- sometimes begged. In Southamp-
ton he got a fireman's job on the Majestic. The work on
this ship was the hardest he had ever experienced; pay was
six pounds a month with board. When the Majestic came to
New York in May of this year he deserted the ship. He
wanted to see if he could "make a stake" -- money, or a
fortune, in America; at first to earn and save money, then
to try some business enterprise. "Money is bigger here than
anywhere else in the world." At first he wanted to come to
the Great Lakes and to try a fireman's position here; he was
told that the pay was good and work was easy. But he had
not the money for the railway ticket. Wanting to earn it,
he applied to an Italian private employment office, to which
he paid $2 in advance; he was shipped to Middletown, N.Y.
Here he was employed by Jackson Bros., contractors in
making new roads. His work consisted of shoveling and
digging earth, loading cars, etc.; hard and exhausting work;
nine hours a day; $1.75 a day; lived in the company's shack,
for which he paid 25 cents a week; prepared his own meals;
bought the material from the commissary store of the same
Italian private employment bureau; prices were moderate;
mostly "canned stuff." This store also sold bottled beer.
Very little money was left after a week's work; worked four
weeks to earn and save money for railway ticket to the Great
Lakes. Seeing that no money could be saved and becoming
exhausted by hard labor, all the "white men" -- a dozen of
them -- including this man, left the work.

He went back to New York. Here he applied to another
private employment office, paid $2 for fees in advance, and
was shipped free to Buffalo to work on a railway in an
"extra gang"; work in replacing ties and rails; hard work;
ten hours a day; $1.65 a day. He refused to work because
there would not be money left, and the work was a "horse's
work." He went to the Seamen's Institute and applied for a
job as a fireman on a ship, but he did not get it. He then
jumped a freight train to Conneaut, Ohio. There he hired
out to a farmer to plant potatoes; worked twelve hours a
day; got $1.50 a day and board; it was fine work and the
farmer was a good man. The work was finished in three days.
He then went to Ashtabula, Ohio. He got work at once on the
street, laying blocks, cement, etc.; ten hours a day; pay
$2.25; the work was hard and tiresome; worked one week.
Then to save money he jumped a freight train to Cleveland.
Seeing that there was nothing doing, he jumped the freight
train again and went to Lorain, a small factory town. The

303

next afternoon he jumped another freight train to Bellevue; again he found no work; he then "freighted" out to Fort Wayne, Ind. There he shoveled coal a day – 10 hours – and got $2.

The next day he saw an advertisement in the newspaper that the circus of Ringling Bros. wanted men. He applied and got a job which consisted of putting up and taking down a big tent and all sorts of other work; worked day and night; had little sleep; the worst job he ever had in his life; pay $30 a month with board. After three weeks he quit in LaSalle, Ill. He took a freight train to Rock Island, Ill. where he got work on the street; 10 hours; $2.25 a day; very hard work. After five days he quit again. As he was looking for easier work he got a job at throwing coal out of cars; pay was 10 cents per ton; earned $1.50 a day. He was then put to work on an ice wagon for $2.25 a day; as he was on another man's place his job continued for only three days. He then got a job as a deck hand on the excursion steamer <u>Mississippi</u>; but there was no sleeping place or other accomodation; pay was only $1 a day with board. After six days he became sick of this work and quit. The next place was on a freight steamer, <u>The Morning Star</u>, going to St. Paul. He worked for three days, getting $1 a day, until he landed in St. Paul the latter part of August.

From there he walked to Hastings, Minn., which is 18 miles. On the way he picked potatoes on a farm for half a day, for $1. He could have continued but the picking machine broke. While in the street of Hastings a farmer accosted him in front of a saloon and hired him as a farm-hand for $1.75 a day; to do the chores and all sorts of farm work. Although the job was a good one the whiskey fever got hold of him and he quit. After two days he applied to a private employment bureau, paying $2 in advance. He then was shipped free to Ambroo, N.D. to work on a farm; he did not go to work on the farm, but found work on the Soo Line, removing ties and rails; 10 hours a day; pay $2.25 a day; he worked slowly and easily and the boss was kind. When four weeks passed the weather became cold and the ground was covered with snow, so he did not care to work there any longer and jumped a train back to Minneapolis. There he applied to an employment office connected with a lodging and boarding house. The fee was only 50 cents, for which two meals were given, besides the job. This bureau shipped him free to Superior to work in repairing railroad; but he was under a bad spell of his "whiskey fever," and his head ached and he did not go to work.

He very soon applied to the State Free Employment Office, which shipped him out to Birchwood, near Spooner, to a railway construction camp, to smooth surface and to lay steel, etc; 10 hours a day; pay $1.25 a day; paid $4.50 for

board furnished by the company. Slept in box car, which was
dirty inside; bedding was dirty and very lousy; he could not
stand the life for more than three days, so he took out his
pay from the commissary store in tobacco; did not get any
money. He then walked to Cameron, 16 miles; there he jumped
a freight train to Presser Junction, where he found work on
a bridge, putting up a new arch; 10 hours for $2 a day.
After two weeks, work was stopped by a shortage of material.
He and other men did not like to waste time waiting, so they
quit. He jumped a train to Minneapolis and waited there for
his earnings two days, in which time he did not eat anything
-- was starving. When he got his money he started to have a
good time, drank heavily, went to moving picture theatres,
courted the girls, etc. When the money was gone he tramped
to Midway and found a job at once on a new building. He
mixed cement, passed materials, etc.; 10 hours a day; 25
cents an hour. Worked nine days and quit because the job
was finished. He then went to St. Paul, where he jumped a
freight train for Chicago, but got "ditched" in LaCrosse.
The "bulls" took him to the police station, from which he
was freed the next morning. From LaCrosse he came to Milwaukee yesterday.

He prefers the old country, England, to America, because here is too much "hustle" and the work is too heavy.
He sometimes considers committing suicide -- to get out of
misery. He has never applied for public charity. He thinks
of going back to the old country to remain there till his
days are over. He has good intentions and ambitions, if it
were not for his wandering spirit and whiskey fever -- he
asserts. In most cases other "wanderers" with whom he works
lure him to drink, and if once he is started he goes to the
limit.

His future plans are as follows: He will pull out of
Milwaukee tomorrow by jumping a freight train towards the
South. He will go through St. Louis to New Orleans and
spend the winter in Louisiana and Texas by "rounding." He
intends to return then to Chicago, Milwaukee and Minneapolis, and to freight to the Pacific Coast, at first to Seattle. He wants to see the far west; he never has been there,
and there may be a "good opening" for him - to start a
"man's life." If not, he will work his way on a steamship
to Australia; if the life is not better there, and he remains still a failure -- "just a human wreckage" -- he will
return to England for the rest of his miserable life.

July 10, 1914, Jungle, Redfern, S. Dakota

Number 3. Age 24 years, Dane.

Seven years in this country. Came to America because
it is the best country in the world. The best opportunities
to better himself.

Latin (High School) education. Started out as a sailor
Learned steamer engineering. Quit it because of the hardships and monotony in the life of a sailor. Pay was from $5
to $20 a month. Worked in various industries in America.
Had a job in the shipyard at Philadelphia, $2 a day, 10
hours; treatment first class. Quit. Started to go sailing
on the Great Lakes -- higher wages, more opportunity of
saving money. Could not get job because of the sailors'
union; entrance fees $25; he had not the money. A job in a
factory -- one day, conditions bad; secured a job in a
rubber works; $1.50, afterwards $1.75; 10 hours a day. Laid
off because of the business depression. Went out to a farm
to pick potatoes at $1 a day, 10 hours; the board was good.
Returned to the East. No work for four or five months. Got
money from home, about $200 -- his own saved money. Went
back to Buffalo, paid his way. Was told that a steel plant
was to be opened there. Did not get work there -- because
nearly all men taken were South European immigrants. Wanted
to enter the union. The union did not let him in because
too many old members were around out of work. The Lake
Carriers' Association declared open shop. Got a job from
this association. It was necessary to sign a statement
declaring loyalty to association or to union. He signed the
union oath, after which he was fired.

Started for the West. Believed that the West was
better. Went broke in Chicago. Went into restaurant asking
for dish washing. Did not get work, but got meals. Went to
Santa Fe. Beat his way down to Missouri. Went over the
country roads not very far from Kansas City. Avoided the
city because of the fear of getting arrested for vagrancy.
Asked farmers for job. Begged. Got one job at 50 cents a
day for five days, when the job was done. After buying some
clothing, 25 cents left. Bought a loaf of bread, ice cream
-- all money gone. Went into Nebraska -- westward. Several
days without eating, except apples. Got a job, with a
German farmer, haymaking, $1.50 a day, 10 to 11 hours. Good
board, slept in the barn. Treatment was fine. Six days,
the job was done. Partner got hurt very badly, trying to
get a freight train and was sent home East. Continued his
way toward West. Freighted. Got a job on a farm in Nebraska, $18 a month. Chores and general farm work, 10 hours.
Board good. Got hurt after three months. Right foot was
hurt by mowing machine. Two weeks ill. Doctor's bill $15.
Paid it himself. Was young, no company for him, the life

was too monotonous on the farm. Working all the time in the
fields, wages low, hours long. Quit, although the farmer
promised $30 a month; he could buy calves and pasture them,
free of charge, and market them for his own benefit. Perhaps this was a little opportunity for him, but for the
reasons stated he left.

Went to Denver -- westward. Two weeks. Looked for
jobs through private employment agencies. Paid for fees
$1.50. Was shipped to Moffatt Road; in railway construction
camp; $2 a day or 20 cents an hour, 10 hours; two days.
Quit. Got work in a coal mine. Outside night work; $2.25,
9 hours. Mine camp four or six men slept in each room, two
in a bed; dirty mattress, dirty blankets. Lousy. No ventilation, no spittoons. No sanitary rules; no garbage collections. No toilet -- go anywhere in the hills. One week.
Left because snow storm. Went westward, beat his way to
Salt Lake City. Broke. Two days in Salt Lake City. Asked
a fellow in the street where a man without money could get a
bed. Slept in a saloon. Begged. Sold his razor. Was
shipped out with 800 men to the Western Pacific construction
camp in Nevada. On the road two days and two nights without
meals. Some fellows ate raw potatoes picked up. Were taken
to the end of the new track. Box cars. Some with provisions. The men stormed the cars with provisions and took
cheese, bread, and a few canned stuffs. He got several
cans. Hiked 20 miles into the desert. Wanted to go to the
Southern Pacific. Took a train down the line. Got a job on
a construction camp on Western Pacific, $1.75 a day, 10
hours. The board was poor. It was a slave-driving job;
lousy bunks in tents; 12 days; quit. Went South into another camp, conditions were slightly better, $2 a day, better
work. Quit. Got sick from cold. No medical aid. Went to
California, to San Francisco; 50 cents in pocket; 3 weeks.
Was on Barbary Coast. Hung around the red-light district.
Down-and-outs hang around there for the "Sports" (rich
people) come there, spend money lavishly. He did begging.
Entered a mission called "Whosoever Will." He wanted to
have a Christmas breakfast. Promised by the mission. About
2,000 people had gathered, the street was full; almost a
riot occurred. The hungry people were waiting for that
breakfast the whole night. He got inside. Got for breakfast rotten fish, could not eat it; two slices bread and
coffee -- bread was all right. The mission wanted the men
to come for dinner, for parading through the streets. He
refused, his self-respect was against it. (The men conduc-
ting the "Holy Mission" had made $300,000 out of these poor
people through their work, donations, and any kind of manipulation. The mission crooks were afterwards arrested.)

He left for the South to pick oranges; put to work by
police on street cleaning in a small town. Worked a day
then told to get out of town. No trial. Went to Los An-

geles. A job for the city, pick and shovel, $2.25 a day, 8 hours. Worked five months. Quit -- too hot. Went sailing. One year sailing. Got sick. Thought he had consumption, but had only cold. Went to Portland, Oregon. Went to work in Columbia Digger Co., $50.00 a month. Board and room all were good. Worked 8 months as second engineer. No more work. Laid off in the winter time. $125 saved. Went to Los Angeles.

Joined I.W.W. in Portland. In Los Angeles was elected secretary of this organization, but he did not get any pay. Took part in the Madero Revolution in Mexico. Three months on the battle-ground. The command had about 200 men; about half were Americans. It had control over several towns. He did shooting. He is sure he killed one federal. Was selected financial secretary of a town. No pay. Was handed about $1900. Bought ammunition. Had machine guns made in Los Angeles. Their command got defeated by Federals who had 1500 men. The command in which he was fighting lost three or four men. Retreated to the United States, surrendered to the United States troops. He beat his way across the line. Went to Los Angeles. Was hidden there for a time. Went to San Pedro. Got a steam schooner. Went to San Francisco. Then to Portland. Had a little money, about $10. Could steal in Mexico -- big money, but did not -- the money belonged to his fellow workers. Went to work right away in Portland for the same company as before. Conditions the same. Worked there six months. Job done in winter; $150 saved. All winter there in Portland. Got a job of dishwashing; $8 a week and meals, 12 hours, two weeks. Quit. Too long hours, not enough money; out of work two months. Got a secret disease.

In 1913 went to a lumber camp near Seattle, Washington, to drive donkies, $3.25. Board good. Slept in bunks. One-man bunks in two layer tiers. Bedding straw, own blankets, vermin. No laundry, washing, bathing, toilet facilities, no screens, no sanitary rules. Worked 11 hours; had 1-1/2 miles to hike out to the work place each day. Got up about 5 o'clock; stopped at 5:45 at night. Worked 2 weeks. Quit. Long hours. Bad conditions. Went to Portland to work for the same company. Later he worked on a boat of the same company. Joined the new Longshoreman's Union. This fought another union but lost out. Went to work for the Columbia Digger Company. Conditions the same. Work the same. Worked to the first of January 1914. Got laid off. No work. Took a contract to chop cordwood; 500 cords; $1 a cord. Spent all his money for tools and provisions and shipment out to the place -- spent about $100. When he, with his partner, got there, they discovered they were cheated by a crooked contractor. No work.

Returned to Portland. Was broke. Partner got $10 from

his father. Took another contract to clear land, two acres, $50 an acre; and to cut 100 cords of wood, $1 a cord; got cheated also; the land was harder to clear than the owner told. It rained and snowed also. Left. Did not earn a cent during 1-1/2 months of work. Were broke, absolutely -- provisions all gone, the farmer did not even take their tools to the depot, because he had not time; he really wanted to have their tools. Got another job on a farm, 20 cents an hour to clear land; got potatoes, apples and milk free. Made about $10. Work done. Went to Portland. Beat his way to Seattle. Nothing doing in the woods. In Seattle about a week. Stayed with a friend. Went back to Portland, beat it. Broke. Stayed down on the dredge, even slept there. Went hungry. Went to work for that company -- again $60 a month and own board. Worked until the latter part of May. No work. Laid off. Got another job for another company as a deck hand, $45 a month; good board; too long hours, 14 to 15 hours, sometimes only four hours for slee- ping; slept in the "dog hole." Worked 20 days. Quit -- could not stand it. Went to Seattle, June 21; no work in Seattle. Started for harvest in Montana, beating his way. Got ditched lots of times. Paid to carmen, for the tips, from 25 cents to 50 cents every time. He had some money, bought some stuff. Made tramp mulligan in jungles. No jobs in Montana. Thousands of idle men there; you could not even buy a job there. Came to Aberdeen, then to Redfield; 10 days here, out of work. Had money for first two or three days. Now about seven days broke. Begging of farmers, asking for work; these give meals anyhow. Sleeps in box cars and haystacks.

Immediate plans: to work here in the harvest fields, then in North Dakota, then elsewhere to save money, to go home to his mother in Denmark, and to stay there more or less permanently. In Los Angeles lived with a girl for four months like married people; she got $5 in a department store; he got $13.50 a week. The best time he ever had in this country. Loved each other. Could not marry. Wages were low; were afraid.

In addition to works cited, this bibliography includes items
that either corroborate the illustrations selected for the
text, or contribute to an understanding of the cultural
background of violence and industrialization in the Progressive Era. Several collections of primary source materials
have been indexed from this point of view: the Commission on
Industrial Relations' Final Report and Testimony, and its
unpublished reports in the National Archives; Wayne State
University Labor History Archives' Industrial Workers of the
World Collection; and the State Historical Society of Wis
consin's Collection of Material on or about the Industrial
Workers of the World. Because the focus was on attitudes
and perceptions of contemporaries of the IWW, "Primary Sources" include any work written before 1940; "Secondary Sources" refer (with a few exceptions) to later works.

PRIMARY SOURCES: BOOKS

Adamic, Louis. Dynamite: The Story of Class Violence in
    America. Rev. ed. New York, 1934.

American Civil Liberties Union. The Police And The Radi-
    cals: What 88 Police Chiefs Think and Do About Radical
    Meetings. New York, March 1921.

_____. Who May Safely Advocate Force and Violence?.
    New York, 1922.

Anderson, Nels. The Hobo: The Sociology of the Homeless
    Man. Chicago, 1923.

_____. Men on the Move. Chicago, 1940.

Bellamy, Edward. Looking Backward, 2000-1887. New York,
    1917.

Bonnett, Clarence E. Employers' Associations in the United
    States: A Study of Typical Associations. New York,
    1922.

Brissenden, Paul F. The I.W.W.: A Study of American Syndicalism. New York, 1919.

_____. "Underemployment." In Business Cycles and Unemployment. New York, 1923.

Carnegie, Andrew. Autobiography of Andrew Carnegie. New York, 1920.

_____. The Gospel of Wealth, And Other Timely Essays. Ed. Edward C. Kirkland. Cambridge, Mass., 1962.

_____. The Empire of Business. New York, 1902.

_____. Triumphant Democracy; or, Fifty Years' March of The Republic. New York, 1886.

Chapin, Robert C. The Standard of Living Among Workingmen's Families in New York City. New York, 1909.

Chaplin, Ralph. Wobbly: The Rough-and-Tumble Story of an American Radical. Chicago, 1948.

Commons, John R. History of Labour in the United States. 4 vols. New York, 1918-35.

Conwell, Russell H. Acres of Diamonds. New York, 1915.

Croly, Herbert. The Promise of American Life. New York, 1909.

Delaney, Ed and M. T. Rice. The Bloodstained Trail. Seattle, 1927.

Dos Passos, John. The Big Money. New York, 1937.

Douglas, Paul H. Real Wages in the United States, 1890-1926. Boston, 1930.

Faulkner, Harold U. The Quest For Social Justice, 1898-1914. New York, 1951.

Fitch, John A. The Causes of Industrial Unrest. New York, 1924.

Flynn, Elizabeth Gurley. I Speak My Own Piece: Autobiography of the Rebel Girl. New York, 1955.

Gambs, John S. The Decline of the I.W.W. New York, 1932.

Goldman, Emma. Living My Life. New York, 1934.

Hapgood, Norman. ed. Professional Patriots. New York,

1927.

Hanson, Ole. *Americanism Versus Bolshevism*. New York.
1920.

Harré, T. Everett. *The IWW an Auxiliary of the German
Espionage System. History of IWW anti-war activities,
showing how the IWW program of sabotage inspired the
Kaiser's agents in America*. With introduction by
R[alph] M. Easley. N.P. [1918].

Hayes, Carleton J. *Essays on Nationalism*. New York, 1926.

_____. *Nationalism: A Religion*. New York, 1960.

Haywood, Bill. *Bill Haywood's Book*. New York, 1929.

Howard, Sidney. *The Labor Spy*. New York, 1924.

Hoxie, Robert F. *Trade Unionism in the United States*. New
York, 1921.

Hubbard, Elbert. *A Message To Garcia*. East Aurora, N.Y.,
1899.

Hunter, Robert A. *Poverty*. New York, 1917.

_____. *Violence and The Labor Movement*. New York,
1922.

LeBon, Gustave. *The Crowd: A Study of the Popular Mind*.
London, 1952 [1896].

Martin, Everett Dean. *The Behavior of Crowds: A Psychological Study*. New York, 1920.

Mereto, Joseph J. *The Red Conspiracy*. New York, 1920.

Mitchell, John. *Organized Labor*. Philadelphia, 1903.

Mott, George F., Jr. *San Diego -- Politically Speaking*.
San Diego, 1932.

National Civil Liberties Bureau. *War-Time prosecutions and
Mob Violence, involving the rights of free speech, free
press and peaceful assemblage. From April 1, 1917 to
March 1, 1919*. New York, 1919.

Nearing, Scott. *Financing The Wage Earner's Family*. New
York, 1913.

Orth, Samuel P. *Armies of Labor: A Chronicle of the
Organized Wage-Earners*. The Chronicles of America

Series, Vol. XL, Abraham Lincoln Edition. New Haven, Yale University Press, 1919.

Parker, Carleton H. The California Casual. New York, 1920.

_____. The Casual Laborer and Other Essays. New York, 1920.

Perlman, Selig, and Phillip Taft. The History of Labor in the United States: 1896-1932. New York, 1935.

Riis, Jacob A. A Ten Year's War. Boston, 1900.

_____. The Battle With The Slums. New York, 1902.

_____. How the Other Half Lives. New York, 1957 [1890]

Ryan, John A. A Living Wage. New York, 1912.

Schroeder, Theodore. Free Speech for Radicals. New York, 1916.

Smith, Walker C. The Everett Massacre: A History of the Class Struggle in the Lumber Industry. Chicago, 19[17]

Sorel, Georges. Reflections on Violence. Tr. T. E. Hulme and J. Roth. New York, 1961 [1908].

Steiger, John H. The Memoirs of a Silk Striker; an Exposure of the Principles and Tactics of the I.W.W. [Paterson, N.J.], privately printed, 1914.

Streightoff, Frank H. The Standard of Living Among The Industrial People of America. Boston, 1911.

Symes, Lillian and Travers Clement. Rebel America: The Story of Social Revolt in the United States. New York, 1934.

Taylor, Albion Guilford. Labor Policies of the National Association of Manufacturers. Urbana, 1928.

Todes, Charlotte. Labor and Lumber. New York, 1931.

VanCleave, James W[allace]. Americanism, The True Solution of the Labor Problem. National Association of Manufacturers Pamphlet no. 10. New York, 1908.

_____. Industrial Education As An Essential Factor in Our National Prosperity. National Association of Manufacturers Pamphlet no. 9. New York, 1908.

Veblen, Thorstein. <u>Essays in Our Changing Order</u>. New York, 1934.

Whitman, Walt. <u>Leaves of Grass</u>. New York, 1914.

_____. "The Tramp and Strike Question." In <u>Complete Prose Works</u>. Boston, 1907.

Witte, Edwin E. <u>The Government in Labor Disputes</u>. New York, 1932.

Wolman, Leo. <u>The Growth of American Trade Unions, 1880-1923</u>. New York, 1924.

PRIMARY SOURCES: ARTICLES

"The Acquittal of William D. Haywood." <u>Arena</u>, 38 (September 1907), 332-33.

"After the Battle." <u>Survey</u>, April 6, 1912, 1-2.

"Attacking National Self-Respect." Editorial. <u>American Industries</u>, 14 (May 1914), 8-9.

"Bands of Men who Disregard the Law." Editorial. <u>American Industries</u>, 14 (January 1914), 33.

Bent, George P. "Cooperation and the Invisible Government." <u>Am. Industries</u>, 14 (August 1913), 18.

Blyth, Samuel G. "Our Imported Troubles and Trouble Makers." <u>The Saturday Evening Post</u>, 190, no. 45 (May 11, 1918), 3-4, 41-45.

Booth, Edward Townsend. "The Wild West." <u>Atlantic Monthly</u>, 120 (December 1920), 785-788.

Brooks, John Graham. "The Shadow of Anarchy: The Industrial Workers of the World." <u>Survey</u>, 28, no. 1, April 6, 1912, 80-82.

Bruere, Robert W. "Following the I.W.W. Trail." <u>New York Evening Post</u>, Sunday Supplements, November 1917-March, 1918.

_____. "Notes on the I.W.W. in Arizona and the Northwest." In <u>Reconstruction after the War. Journal of the National Institute of Social Sciences</u>, vol. 4 (April 1, 1918), 99-108.

Bryce, Joseph W. "The Establishment of Industrial Peace."
    Am. Industries, 12 (June 1912), 35.

Coleman, N. F. "The I.W.W. and the Law: Everett." Sunset
    Magazine, The Pacific Monthly, 39 (July 1917), 35, 68-7(

Currie, B. W. "How the West Dealt with the Industrial Work-
    men [sic] of the West." Harper's Weekly, 51 (June 22,
    1907), 908-10.

Darrow, Clarence. "Darrow's Speech in the Haywood Case."
    Wayland's Monthly (October 1907).

Dosch, Arno. "What the I.W.W. is." World's Work, 26
    (August 1913), 406-420.

Dowell, Eldridge Foster. "A History of Criminal Syndicalism
    Legislation in the United States." Johns Hopkins Uni-
    versity Studies in Historical and Political Science, 57
    (1939).

Dueberg, Helmuth. "I.W.W.'s Attempt to Organize
    Discontent." Los Angeles Times, August 16, 1914,
    pt. vi, p. 4.

Duff, Hezekiah N. "The I.W.W.'s: What They Are and What
    They Are Trying to Do." Square Deal, 10 (May 1912),
    297-310.

Eastman, Max. "I.W.W.: The Great American Scapegoat." New
    Review, 2 (August 1914), 465-470.

Edwards, George. "Free Speech in San Diego." Mother Earth,
    10 (July 1915), 182-85.

Emery, James A. "Shall the Decalogue Be Repealed?" Am.
    Industries, 13 (June 1913), 17.

"Enemy Within Our Midst." The Gateway. 29 (December 1917),
    13-16.

Fitch, J[ohn] A. "Baiting the I.W.W." Survey, 33 (March 6,
    1915), 634-35.

_____. "Class Fighters and a Hobo Who Solved A
    Problem." Survey, 32 (September 5, 1914), 558-560.

_____. "The I.W.W., an Outlaw Organization." Survey,
    30 (June 7, 1913), 355-362.

Flynn, Elizabeth Gurley. "The Fight for Spokane Justice."
    International Socialist Rev., 10 (December 1909), 483-
    89.

_____. "The Shame of Spokane." International Social-
    ist Rev., 10 (January 1910), 610-619.

Gannett, Lewis S. "The I.W.W." Nation, 111 (October 20,
    1920), 448.

Gilmore, Inez Haynes. "At the Industrial Hearings."
    Masses, 6 (March 1915), 8-9.

Goldman, Emma. "The Outrage in San Diego." Mother Earth, 7
    (June 1912), 116-118.

Gompers, Samuel. Editorial. "Destruction the avowed pur-
    pose of the I.W.W." American Federationist, 20 (July
    1913), 533-537.

Grant, Luke. "The Haywood Trial: A Review." Outlook, 86
    (1907), 855-862.

_____. "Idaho Murder Trial." Outlook, 85 (1907), 805-
    811.

Griswold, Alfred Whitney. "New Thought: A Cult of
    Success." Am. J. of Soc., 40, no. 3 (November 1934),
    309-318.

Heaton, James P. "The Legal Aftermath of the Lawrence
    Strike." Survey, 28 (July 6, 1912), 503-10.

_____. "The Salem Trial." Survey, 29 (December 7,
    1912), 301-04.

Heslewood, Fred. "Barbarous Spokane." International
    Socialist Rev., 10 (February 1910), 705-13.

Hill, Mary A[nderson]. "The Free Speech Fight at San
    Diego." Survey, 28 (May 4, 1912), 192-94.

Hopkins, Ernest Jerome. "The San Diego Fight." The Coming
    Nation (May 4, 1912), 8-9.

"Industrial Relations Commission Reports." Editorial. Am.
    Industries, 16 (September 1915), 12-14.

"The Industrial Workers of the World." The New York Evening
    Post, November 2, 1912, Saturday supplement, pp. 1, 2;
    November 9, 1912, Saturday supplement, pp. 1, 3; Novem-
    ber 16, 1912, Saturday supplement, p. 2.

"The I.W.W." Resolution Adopted in Convention. Am.
    Industries. 13 (June 1913), 12.

"I.W.W. Beaten in Dominion [of British Columbia]." Los

Angeles Times, June 6, 1915, Pt. vi. p. 3, columns 1,
2. 3.

"The I.W.W. Develops Into A National Menace." Current
Opinion 63 (1917), 153-4.

"The Industrial Workers of the World Make Confession."
Square Deal, 13 (October 1913), 236-238.

Kirby, John, Jr. "A Disloyal and Unpatriotic Organization."
Am. Industries, 12 (August 1911), 10.

_____. "The Political Factor in the Industrial
Unrest." Am. Industries, 13 (June 1913), 14.

_____. "Tolerance and Consequence." Am. Industries,
13 (November 1912), 10.

"'Knights of Liberty' in Oklahoma." The Class Struggle, 2,
no. 3 (May-June 1918), 371-375.

"The Larger Aspects of the McNamara Case." Survey, 27
(December 30, 1911), 1413-29.

Luepp, Constance D. "The Lawrence Strike Hearings."
Survey, 27 (March 23, 1912), 1953-1954.

Lippman, Walter. "The I.W.W. - Insurrection or Revolution?"
New Review, 1 (August 1913), 701-706.

Lovejoy, Owen R. "Right of Free Speech in Lawrence."
Survey, 27 (March, 9, 1912), 1904.

Marcy, Leslie H. "800 percent and the Akron Strike." Int.
Soc. Rev., 8 (April 1913), 711-724.

"Menace of the I.W.W." Houston Labor Journal (November 2,
1912), 1.

"Mollie Maguires in the West," Independent, 60 (March 8,
1906), 536.

Nevin, A. Parker. "Some Problems of American Industry."
Am. Industries, 14 (March 1914), 13.

"The New Socialism That Threatens the Social System." New
York Times, Sunday, March 17, 1912, Pt. V, pp. 1, 2.

"Organization or Anarchy." Editorial. The New Republic, 11
(July 21, 1917), 320-322.

Parker, Carleton. "The California Casual and His Revolt."
Quart. Journal of Economics (November 1915), 110-126.

_____. "The I.W.W." Atlantic Monthly, 120 (November 1917), 651-662.

"Patriotism in the Middle West." The Masses, 9 (June 1917), 19-21.

"The Perversion of the Ideal. A Reply to the Doctrine of Syndicalism as Advocated by the I.W.W." International Molders' Journal (August 1913), 635-38.

Pope, George. "A Message From Colonel Pope." Am. Industries, 13 (June 1913), 7.

Randolph, H. S. "The I.W.W." The Common Cause, 1, no. 5 (May 1912), 1-9.

"The Real Menace to Unionism." Labor Digest (April 1912), 1-7.

"Salvaging the Unemployable." Editorial. The New Republic, 4 (October 15, 1915), 221-223.

Short, Wallace M. "How One Town Learned A Lesson in Free Speech." Survey, 35 (October 30, 1915), 106-108.

"Socialism in the Colleges." Am. Industries, 13 (July 1913), 11. (Reprinted from The Century Magazine, July 1913.)

Speek, Peter Alexander. "The Psychology of Floating Workers." Annals of the American Academy of Political and Social Science, 69 (January 1917), 72-78.

Stevenson, Frederick Boyd. "The I.W.W. - A World Menace to Civilization." Brooklyn Eagle, Sunday, April 28, 1912, Magazine section, pp. 1, 2, illustrated.

Thompson, Chas. W. "The New Socialism that threatens the social system." New York Times, Sunday, March 17, 1912, pt. v., pp. 1-2.

Tucker, Irwin St. J[ohn]. "The Church and the I.W.W." Churchman (August 30, 1913), 278-290 [New York].

"The Unemployable." Editorial. Am. Industries, 14 (April 1914), 10.

Wernicke, O. H. L. "Sorry for the Boy." Am. Industries, 12 (October 1911), 10.

West, George P. "The Mesabi Range Strike." The New Republic, 8 (September 2, 1916), 109.

Weston, Edmund. "Some Principles of the I.W.W." American Employer (July 1913), 713-718.

"Why the I.W.W. is Dangerous." Labor Clarion (April 5, 1912) [San Francisco].

Woehlke, Walter V. "The I.W.W. and the Golden Rule." Sunset, The Pacific Monthly, 38 (February 1917), 16-18, 62-65.

_____. "Porterhouse Heaven and The Hobo." Technical World (August 1914), 808-813.

_____. "Red Rebels Declare War." Sunset (September 1917), 20-21.

_____. "San Diego I.W.W." Outlook, 101 (July 6, 1912), 531-536.

"Work and the police mortal foes of the I.W.W." New York Tribune, April 12, 1914, Part V, special feature section - full page article, illustrated.

PRIMARY SOURCES: PUBLISHED DOCUMENTS

Cong. Rec. Ashurst, H. F. "The I.W.W. Menace." August 17, 1917, p. 6104.

Cong. Rec. Bryan, J. W. "Seattle Riots." July 29, 1913, p. 2904.

Cong. Rec. Humphrey, William E. "Riots in Seattle, Wash., in [July] 1913 between Industrial Workers of the World and United States soldiers and sailors." (Includes newspaper clippings on the subject). September 4, 1913, pp. 4192-4204.

Proceedings, First Convention of the Industrial Workers of the World. Chicago, 1905.

Report of the President's Mediation Commission to the President of the United States. GPO, 1918.

San Francisco Labor Council. San Diego Free Speech Controversy: Report to the San Francisco Labor Council by Special Investigating Committee. San Francisco, Cal., April 25, 1912.

U.S. Dept. of Labor. Howd, Cloice R. "Industrial Relations in the West Coast Lumber Industry." Bulletin of the

U.S. Department of Labor Statistics No. 349, Misc. series. GPO, 1923.

U.S. House. Hearings on the Lawrence Strike. Document 671, 62nd Cong., 2nd Sess. (1912), 138:6320.

U.S. House. Industrial Commission Hearings. Committee on Labor of the House of Representatives, H.R. 21094, to create a Commission on Industrial Relations, March 22, 1912. 62nd Cong., 2nd Session (1912).

U.S. National Commission on Law Observance And Enforcement. Report On Police, No. 14. GPO, 1931. (The Wickersham Commission Report).

U.S. Senate. Industrial Relations: Final Report and Testimony Submitted to Congress by the Commission on Industrial Relations Created by the Act of August 23, 1912. 11 Vols. Document no. 415, 64th Cong., 1st Session (1916). These volumes are invaluable for information on events and attitudes of pre-World War I America. The testimony of the following individuals has been drawn on directly or indirectly:

Andreani, F. M. Italian Immigration Office and Legal Bureau. 6:5122-5125.

Atwood, Sarah J. Employment Agency Director (New York City). 1:1260-1263.

Banfield, M. C. Vice President, Employer's Association of the Pacific Coast. 5:4643-4653.

Bell, George L. Attorney, Commission of Inmigration and Housing of California. 5:4979-4982.

Blethen, Col. Alden J. Publisher of Seattle Times. 5:4224-4229.

Brandeis, Louis. Attorney. 1:63-64.

Brown, J. G. President, International Union of Timber Workers (AFL). 5:4208-4223.

Byrd, Rev. J. W. Pastor, Grace Methodist Church. 5:4892-4895.

Clark, Judge Walter. Chief Justice No. Carolina State Supreme Court. 11:10454-10455.

Cleland, Alexander. State Commission of Immigration of New Jersey. 2:1338-1343.

Constantine, Earl. Manager, Employer's Association of
    Washington [State]. 5:4150-4153.

Cooke, James W. Treasurer, Ferguson Building Construc-
    tion Co., Paterson, N.J. 3:2610-2611.

Cooney, Neil. Manager, Gray's Harbor (Wash.) Commer-
    cial Co. 5:4278-4279.

Darrow, Clarence S. Attorney. 11:10769-10809.

Distler, Rudolph. Working conditions in lumber indus-
    try. 5:4377-4379.

Ferguson, John. Contractor, Paterson, N.J. 3:2578-
    2583.

Francis, W. C. Manager, Employer's Association of
    Portland (Ore.). 5:4728-4731.

Gilbert, Ed. Portland (Ore.) Unemployed League.
    5:4721-4723.

Gill, Hiram C. Progressive Mayor of Seattle at Time of
    Everett Massacre, 1916. 5:4100-4112.

Halbert, L. A. Superintendent of the Kansas City Board
    of Public Welfare. 1:368-369.

Harriman, Job. Labor Attorney. 6:5808-5811.

Haywood, Bill. IWW Leader. 11:10588-10589.

Irish, John P., Jr. Secretary, Stockton (Cal.) Chamber
    of Commerce. 5:4776-4781.

Johannsen, Anton. Organizer, Union Brotherhood of
    Carpenters and Joiners. (Stockton). 5:4792-4793;
    11:10674-10679, 10702-10703.

Kincaid, Fred L. Land Speculator, Stockton (Cal.).
    5:4868-4871.

Lane, Warren D. Commissioner, Seattle Commission of
    Unemployment. 5:4374-4377.

Larson, A. H. National Employment Gxchange (New York
    City). 2:1268-1272.

Lessig, Adolph. Secretary, National Industrial Union
    of Textile Workers (I.W.W.). 3:2462-2463.

Lewis, Austin. Defense Attorney in Wheatland Riot

322

Case. 5:4999-5010.

McGill, Rev. Oscar. Social Worker, Seattle. 5:4382-4390, 4552-4553.

McKenzie, A. B. District Attorney, Contra Costa County, Cal. 5:4994-4999.

Mack, Wm. B. Manager, S. E. Slade Lumber Co., Slade-Wells Logging Co., Hump-Tulips Logging Co., Aberdeen, Wash. 5:4294-4297.

Magnet, Louis. Silk ribbon weaver, Paterson, N.J. 3:2572-2573.

Marelli, Henry. Defense Attorney, Paterson Strike. 3:2529-2543

Martin, Irving. Publisher, Stockton Record. 5:4876-4891.

Mathews. John L. Editor, Paterson Press (N.J.). 3:2583-2585.

Mayper, Joseph. Chief Investigator, New York State Bureau of Immigration and Industry; General Secretary of the Legislative Committee of the North American Civic League for Immigrants. 2:1358-1361.

Miller, Rodney. Railroad Labor Administrator. 3:2498-2499, 2516-2519.

Older, Fremont. Editor, San Francisco Evening Bulletin. 6:5442-5443.

Olson, Edward W. Washington State Labor Commissioner. 5:4120-4121.

Page, Paul E. President, Page Lumber Co., Buckley, Wash. 5:4249-4251.

Parker, Dr. Carleton H. Executive Secretary of the California State Commission of Immigration and Housing. 5:4932-4935.

Paterson, J. V. Businessman. 5:4311-4325.

Pauly, Henry. Chairman, International Order of Itinerant Workers. 5:4242-4248.

Roe, Gilbert E. Labor Attorney. 11:10474-10475.

Rossenheim, Ralph. Silk manufacturer, Augusta Silk
    Works; Secretary of the Silk Association, Pater-
    son, N.J. 3:2624-2626.

Royce, Robert M. Defense Attorney in Wheatland Riot
    Case. 5:5019-5024.

Rucker, W. J. Seattle Lumberman. 5:4304-4311.

St. John, Vincent. IWW Publicist. 2:1450-1453.

Schroeder, Theodore. Author and Attorney for Free
    Speech League. 11:10850-10896.

Scott, Alexander. Former editor Paterson Daily Issue
    (during 1913 IWW Strike). 3:2519-2529.

Stanwood, Edward B. District Attorney in Wheatland
    Riot Case. 5:5025-5026.

Swett, Isaac. Executive Secretary, Oregon Civic
    League. 5:4595-4605.

Taylor, J. A. IWW Organizer; Agent for Pacific N.W.,
    International Union of Machinists. 5:4336-4343.

Thompson, James P. IWW Organizer. 5:4236-4239.

Tyler, John G. Manager, San Francisco Office of Utah
    Construction Co. 6:5106-5109.

Walsh, Frank P. Chairman, Commission on Industrial
    Relations. Supplemental Statement. 1:153-157.

Wolfe, Frank E. Editor, Western Comrade (Los Angeles).
    6:5845-5853.

Wollner, William S. Labor Administrator, Northwestern
    Pacific Railroad Co. 6:5095-5106.

Wood, Dr. A. E. Instructor in Social Science, Reed
    College, Portland. Exhibit. 5:4762-4763.

Zversher, Edward. Secretary-treasurer I.W.W., Pater-
    son, N.J. 3:2585-2597.

U.S. Senate. Report on the Strike of Textile Workers in
    Lawrence, Massachusetts. Senate Doc. 870, 62nd Cong.,
    2nd Sess. (1912), 31:6170.

Weinstock, Harris. Report of Harris Weinstock, Commissioner
    To Investigate The Recent Disturbances In The City of
    San Diego And The County of San Diego, California.

Sacramento, Superintendent of State Printing, 1912.

PRIMARY SOURCES: UNPUBLISHED DOCUMENTS

The Archives of Labor History and Urban Affairs. University Archives, Wayne State University. The Industrial Workers of the World Collection. 181 Boxes. In this collection, the following items were of particular interest:

Bourg, G. J. 1918 Chicago Trial Testimony, pp. 8279-8283. (Harrassment of Wobblies in Aberdeen, S.D.). Box 113, folder 3.

Brazier, Richard. "Looking Backward To The Spokane Free Speech Fight." Box 46, folder 13.

Federal Writers Project. "The I.W.W. in California Agriculture." [1938?]. Box 149, folder 5.

Foy, James. "A Migratory Worker's Diary." February 1924. Box 148, folder 8.

French, Joe. 1918 Chicago Trial Testimony, pp. 11812-11828. (Harrassment of Wobblies in Aberdeen, S.D. and Tulsa. Okla.). Box 117, folder 6.

Plahn, Charles. 1918 Chicago Trial Testimony, pp. 8311-8316. (Re: Harrassment of Wobblies in the Gogebic Range Country of Michigan and Wisconsin). Box 113, folder 3.

Rowan, James. 1918 Chicago Trial Testimony, pp. 6907-6909, 6922-6927 (on Company hospitals and the Everett Massacre). Box 111, folder 6.

Sheridan, Don. 1918 Chicago Trial Testimony, pp. 6849-6850. Box 111, folder 6.

"Stenographic Report of Meeting of County Council of Defense, Labor and Financial Interests, Butte, Montana, Feb. 13, 1919." (A meeting to discuss declaring martial law.) Box 99, folder 24, 23 pp. (See Appendix I of present work for reprint.)

Thompson, James P. 1918 Chicago Trial Testimony, pp. 5009-5028, 5069-5083. (IWW Organizer on Everett Massacre and Wheatland Riot). Box 109, folder 2.

State Historical Society of Wisconsin. Collection of Ma-

325

terials on and about the Industrial Workers of the
World. Microfilm P34898. Of special interest were the
following:

Brissenden, Paul F. Justice and the I.W.W. Chicago,
[1920?]. Sec. IV, no.3. (An excellent constitutional analysis of the 1918 Chicago trial.)

Bruere, Robert. "Following the I.W.W. Trail." Misc.
end of reel.

"The I.W.W. and The Iron Heel." (1919). Sec. 1, no.
19.

National Civil Liberties Bureau. The Truth About the
I.W.W. New York, April, 1918. Sec. IV, no. 18.

_____. More Truth About the I.W.W. New York,
n.d. Sec. I, no. 34.

Nelles, Walter. Analysis of the Indictment. Chicago,
[1920?]. Sec. IV, no. 3. Re: 1918 Chicago trial.

Parker, Carleton H. "The Economic Basis of the I.W.W."
Sec. I, no. 34, p. 10.

U.S. Dept. of Justice. General Records. National Archives
Record Group 60. File no. 150139. (A copy of this
file, on the IWW 1910-1916, is now in the University of
Minnesota Library Microfilm Collection.)

U.S. Dept. of Labor. General Records. "Report of the United States Commission on Industrial Relations, 1912-
1915." National Archives Record Group 174. Microfilm
publication T4, 15 Rolls. (Also available from State
Historical Society of Wisconsin). Among other useful
materials, these unpublished reports of the Commission's staff include:

Duffue [Duffus?], William A. "Labor Market Conditions
in the Harvest Fields of the Middle West." HF145,
D9.

Fielde, Adele M. "A Scheme for Labor Colonies Under A
State Board," (published in Western Woman's Outlook, January 23, 1915, p. 15). HF1452.

Grant, Luke. "Violence in labor disputes and methods
of policing industry." HF14464, G7.

"I.W.W. Letters received in regard to free speech Oct.
1910-March 1911." ("Fresno Free Speech Fight by
H. Minderman, one of the boys who went through the

whole fight"). HF1424, M6.

Lauck, W. J. "Analysis of the economic causes of
industrial unrest." HF1423, L3.

Leiserson, W. M. "The Labor Market and Unemployment.
Feb. 15, 1915." HF1452, L5.

O'Regan, Daniel. "Free Speech Fights of the I.W.W.'s."
HF1424, O6.

O'Sullivan, M. "Is There Opposition on the Part of
Large Industrial Corporations to Labor Unions? If
So, What Are the Reasons Therefor? Dec. 12,
1914." HF1458, O8.

Parker, Carleton. "Preliminary report on tentative
finding and conclusions on investigations of seasonal, migratory, and unskilled labor in California. 1914." HF145, P2.

Perlman, Selig. "Preliminary report of an investigation of the relations between labor and capital in
the textile industry of New England." HF1423, P4.

Richardson, N. A. "Committee Report to the Socialist
Party of California State Executive Board on the
Labor Troubles of San Diego, California, May,
1912." HF1424, S6.

Socialist Party. Free Speech, Violation of the Right
of Free Speech, 1905-1914. "Riot in Minot, North
Dakota, July, 1913." Information furnished by
Arthur LeSueur, Attorney, Minot, North Dakota, to
the Information Department of the Socialist Party,
Chicago. HF1424, S6.

Speek, Peter S. "Report on cheap lodging houses in
the cities, July 25, 1915." HF145, S7.

_____. "Report on Conditions in Labor Camps, June
4, 1915." HF145, S7.

_____. "Report on the preliminary investigation
of the harvest hand situation in the states of
Kansas and Missouri, June 25-July 5, 1914."
HF145, S7.

_____. "Report on the Psychological Aspect of the
Problem of Floating Laborers (An Analysis of Life
Stories), June 25, 1915." HF145, S7.

_____. "Report on Transportation of Laborers,

PRIMARY SOURCES: NEWSPAPER FILES

Evening Tribune. Lawrence, Mass. January 1912 - May 1912.

Everett Daily Herald. Everett, Wash. Sept. 1916 - April
1917.

New York Evening Post. Nov. 1917 - March 1918.

San Diego Evening Tribune. San Diego, Cal. Jan. 1912 -
June 1912.

San Diego Sun. San Diego, Cal. Jan. 1912 - June 1912.

San Diego Union. San Diego, Cal. Jan. 1912 - June 1912.

The Socialist: The Workingman's Newspaper. Seattle. Wash.
Jan. 1910 - Mar. 1910.

Spokane Daily Chronicle. Spokane, Wash. Jan. 1910 - Mar.
1910.

Spokane Inland Herald. Spokane, Wash. Jan. 1910 - Mar.
1910.
The Spokesman-Review. Spokane, Wash. Nov. 1909 - Dec.
1909.

SECONDARY SOURCES: BOOKS

Adams, Graham Jr. Age of Industrial Violence, 1910-1915:
The Activities and Findings of the U.S. Commission on
Industrial Relations. New York, 1966.

Allport, Gordon Willard. The Nature of Prejudice. Reading,
Mass., 1979.

Andreano, Ralph, ed. New Views On American Economic
Development. Cambridge, Mass., 1965.

Apter, David E. Choice and the Politics of Allocation: A
Developmental Theory. New Haven, 1971.

_____, ed. Ideology and Discontent. New York, 1964.

_____. "Ideology and Discontent." In Reader in Poli-
tical Sociology. Ed. Frank Lindenfeld. New York,
1968, pp. 470-485.

_____. Some Conceptual Approaches to the Study of
Modernization. Englewood Cliffs, 1968.

Arendt, Hannah. On Violence. New York, 1970.

Bain, Joe S. "Industrial Concentration And Anti-Trust Policy." In The Growth of The American Economy. Ed.
Harold Williamson. Englewood Cliffs, N.J., 1951.

Baltzell, E. Digby. The Protestant Establishment: Aristocracy and Caste in America. New York, 1964.

Barnes, Samuel. "Political Ideology and Political Behavior." In Ideology, Politics, and Political Theory.
Ed. Richard H. Cox. Belmont, Cal., 1969.

Bell, Daniel. The End of Ideology. New York, 1965.

Bendix, Reinhard. Work and Authority in Industry: Ideologies of Management in the Course of Industrialization.
New York, 1956.

Berger, Peter L. and Thomas Luckman. The Social Construction of Reality: A Treatise in the Sociology of Knowledge. New York, 1966.

Berkhofer, Robert F. A Behavioral Approach to Historical
Analysis. New York, 1969.

Blauner, Robert. Alienation and Freedom: The Factory Worker
and His Industry. Chicago, 1964.

Brown, Richard Maxwell, ed. American Violence. Englewood
Cliffs, N.J., 1970.

_____. Strain of Violence: Historical Studies of
American Violence and Vigilantism. New York, 1975.

Cagan, Phillip. "The First Fifty Years of the National
Banking System -- An Historical Appraisal." In Banking
And Monetary Studies. Ed. Deane Carson. Homewood,
Ill., 1963.

Carlson, Peter. Roughneck: The Life and Times of Big Bill
Haywood. New York, 1983.

Caughey, John W. Their Majesties The Mob. Chicago, 1960.

Cawelti, John G. Apostles of the Self-Made Man. Chicago,
1965.

Clark, Norman. Mill Town: A Social History of Everett,
Washington. Seattle, 1970.

Cochran, Thomas and William Miller. The Age of Enterprise:
A Social History of Industrial America. New York,

1942.

Cole, Donald B. Immigrant City: Lawrence, Massachusetts, 1845-1921. Chapel Hill, 1963.

Coleman, James S. Community Conflict. Glencoe, Ill., 1957.

Conlin, Joseph R., ed. At the Point of Production: The Local History of the IWW. Westport, Conn., 1981.

_____. Bill Haywood and the Radical Union Movement. Syracuse, 1969.

_____. Bread and Roses Too: Studies of the Wobblies. Westport, Conn., 1969.

Coser, Lewis. The Functions of Social Conflict. London, 1956.

Cox, Richard H. Ideology, Politics, and Political Theory. Belmont, Cal., 1969.

Dahrendorf, Ralf. Classes and Class Conflict in Industrial Society. Rev. ed. Stanford, 1959.

Davies, Wallace E. Patriotism on Parade: The Story of Veteran's and Hereditary Organizations in America, 1783-1900. Cambridge, Mass., 1956.

Davis, David Brion, ed. The Fear of Conspiracy: Images of Un-American Subversion From the Revolution to the Present. Ithaca, 1971.

_____. The Slave Power Conspiracy and the Paranoid Style. Baton Rouge, 1969.

Demerath, N. J., III and Richard A. Peterson, eds. System, Change, and Conflict: A Reader on Contemporary Sociological Theory and the Debate Over Functionalism. New York, 1967.

Destler, Chester McArthur. American Radicalism, 1865-1901. Chicago, 1966.

Diamond, Sigmund. Reputation of the American Businessman. Cambridge, Mass., 1955.

Dollard, John. Caste and Class in a Southern Town. Garden City, 1957.

Draper, Theodore. The Roots of American Communism. New York, 1953.

Drinnon, Richard. <u>Rebel in Paradise: A Biography of Emma Goldman</u>. Chicago, 1961. (See also diss. citation.)

Dubofsky, Melvin. <u>Industrialism and the American Worker, 1865-1920</u>. Arlington Heights, Ill., 1975.

_____. "Socialism and Syndicalism." In <u>Failure of A Dream? Essays in the History of American Socialism</u>. (With a comment by Robert Tyler.) Eds. John H. M. Laslett and Seymour Martin Lipset. Garden City, New York, 1974.

_____. <u>We Shall Be All: A History of the Industrial Workers of the World</u>. Chicago, 1969.

Elson, Ruth Miller. <u>Guardians of Tradition: American Schoolbooks in the Nineteenth Century</u>. Lincoln, Neb., 1964.

Erickson, Charlotte. <u>American Industry and the European Immigrant, 1860-1885</u>. Cambridge, Mass., 1957.

Erikson, Erik H. <u>Young Man Luther: A Study In Psychoanalysis and History</u>. New York, 1958.

Fanon, Franz. "The Wretched of the Earth." In <u>Reader in Political Sociology</u>. Ed. Frank Lindenfeld, New York, 1968, pp. 486-505.

Foner, Philip S., ed. <u>Fellow Workers and Friends: I.W.W. Free Speech Fights as told by Participants</u>. Westport, Conn., 1981.

_____. <u>History of the Labor Movement in the United States</u>. Vol. 4. New York, 1965.

Fraser, John. <u>Violence in the Arts</u>. Bristol, Eng., 1974.

Friedman, Milton and Anna Schwartz. <u>A Monetary History of the United States, 1867-1960</u>. Princeton, N.J., 1963.

Freud, Sigmund. <u>Civilization and Its Discontents</u>. Tr. and ed. James Strachey. New York, 1961.

_____. <u>Group Psychology and the Analysis of the Ego</u>. Tr. and ed. James Strachey. New York, 1967.

_____. <u>Totem and Taboo</u>. Tr. and ed. James Strachey. New York, 1950.

Garraty, John A., ed. <u>The Transformation of American Society: 1870-1890</u>. New York, 1968.

331

Goffman, Erving. The Presentation of Self in Everyday Life. Garden City, New York, 1959.

Goldman.Eric. Rendezvous with Destiny: A History of Modern American Reform. New York, 1952.

Goldstein, Robert Justin. Political Repression in Modern America: 1870 to the Present. Cambridge, Mass., 1978.

Goodman, Paul. Speaking and Language: A Defence of Poetry. New York, 1971.

Graham, Hugh Davis, and Ted Robert Gurr. Violence in America: Historical and Comparative Perspectives. (A Report to the National Commission on the Causes and Prevention of Violence). GPO, June 1969. Vol. I.

Gras, N. S. B. and Henrietta M. Larson. Casebook In American Business History. New York, 1939.

Green, Marguerite. The National Civic Federation and the American Labor Movement, 1900-1925. Washington, D.C., 1956.

Grob, Gerald. Workers and Utopia. Evanston. Ill., 1961.

Grover, David H. Debaters and Dynamiters: The Story of the Haywood Trial. Oregon State Monographs: Studies in History, No. 4. Corvallis, Oregon State University Press, 1964.

Gurr, Ted Robert. Why Men Rebel. Princeton, 1970.

Gutman, Herbert G. Work, Culture, and Society in Industrializing America. New York, 1976.

Haber, Samuel. Efficiency and Uplift: Scientific Management in the Progressive Era, 1890-1920. Chicago, 1964.

Halle, Louis. "Strategy Versus Ideology." In Ideology, Politics, and Political Theory. Ed. Richard H. Cox. Belmont. Cal., 1969.

Hauser, Phillip. "The Social, Economic, and Technological Problems of Rapid Urbanization." In Industrialization and Society. Eds. Bert Hoselitz and Wilbert Moore. UNESCO, 1963, pp. 199-217.

Hawley, Lowell S. and Ralph Bushnell Potts. Counsel for the Damned: A Biography of George Francis Vanderveer. New York, 1953.

Hays, Samuel P. The Response to Industrialism, 1885-1914.

Hyman, Harold Melvin. _Soldiers And Spruce: Origins of the Loyal Legion of Loggers and Lumbermen_. Los Angeles, 1963.

_____. _To Try Men's Souls_. Berkeley and Los Angeles, 1959.

Jaffe, Julian F. _Crusade Against Radicalism: New York During the Red Scare, 1914-1924_. Port Washington, N.Y., 1972.

Jeffreys-Jones, Rhodri. _Violence and Reform in American History_. New York, 1978.

Jensen, Joan M. _The Price of Vigilance_. Chicago, 1968.

Jensen, Vernon H. _Heritage of Conflict_. Ithaca, N.Y., 1950.

Jones, Gareth Stedman. _Outcast London: A Study in the Relationship Between Classes in Victorian Society_. Oxford, 1971.

Jones, James. _From Here to Eternity_. New York, 1952.

Karson, Marc. _American Labor Unions and Politics, 1900-1918_. Boston, 1958.

Kevfitz, Nathan. "The Impact of Technological Change on Demographic Patterns." In _Industrialization and Society_. Eds. Bert F. Hoselitz and Wilbert E. Moore. UNESCO, 1963, pp. 218-236.

Kirkland, Edward Chase. _Dream and Thought in the Business Community, 1860-1900_. Chicago, 1964.

Klapp, Orrin E. _Collective Search For Identity_. New York, 1969.

Kolko, Gabriel. "Max Weber on America: Theory and Evidence." In _Studies in the Philosophy of History_. Ed. George H. Nadel. New York, 1965.

_____. _The Triumph of Conservatism: A Reinterpretation of American History, 1900-1916_. New York, 1963.

_____. _Wealth And Power In America: An Analysis of Social Class and Income Distribution_. New York, 1962.

Kornbluh, Joyce. _Rebel Voices: An I.W.W. Anthology_. Ann Arbor, 1964.

Kraditor, Aileen S. _The Radical Persuasion, 1890-1917:_

Aspects of the Intellectual History and the Historiography of Three American Radical Organizations. Baton Rouge, 1981.

Landis, Paul H. Three Iron Mining Towns: A Study in Cultural Change. Ann Arbor, 1938.

Lane, Robert E. Political Ideology: Why the American Common Man Believes What He Does. New York, 1962.

Lebergott, Stanley. Manpower in Economic Growth: The American Record Since 1800. New York, 1964.

Letwin, William. Law And Economic Policy in America: The Evolution of the Sherman Antitrust Act. New York, 1965.

Levin, Murray. Political Hysteria in America: The Democratic Capacity for Repression. New York, 1971.

Levine, Daniel. Varieties of Reform Thought. Madison. Wisc., 1964.

Lichtheim, George. The Concept of Ideology and Other Essays. New York, 1967.

Lowenstein, Karl. "Political Ideology and Political Institutions." In Ideology, Politics, and Political Theory. Ed. Richard H. Cox. Belmont, Cal., 1969.

MacPherson, C[rawford] B[rough]. The Political Theory of Possessive Individualism: Hobbes to Locke. London, 1962.

_____. "Revolution and Ideology." In Ideology, Politics, and Political Theory. Ed. Richard H. Cox. Belmont Cal., 1969.

McCloskey, Robert G. American Conservatism in the Age of Enterprise. Cambridge, Mass., 1951.

McKelvey, Blake. The Urbanization of America, 1860-1915. New Brunswick, N.J., 1963.

Mannheim, Karl. Ideology and Utopia: An Introduction to the Sociology of Knowledge. New York, 1964.

May, Henry F. The End of American Innocence: A Study of the First Years of Our Own Time, 1912-1917. Chicago, 1964

Mencken, H. L. The Vintage Mencken. Ed. Alistair Cooke. New York, 1955.

Merton, Robert K. Social Theory and Social Structure. Rev.
    ed. New York, 1957.

Mosier, Richard D. Making the American Mind: Social and
    Moral Ideas in the McGuffey Readers. New York, 1947.

Mowry, George E. The Era of Theodore Roosevelt and the
    Birth of Modern America, 1900-1912. New York, 1958.

Murphy, Paul L. The Meaning of Freedom of Speech: First
    Amendment Freedoms From Wilson to FDR. Westport,
    Conn., 1972.

_____. World War I and the Origin of Civil Liberties
    in the United States. New York, 1979.

Nelson, Ralph L. Merger Movements In American Industry,
    1895-1956. Princeton, 1959.

North, Douglas. Growth And Welfare In The American Past: A
    New Economic History. Englewood Cliffs, N.J., 1966.

Oberschall, Anthony. Social Conflict and Social Movements.
    Englewood Cliffs, N.J., 1973.

O'Connor, Harvey. Revolution in Seattle: A Memoir. New
    York, 1964.

Paul, Rodman. Mining in the Far West, 1848-1880. New York,
    1963.

Pelling, Henry. American Labor. Chicago, 1960.

Peterson, Merrill D. The Jeffersonian Image in the American
    Mind. New York, 1960.

Platt, Gerald M. and Fred Weinstein. "Alienation and the
    Problem of Social Action." In The Phenomenon of
    Sociology, A Reader in the Sociology of Sociology. Ed.
    E. A. Tiryakian. New York, 1969.

Pollack, Norman. The Populist Response to Industrial
    America. Cambridge, Mass., 1962.

Porter, Glenn. The Rise of Big Business, 1860-1950. New
    York, 1973.

Preston, William Jr. Aliens and Dissenters: Federal
    Suppression of the Radicals, 1903-1933. New York,
    1963.

Prochnow, Herbert. The Federal Reserve System. New York,
    1960.

Quint, Howard H. The Forging of American Socialism: Origins of the Modern Movement. New York, 1964.

Rees, Albert. Real Wages In Manufacturing, 1890-1914. Princeton, 1961.

Renshaw, Patrick. The Wobblies. New York, 1967.

Richards, Leonard L. Gentlemen of Property and Standing: Anti-Abolition Mobs in Jacksonian America. New York, 1970.

Rischin, Moses. The American Gospel of Success: Individualism and Beyond. Chicago, 1965.

Roazen, Paul. Erik H. Erikson: The Power and Limits of a Vision. New York, 1976.

_____. Freud: Political and Social Thought. New York, 1968

Samuelsson, Kurt. Religion and Economic Action: A Critique of Max Weber. Tr. E. Geoffrey French. Ed. D. C. Coleman. New York, 1961.

Schreiber, Harry N. The Wilson Administration and Civil Liberties, 1917-1921. Ithaca, 1960.

Seeley, John R., R. Alexander Sim, Elizabeth W. Loosley. Crestwood Heights, A Study of the Culture of Suburban Life. New York, 1956.

Shils, Edward. "Ideology and Civility: On the Politics of the Intellectual." In Ideology, Politics, and Political Theory. Ed. Richard H. Cox. Belmont, Cal., 1969.

Smelser, Neil. A Theory of Collective Behavior. New York, 1963.

Stein, Maurice R. The Eclipse of Community: An Interpretation of American Studies. New York, 1960.

Suggs, George G., Jr. Colorado's War on Militant Unionism: James H. Peabody and the Western Federation of Miners. Detroit, 1972.

Sullivan, Harry Stack. The Interpersonal Theory of Psychiatry. New York, 1953.

_____. "Psychiatry: Introduction to the Study of Interpersonal Relations." In A Study of Interpersonal Relations: New Contributions to Psychiatry. Ed. Patrick Mullahy. New York, 1949.

Sutton, Francis X., Seymour Harris, et al. The American Business Creed. Cambridge, Mass., 1956.

Tawney, R. H. The Acquisitive Society. New York, 1962.

_____. Religion and the Rise of Capitalism: A Historical Study. New York, 1954.

Tenenbaum, Samuel. Why Men Hate. Philadelphia, 1947.

Thernstrom, Stephan. Poverty and Progress: Social Mobility in A Nineteenth Century City. Cambridge, Mass., 1964.

Thompson, Fred. The I.W.W. -- Its First Fifty Years. Chicago, 1955.

Tilly, Charles. "Collective Violence in European Perspective." In Violence in America: Historical and Comparative Perspectives. (A Report to the National Commission on the Causes and Prevention of Violence). Eds., Hugh Davis Graham and Ted Robert Gurr. GPO, June 1969. Vol. I, pp. 5-34.

Tyler, Robert L. Rebels of the Woods: The I.W.W. in the Pacific Northwest. Eugene, Oregon, 1967.

U.S. Bureau of the Census. Historical Statistics of the United States, Colonial Times to 1970. Bicentennial Edition. Part 1. Washington, D. C., 1975.

Walker, Samuel. A Critical History of Police Reform. Lexington, Mass., 1977.

Ware, Norman J. The Labor Movement in the United States: 1860-1890. A Study in Democracy. New York, 1964.

Weber, Max. General Economic History. Tr. Frank H. Knight. New York, 1961.

_____. The Protestant Ethic and the Spirit of Capitalism. New York, 1958.

Weinstein, Fred and Gerald M. Platt. Psychoanalytic Sociology: An Essay on the Interpretation of Historical Data and the Phenomena of Collective Behavior. Johns Hopkins U. Press, Baltimore, 1973.

_____. The Wish to Be Free: Society, Psyche, and Value Change. Berkeley and Los Angeles, 1969.

Weinstein, James. The Corporate Ideal in the Liberal State: 1900-1918. Boston, 1968.

337

SECONDARY SOURCES: ARTICLES

Benson, Lee. "An Approach to the Scientific Study of Past Public Opinion." Public Opinion Quarterly, 3 (1967), 522-67.

Berkhofer, Robert F., Jr. "Time, Space, Culture, and the New Frontier." Ag. Hist., 28 (1964), 21-30.

Betten, Neil. "Riot, Revolution, Repression in the Iron Range Strike." Minn. History, 41 (1968), 82-94.

Botting, David C., Jr. "Bloody Sunday." Pacific Northwest Quarterly, 49 (1958), 162-72.

Chandler, Alfred D., Jr. "The Beginnings of 'Big Business' in American Industry." Business History Review, 33, no. 1 (Spring 1959), 1-31.

Chaplin, Ralph. "Why I Wrote 'Solidarity Forever.'" Am. West, 5, no. 1 (Jan. 1968), 18-27, 73.

Clark, Norman H. "Everett, 1916, and After." Pacific Northwest Quarterly, 57 (1956), 57-64,

Conlin, Joseph R. "The Case of the Very American Militants." Am. West, 7, no. 2 (March 1970), 4-10, 62-63.

Davis, David Brion. "Some Ideological Functions of Prejudice in Ante-Bellum America." Am. Q., 15 (Summer 1963), 115-125.

_____. "Some Themes of Countersubversion: An Analysis of Anti-Masonic, Anti-Catholic, and Anti-Mormon Literature." MVHR, 47, no. 2 (September 1960), 205-224.

Davis, Lance E. "Capital Immobilities And Finance Capitalism: A Study of Economic Evolution In the United States, 1820-1920." Explorations In Entrepreneurial History, 1 (1963), 88-105.

Doherty, Robert W., "Status Anxiety and American Reform; Some Alternatives." Am. Q., 19 (1967), Supp., 329-337.

Drucker, Peter. "A Warning to the Rich White World." Harper's Magazine, 237 (Dec. 1968), 67-75.

Dubofsky, Melvyn. "The Origins of Western Working Class Radicalism, 1890-1905." Labor History, 7, no. 2 (Spring 1966), 131-154.

Erikson, Erik H. "Identity and the Life Cycle." Psychological Issues, 1, no. 1 (1959), monograph 1.

Fischoff, Ephraim. "The Protestant Ethic and the Spirit of Capitalism -- The History of a Controversy." Soc. Research, 2 (1944), 53-77.

Fromm, Eric. "The Erich Fromm Theory of Aggression." The New York Times Magazine, Feb. 27, 1972, pp. 14-15+; April 23, 1972, p. 6.

Genini, Ronald. "Industrial Workers of the World and Their Fresno Free Speech Fight, 1910-1911." California Historical Quarterly, 53 (Summer 1974), 100-114.

Gitelman. H. M. "Perspectives on American Industrial Violence." Business History Review, 47, no. 1 (Spring 1973), 1-23.

Haug, Charles J. "The Industrial Workers of the World in North Dakota, 1913-1917." North Dakota Quarterly, 39 (Winter 1971), 85-102.

Hughes, Everett. "Good People and Dirty Work." Social Problems, 10 (Summer 1962), 3-11.

Johnson, Bruce C. "Taking Care of Labor: The Police in American Politics." Theory and Society, 3, no. 1 (Spring 1976), 89-117.

Johnson, Michael R. "The I.W.W. and Wilsonian Democracy." Science and Society, 28 (Summer 1964), 257-274.

Kennedy, Robert E., Jr. "The Protestant Ethic and the Parsis." Am. Journ. Soc., 68, no. 1 (July 1962), 11-20.

Kirschner, Don S. "The Ambiguous Legacy: Social Justice and Social Control in the Progressive Era." Historical Reflections, 2 (Summer 1975), 69-88.

Kloppes, Clayton R. "The Kansas Trial of the I.W.W., 1917-1919." Labor Hist., 16, no. 3 (Summer 1975), 338-358.

Lane, Robert E. "The Fear of Equality." American Pol. Sci. Rev., 53 (Mar. 59), 35-51.

Lees, Lynn H. "The Study of Cities and the Study of Social Processes: Two Directions in Recent Urban History." Journal of Social History, 7, no. 3 (Spring 1974), 330-337.

LeWarne, Charles Pierce. "The Aberdeen, Washington, Free Speech Fight of 1911-1912." Pacific Northwest

Quarterly, no. 1 (January 1975), 1-12.

Lindquist, John H. and James Fraser. "A Sociological Interpretation of the Bisbee Deportation." Pacific Historical Review, 38 (1968), 401-422.

McIntosh, Donald. "Weber and Freud: On the Nature and
Sources of Authority." Am. Soc. Rev., 35, no. 5 (Octo
ber 1970), 901-911.

Miller, Grace L. "The I.W.W. Free Speech Fight: San Diego,
1912." Southern California Quarterly, 54 (Fall 1972),
211-238.

Montgomery, David. "The 'New Unionism' and the Transformation of Workers' Consciousness in America, 1909-1922."
Journal of Social History, 7, no. 4 (Summer 1974), 509-
535.

Myers, R. C. "Anti-Communist Mob Action: A Case Study."
Public Opinion Quarterly, 12 (Spring 1948), 57-67.

Schlesinger, Arthur M., Jr. "Herbert Croly's The Promise of
American Life." The New Republic (April 8, 1972), 22-
25.

Shanks, Rosalie. "The I.W.W. Free Speech Movement: San
Diego, 1912." San Diego Historical Quarterly, 19 (Win
ter 1973), 25-33.

Sherman, Richard B. "The Status Revolution and Massachusetts Progressive Leadership." Pol. Sci. Q., 78 (March
1963), 59-65.

Shorter, Edward. "Illegitimacy, Sexual Revolution, and
Social Change in Modern Europe." Journ. Interdisc.
Hist., 2 (1971), 237-272.

Sims, Robert C. "Idaho's Criminal Syndicalism Act: One
State's Responses to Radical Labor." Labor Hist., 15,
no. 4 (Fall 1974), 511-527.

Skotheim, Robert. "A Note on Historical Method." Journal
of Southern Hist., 25 (August 1959), 356-365.

Tyler, Robert L. "The Everett Free Speech Fight." Pacific
Historical Review, 23 (1954), 19-30.

_____. "Four L's." MVHR, 47 (1960), 434-51.

_____. "I.W.W. and the Brainworkers." American
Quarterly, 15 (1963), 41-51.

_____. "I.W.W. and the West." <u>American Quarterly</u>, 12 (1960), 175-87.

Van Valen, N. "Bolsheviki and the Orange Growers." <u>Pacific Historical Review</u>, 22 (1953), 39-50.

Westley, William A. "The Escalation of Violence Through Legitimation." <u>Annals of the Amer. Acad. of Pol. and Soc. Sci.</u>, 364 (March 1966), 120-26.

Whitten, Woodrow C. "The Wheatland Episode." <u>Pacific Historical Review</u>, 17 (Feb. 1948), 37-42.

Wirth, L. "Ideological Aspects of Social Disorganization." <u>American Soc. Rev.</u>, 5 (1940), 474-75.

SECONDARY SOURCES: DISSERTATIONS

Barnes, Donald M. "The Ideology of the I.W.W.: 1905-1921." Diss. University of Washington 1962.

Drinnon, Richard. "Emma Goldman: A Study in American Radicalism." Diss. Univ. of Minnesota 1957.

Raff, Willis H. "Coercion and Freedom in a War Situation: A Critical Analysis of Minnesota Culture During World War One." Diss. Univ. of Minnesota 1957.

Villalobos, Charlotte Benz. "Civil Liberties in San Diego: The Free Speech Fight of 1912." M.A. Thesis. San Diego State College 1966.

Ward, Charles Shandrew. "The Minnesota Commission of Public Safety in World War One: Its Formation and Activities." M.A. Thesis. Univ. of Minnesota 1965.

Weintraub, Hyman. "The I.W.W. in California." M.A. Thesis. UCLA 1947.